Alpine Climbing

American Mountain Guides Association

Authors Mark Houston and Kathy Cosley have undergone internationally recognized training and certification exams in the highest levels of professional guiding. Although the content of this book does not officially represent American Mountain Guides Association (AMGA) guiding techniques, the AMGA does endorse the authors, who are certified guides, and the content of this book which provides the most current techniques used in the craft of technical mountaineering.

Outstanding technical guidance . . . concisely written, with little fluff to sidetrack the reader.
—*Reno Gazette-Journal*

Its organized, step-by-step presentation of information on climbing techniques and strategies provides an effective learning experience . . . . Gems of advice on how to maneuver safely and respectfully around other parties on long alpine routes also separate this book from others.
—*Rock & Ice*

An in-depth look at how anyone can become a better mountain climber . . . .
The photography is excellent and the writing is easy to follow.
—*Idaho Falls Post Register*

Alpine Climbing is yet another installment in the excellent Mountaineers Outdoor Expert Series of instructional mountaineering skill books . . . .*Alpine Climbing* is a useful book for inexperienced and experienced alpinists, alpinist wanabees, armchair mountaineers who wish to understand their most serious Krakauer works or laugh harder at movies such as *Cliffhanger,* and rangers involved with the alpine environment as a resource . . . . It just might be the most important work for the alpinist since Darwin's theory of natural selection.
—*Ranger* (**The Journal of the Association of Park Rangers**)

Every backcountry skier and ski mountaineer should have a copy of *Alpine Climbing.*
—*Backcountry Magazine*

MOUNTAINEERS
OUTDOOR EXPERT
series

ALPINE CLIMBING
Techniques to Take You Higher

Mark Houston and Kathy Cosley

THE MOUNTAINEERS BOOKS

Dedication

In fond memory of Bruce, Jill, Randall, and Julie

THE MOUNTAINEERS BOOKS
*is the nonprofit publishing arm of The Mountaineers Club,
an organization founded in 1906 and dedicated to the exploration,
preservation, and enjoyment of outdoor and wilderness areas.*

1001 SW Klickitat Way, Suite 201, Seattle, WA 98134

© 2004 by Mark Houston and Kathy Cosley

First printing 2004, second printing 2005, third printing 2007, fourth printing 2008, fifth printing 2009, sixth printing 2011

Distributed in the United Kingdom by Cordee, www.cordee.co.uk

Manufactured in the United States of America

Project Editor: Mary Metz
Developmental Editor: Erin Moore
Copy Editor: Kris Fulsaas
Cover and Book Design: The Mountaineers Books
Layout: Mayumi Thompson
All photos by the authors unless otherwise noted

Cover photograph: *Climbing on the Petite Aiguille Verte, Mont Blanc Massif, France*
Back cover photograph: *Climber starting the southwest face route of the Dent du Géant, Mont Blanc Massif, France*
Frontispiece: *Climber on the Zinal Rothorn, Switzerland. The North Face of the Matterhorn is in the background.*

Library of Congress Cataloging-in-Publication Data
Houston, Mark, 1956-
    Alpine climbing : techniques to take you higher / Mark Houston and Kathy Cosley.— 1st ed.
        p. cm. — (Mountaineers outdoor expert series)
    Includes bibliographical references and index.
    ISBN 0-89886-749-5
    1. Mountaineering—Handbooks, manuals, etc. I. Cosley, Kathy, 1957- II. Title. III. Series.
    GV200.H68 2004
        796.52'2—dc22
                                                    2004013210

♻ Printed on recycled paper
ISBN (paperback): 978-0-89886-749-7
ISBN (ebook): 978-1-59485-268-8

Contents

CHAPTER 4

Routefinding and Navigation

CHAPTER 5

Alpine Rock

CHAPTER 6

Snow and Ice

CHAPTER 7

Glaciers

Acknowledgments

We would like first and foremost to thank Peter Lewis, without whom this book would never have come to be. We also are deeply grateful for the wise counsel, criticism, and careful reading of a handful of generous friends: Christopher Kulp, Leigh McGuigan, and Margaret Willson. We owe a great debt as well to Erin Moore and Kris Fulsaas for their tremendous help and clear guidance.

Special thanks and credit (or blame) are due to Ira Kalet and Bruce Sherman, for providing our first introduction to mountaineering. Our many other teachers are too numerous to mention individually here, but we sincerely thank and acknowledge all the many friends and climbing partners who have taught us over the years how to climb and how to live.

Most of all we thank our parents, who set our feet upon the path and encouraged us every step of the way.

Introduction

"Because they're too big to eat!" is how Bruce Pratt, an old friend and early climbing partner of ours in the North Cascades, used to "explain" his enthusiasm for climbing mountains. We all have our own reasons for climbing. Most of us, when pressed, wax lyrical about the wild and beautiful settings; the shared intense experiences; the way mountains challenge us physically, mentally, and emotionally; and the sense of freedom that comes from moving efficiently and comfortably in an inhospitable realm.

Alpine Climbing: Techniques to Take You Higher is about gaining the skills and knowledge that will open the door to all the rewards the mountains can offer. In this book we hope to take the reader beyond the basics to focus on the special skills and particular techniques required to successfully negotiate the varied terrain found in the mountains. Over our combined fifty years of climbing and guiding, we've worked with aspiring alpinists coming from backgrounds in hiking, scrambling, and crag climbing who wished to learn what is needed to get farther into the wild and technical terrain of the mountains. In this book, as in our approach to these students in the field, our aim is to focus on the special conditions, tools, techniques, tips, and decision-making processes specific to alpine—as opposed to crag or hill—climbing.

To make this book as broadly useful as possible, we have tried to zero in on the following questions: What special tools are needed to climb in the mountains? What special knowledge is demanded by a landscape that varies greatly in difficulty

Opposite: Climbing the Voie Suisse on the Grand Capucin, Mont Blanc Massif, France

and that includes rock, snow, ice, and even glaciers? What skills enable a climber to move quickly and efficiently over this varied terrain and to cover the often great distances involved? Above all, how can we help developing alpinists learn to make complex, timely decisions in a complex environment?

Although technical protective systems are often necessary, in the final analysis they are not what keep us safe. Safety and success in mountaineering depend on a few acquired skills and qualities: good, strong climbing ability emphasizing precise and confident movement skills; and good decision-making allowing safe and efficient travel over long distances of rough and often exposed terrain. Physical fitness and toughness are also essential to alpine climbing. The main purpose of this book is to help you acquire the physical, technical, and mental skills needed to move well in alpine terrain and come home safely.

The technical protective systems commonly used in the mountains are few in number and not hard to learn. Mastery lies in the far more difficult task of knowing which techniques to use where and when. The ability to choose the best option among many implies more than mere familiarity with those options. It requires flexibility and creativity in decision making, which itself demands a thorough understanding of the complicated circumstances surrounding one's choices and the consequences of those choices.

WHAT IS COVERED IN THIS BOOK

This book addresses alpine terrain—including rock, snow, ice, and glaciers—at moderate altitude: around 5000 meters (16,000 feet) and lower; for example, the mountains of the continental United States, the Canadian Rockies, the European Alps, and New Zealand's Southern Alps. The tools, skills, and techniques covered here are specially selected as they apply to this terrain.

We begin with a discussion in Chapter 1 on decision making and risk. The concepts laid out here form the basis for correctly applying the techniques and skills covered in subsequent chapters. Chapter 2 concerns the alpine environment, its hazards (both human- and mountain-generated), mountain weather, and preservation of the alpine environment. Chapter 3 offers advice on various aspects of preparing for an alpine climb, including equipment selection. Chapter 4 deals with the elusive art of routefinding and also what it takes to navigate in whiteout conditions using instruments such as map, compass, altimeter, and global positioning system (GPS). Chapter 5 covers efficient movement on alpine rock by means of a variety of protective tactics ranging from unroped climbing to moving together on a shortened rope to steep, technical rock climbing. Chapter 6 is about snow and ice climbing, including movement skills as well as protective systems and strategies. Chapter 7 discusses glaciers and glacier travel, emphasizing an understanding of how to match a continuum of protective tools to changing hazards on a glacier.

Because we hope the reader will travel widely in pursuit of a life in the mountains, we believe familiarity with the metric system will be helpful. Therefore, we have chosen to use the metric system of measurement in this book (with conversions to Anglo measurements, where applicable, in parentheses). Where conversions are not supplied, multiply meters by 3.28 to find the equivalent in feet.

WHAT IS NOT COVERED IN THIS BOOK

This book is intended for intermediate alpinists with previous climbing experience. We assume the reader has some prior knowledge, mostly in the area of rock climbing skills and techniques. Basic knots, belaying, rappelling, rock anchor construction, leading, placing rock protec-

tion, and movement skills on high-angle rock are best learned in the relatively controlled environment of the local rock-climbing crag. There are invaluable how-to guides on this topic available (see the bibliography at the end of this book). However, variations of these skills that are of particular value in the alpine environment are addressed in this book.

We also assume that the reader has a general knowledge of outdoor travel, including backpacking and camping, and some basic experience with mountain navigation using map, compass, and altimeter.

Certain topics of importance to climbers are excluded from this book, notably winter mountaineering and high-altitude expeditionary mountaineering. Where other authors provide comprehensive and up-to-date coverage of these topics, we refer the reader to resources listed in the bibliography.

NOTE FROM THE PUBLISHER

Climbing is a dangerous sport that carries with it the risk of injury or death. Climbing safely requires good judgment based on experience, competent instruction, and a realistic understanding of your personal skills and limitations. You cannot rely on this or any other book to alert you to every hazard or anticipate the limitations of every reader. You must assume responsibility for your own safety.

The techniques, procedures and directions described in this book are intended to provide general information. This is not a complete text on outdoor climbing technique, and not all the techniques described here are appropriate for every climber or climbing situation. Nothing substitutes for formal instruction, routine practice, and plenty of experience. Use this book as a general guide to further information. No warranties, express or implied, are given by either the author or publisher as to the information published in this book.

—*The Mountaineers Books*

CHAPTER 1

Climbers on an unnamed summit below
Jirishanca and Yerupaja Chico, Cordillera
Huayhuash, Peru

The Making of an Alpinist

What makes mountaineering so compelling is that it demands so much of us. The simplest climb of the smallest peak requires complex decision making and judgment; it also inevitably entails risk. How we rise to this challenge matters to our survival, and so it engages our whole being: body, mind, and emotions.

We vividly recall an afternoon many years ago, returning from a climb of the Ice Cliff Glacier route on Mount Stuart in the North Cascades. This was certainly not the first climb of this difficulty that we had done together, but as we walked through the forest, relaxed, happy, looking back over our day, we realized it was the first that had gone almost exactly as planned. There had been no nasty surprises, no unforeseen risks. We had used our knowledge and abilities to successfully negotiate difficult terrain in a wild and forbidding world. This realization brought a sense of mastery that was intensely rewarding.

Our return from an ascent of the North Face of the Eiger could not have been more different. We had reached the summit via a difficult, famous, and historic route and were safely down in the alpine meadows looking forward to a beer and a good night's sleep. But our thoughts circled gloomily around recollections of the many ways we had failed to measure up to the demands of this climb. Underestimating the difficulty, we had taken much too long on the route and exposed ourselves to unnecessary risk. We generally felt that luck had played too great a role in our safe return.

What these two different experiences show is that the lure of mountain climbing is not just wilderness, comradeship, or the use of physical strength, athletic skill, and courage. Mountaineering draws on many aspects of our character, including sound judgment, boldness, intelligence, great effort, and faith in ourselves. This total engagement is the source of our greatest reward, and it is where both the joy and the challenge of alpinism lie. We want to feel we have earned our success and survival, that we didn't just roll the dice and let outer circumstances determine our fate.

This chapter deals with decision making, risk, and personal challenge in alpine climbing—fairly theoretical concepts to begin with, but as we move on to the more concrete issues surrounding in-the-field decisions in subsequent chapters, it will become clear how specific, individual decisions are ultimately based on the overarching concepts presented here.

MAKING DECISIONS

To climb mountains is to make decisions: where to go next, when to rope up, when to belay, whether to rappel or downclimb, whether to turn around or push on. Alpinists are faced with such questions at every step, and the quality of their decisions can obviously have extremely serious consequences.

Decision making is complex in the mountains because the terrain is so varied—in difficulty, in exposure, and in medium: rock, ice, snow. Transitions, from one medium to another or from easy to difficult ground and vice versa, entail critical choices regarding team movement, rope management, and protective strate-

gies. The sheer amount of ground to cover introduces often-severe time constraints. Further complicating the task, some factors such as weather and snow stability can undergo sudden or extreme changes.

Good decisions are contextual, based on actual circumstances, and cannot be reduced to a set of rules, such as "always travel in groups of three" or "always belay on exposed terrain." In fact rules, guidelines, and codes, although useful for introducing concepts, ultimately become counterproductive when it comes to actually making choices in the mountains. The simplest climb involves circumstances far too complex to be adequately addressed by rules. The mountain environment itself forces you to rely on your own skills of observation, your understanding of what you observe, and an accurate assessment of risks and of your own abilities.

Rules must be replaced by that mysterious quality called judgment. The acquisition of judgment begins with a mountaineer's very first climb and continues throughout the climber's entire career. It is a process that cannot be bypassed nor ever be considered complete. Over the years, we have found a handful of concepts helpful in guiding our decision making when faced with various options for action.

Anticipate changes. Continually look forward. Every change in terrain, route difficulty, or hazard may require a new strategy, mode of movement, or protective system to deal with new circumstances. These transitions can eat up a lot of time, but to a much lesser degree if you can see them coming and plan ahead.

Keep options open. Any given decision can either maximize or limit other possible options in the future. For example, your decisions about when to put on harnesses and rope up, how to rope up, and how to proceed once you are roped up will influence not only your current pace and efficiency but future choices as well.

Analyze benefits and costs. Addressing one risk or solving one problem often entails introducing other risks or aggravating other problems. Successful alpine climbing means coming up with solutions to address the primary problems while aggravating other problems as little as possible. A good example of this is belaying. While belaying is a sensible response to technical difficulty and exposure, it does take time and could increase the climbers' chance of being trapped by nightfall or deteriorating weather. In this situation, one has to weigh the relative risk of falling against the need to move quickly.

Maintain momentum. In our guiding, we try to minimize time spent on too many or too lengthy breaks. Failing to maintain momentum is a major reason for parties becoming benighted, caught by weather, returning late, or rushing to avoid these problems. Of course, everyone must pause occasionally to eat, drink, adjust clothing, or even simply rest. However, each pause should be no longer than necessary to fulfill its purpose, and each should fulfill multiple purposes if possible.

Staying focused on forward movement means always being a little bit stressed, but in such a potentially dangerous environment, some level of stress is, arguably, appropriate. There certainly are times when one can dawdle, loll in the sun, daydream even, but clearly this is not always the case!

Gather information. Generally speaking, the more information you have, the better your decisions. Preparing ahead of time will give you a head start. Study your route in guidebooks, on topographic maps, in photographs, and during the approach. Get advice from knowledgeable locals. Once on the route, constantly look around, look ahead, compare what you see to what you expected. Above all, remember what you see. Every glimpse is a new piece of the puzzle. Realize, however, that you cannot possibly know everything that there is to know, and that you will see more up ahead as you climb. When in doubt, check it out, but all the while try to keep moving.

Recognize and correct errors. In the mountains, many decisions must be made with limited information, and mistakes are inevitable. Rather than expecting perfection, strive to recognize errors as early as possible, and take steps to correct the situation. Do not carry on blindly, hoping that everything will work out. Denial causes delay, piling error upon error until only good luck can prevent things from spiraling out of control. Error recognition is an essential component of judgment.

Assess your own skill and knowl-

edge. You cannot always have the same level of confidence in your decisions under all circumstances. An honest and dispassionate self-critique is indispensable. For example, the capacity to observe, predict, and respond to cues improves over time, just as movement skills and climbing ability improve with practice; but on the other hand, competence can be degraded temporarily by states such as fear or fatigue or by inadequate information and inaccurate perception. Frequently address questions such as these: How confident are you in your decisions and assessments? Is your confidence (or lack of it) justified by your level of skill and experience? What is your state of mind? What inner and outer factors might be affecting you at this moment, and might they threaten the quality of your decision-making ability?

The following three examples involve the often puzzling decision of whether or where to rope up or unrope. These examples illustrate ways in which many of the preceding concepts—specifically, anticipating changes, keeping future options open, analyzing costs and benefits, and moving as efficiently as possible—are considered in making specific choices.

Example 1. You are on exposed but easy rock terrain with very little probability of falling, given your level of ability and confidence and that of your partner. However, you can see that more difficult rock climbing lies several hundred yards beyond and continues for several pitches. The angle of the slope gradually increases as you approach the more difficult section,

and you are currently in a good, safe place to stop. You decide that the transition into belayed climbing will be quicker and safer if you harness and rope up together now, while still on easy terrain, and move together on a shortened rope (see Chapter 5) until you reach the point where a belay seems necessary. Waiting until the going gets tough enough to warrant harness and rope would in this case be more risky and time consuming, since you would be forced to make the transition in a more precarious position.

Example 2. As in Example 1, you are on exposed but easy rock, neither of you concerned about falling. The ground above looks as though it will continue to be easy, but it is very broken and you cannot see very far. You cannot assess whether the climbing will become more difficult or tenuous anytime soon. You decide to take advantage of a rest break to harness and rope up, moving together with coils so that you can smoothly and quickly transition into belayed climbing at any point that either of you starts to feel insecure. Your skill in moving together while roped offsets the potential disadvantage of the rope encumbering your movement. You gain the added advantage that, should the climbing become harder, the decision to belay any short sections is made easier and quicker because you are already set up for it. As a result, you are more likely to belay where appropriate than you would be if you had to stop and rope up or unrope every time the difficulty changed. This is especially helpful when such changes are likely to be frequent and for short distances.

Example 3. You have just finished belaying several pitches of difficult rock and have a great deal of much easier ground to cover before the summit. You can see almost the entire route ahead, and though the exposure is still great, you and your partner are both confident that it will be no problem for you and that the likelihood of falling is very small. You decide to put away the rope rather than moving together roped and carrying coils, for two reasons: you think that on the whole you will be able to move more quickly that way, and you still have a long way to go.

Common Problems with Decision Making

When aspiring alpinists have difficulties making decisions, their problems often follow certain patterns, which we describe here with the goal of improving understanding and avoidance of these patterns.

Inexperience and second-hand "knowledge." Reliance on preconceived notions, rules of thumb, or the opinions of other climbers can interfere with understanding present circumstances. Such so-called knowledge can lead to missed cues or to the belief that the risk is greater or less than it actually is. This problem is particularly tricky early in a climbing career. A novice climber with limited experience and observation skills has little choice but to rely more heavily on information gathered from courses, books, or other sources. Lack of experience makes it hard to evaluate such information, which leads to a feeling of uncertainty. Mileage in the mountains tends to sort out a lot of this, by building confidence and sharpening the senses to better "hear" what the mountain itself has to say.

Of course, occasional uncertainty is an inherent part of climbing in the mountains, which must be measured and factored in along with all other information available. It will influence the margin for error that you allow for in your decisions.

Stubbornness. The desire to appear always in control can cause excessive attachment to previous decisions or theories despite mounting contrary evidence. Climbers must be alert and flexible in order to perceive and make sense of new observations, to take advantage of opportunities, and to avoid tunnel vision. It is necessary to make decisions and form opinions, but these should be recognized as provisional, needing frequent revisiting and revision as the day goes on.

Fear. This is a natural response that helps to keep us safe. But such a powerful emotion can easily distort perceptions and lead to muddled thinking. Feeling fear to the point of discomfort is neither inherent in nor necessary to climbing; to accept it as such would be a mistake. Fear, like doubt, should not be ignored. It needs to be addressed.

In the mountains, fear is usually the result of risk that is perceived but not adequately managed. This may be due to neglect and unawareness or simply because the risk is impossible to manage in your situation. When it is possible to manage the risk, fear is managed at the same time and in the same way: by reducing exposure to the hazard.

Fear either is justified by your current predicament or is the result of a distortion. Rather than spending precious time struggling and wondering whether your fear is justified, perhaps you had better assume that it is. After all, fear itself, whatever its source, clouds your judgment. You have to bring your fear back under control. Try to think dispassionately. Discuss your unease with your partner. Identify what needs to change to alleviate your discomfort, and then take any action within your power to make that change. The key is to act.

Group dynamics. Mountaineering often involves climbing with a partner or a larger group of climbers, complicating decision making still further. A group of people will often unthinkingly take on a higher level of risk than any individual within it would normally be willing to accept alone. This distressingly common phenomenon is more likely in larger groups or between new climbing partners, particularly those with less experience. The problem arises when a climber chooses not to express concerns out of a reluctance to imply criticism of another's decisions or for fear of appearing negative, uncertain, or even cowardly. Without realizing it, the individual abdicates responsibility for risk management to no one in particular. No one is in charge and no one takes on this responsibility, either for themselves or on behalf of anyone else.

This is a tough nut to crack. You can simply resolve to speak up or stick to a policy of "better safe than sorry"—this is, after all, the right idea. But in practice, for most people this is not very effective advice. Nobody wants to be perceived as a wimp, and nobody wants to turn back from a good climb unless absolutely necessary. A better solution is to become more opinionated. If you really believe you are right, then you are more likely to argue your point, more likely to speak out, and more convincing when you do so. Even if you fail to convince the others, taking individual action such as turning back on your own will be much easier if your decision is based on a strong and well thought-out opinion rather than just a feeling. The way to become more opinionated is to learn as much as possible and get lots of experience.

Nonetheless, you still must voice concerns, even if they are based simply on a dodgy feeling that you cannot articulate even to yourself. When you are in a group, always try to think and observe as if you were the leader or as if you were alone. This can be surprisingly difficult, but it is necessary to prevent you from being surprised by situations or risks you weren't alert enough to anticipate. If you assign responsibility for risk management to one member of the group, be sure that individual is willing and able to shoulder that responsibility.

GROUPTHINK: A LEARNING EXPERIENCE

We had teamed up informally with five of our friends, all guides, for a short day trip to ski a local peak in the Sierra Nevada. A big storm had just dumped at least half a meter of new snow, and we were eager to enjoy the powder but also concerned about snow stability. We stayed on ridges and in thick forest to approach our goal: an open 35-degree slope in a clear glade. Near the top of the slope, we stopped to dig a small pit, to see if we could learn anything useful about the bonding between the old snowpack and the storm snow just laid down.

As one of our number began to dig, others of us stopped nearby, laid down our packs, and began preparing to help him. When the last of us approached the pit, the slope finally settled with a loud *whump*. Alarmed, we all cringed and looked up to see a crack snaking across the top of the slope through the upper pit wall. Looking at each other, we all read the same thought in every wide-eyed face: how could we have been so stupid? We all knew better than to stack up a big group on the very terrain we were trying to assess, even if it was near the edge.

The answer was, yes, we all knew better, but none of us questioned anyone else's action by word, deed, or perhaps even thought. No one made a risk-management decision for the group as a whole. This story shows that even very experienced and trained individuals can succumb to a classic case of groupthink.

CONSIDERING RISK

You often hear that alpinism is an inherently risky sport. It is more accurate to say that the potential for risk is inherent. The real potential of exposure to risk keeps us engaged as few other activities can—in this sense, risk and alpinism are intertwined. We do not climb in order to expose ourselves to risk, but we do climb partly in order to put ourselves in a position where we have to deal with risk: we have to manage it. What we do enormously influences how much risk we run, and this fact is what makes the game interesting.

Risk Management

To manage risk is to reduce it to acceptable levels by skill and technique. The challenge is to move through potentially dangerous terrain in a way that makes us less likely to be harmed. The mountains present the same threats to all climbers; the best climbers stay safe because of their behavior. They foresee and avoid areas of ice- and rockfall; their physical strength and routefinding and climbing skills reduce the likelihood of slips and mistakes.

More-skilled climbers can take on harder or potentially more dangerous routes without increasing their risk. Less-skilled climbers have plenty of risk to manage on easier climbs. Because the sense of accomplishment comes from the management of risk, both beginners and experts alike experience the same rewards.

Managing risk should not be confused with minimizing risk. In some situations the two may coincide—rockfall hazard in a nasty gully may be manageable only by staying out of the gully altogether. But consider that the greatest mountaineering risk is falling. While this risk can be truly minimized only by staying out of the mountains—an unacceptable solution to a mountaineer—it can be managed by being a better climber. Below are some steps to managing risk.

Be observant. The first step in risk management is good observation, the ability to see and evaluate the terrain, difficulty, route options, weather, conditions, time of day, and things that might fall on you. It is equally important to observe internal factors such as your own energy level, alertness, distractions, and confidence. The difficulty lies in identifying and prioritizing all the potential hazards and keeping track of those that may change over time. Take advantage of ongoing opportunities for clear

The summit of the Matterhorn

views to assess route possibilities, descent options, or incoming weather, as well as for breaks, which allow you to assess your party's strength.

Analyze probability and severity of risks. In order to manage risk, one must form opinions about its probability and severity. To analyze risk is, in the most basic terms, to gauge both the likelihood of a bad thing happening and the consequences if it does. Consider the following:

■ The *probability* of a bad thing happening to you is a function of the chance of it happening at any given moment, multiplied by the amount (time) of your exposure.

■ The *severity* of risk (how bad is it, really?) is a function of its probability multiplied by the consequence to you.

For example, consider the probability of being hit by falling ice while passing beneath an area of unstable seracs on a glacier. The severity of this risk—being crushed under several tons of falling ice—is high. However, seracs fall randomly and only occasionally, in response to slow glacier movement. Therefore, if we assume the exposure time is short, the probability of being hit remains low at any given moment. Clearly, the more time spent exposed to such a hazard, the greater the chances of being in the wrong place when the ice block does eventually fall.

Contrast this with the risk caused by poor routefinding. A climber lacking routefinding skill will get off route, into more difficult or poor rock, forcing harder climbing or greater exposure to rockfall

hazard. The probability of risk is high because the chances of getting off route are great, and the climber has ample opportunity to do so. The severity may also be high; the potential consequences of getting off route are various, including getting lost, falling, or being hit by falling rock.

So which of these scenarios involves the greater hazard? As guide instructors love to say, "It depends . . . " Personally, we'd rather walk under the serac.

Anticipate risks. Many risks change throughout the day. It is important to anticipate these changes and track them as you climb, watching the weather, your energy level, the clock, and changes in snow and ice conditions as the day warms. Think ahead to your descent route. How long will it take? What hazards might you encounter?

Balance multiple risks. The mountains rarely present a simple situation with just one risk. A chosen solution to one problem must take other problems into account.

Imagine, for example, a stretch of delicate and exposed climbing that crosses an area also exposed to rockfall. Belaying protects a potential fall but slows the climb, increasing the amount of time spent in the rockfall zone. Yet the risk of falling and the risk of being hit by a rock must both be managed. Choosing a different route would be the best option. If this is not possible, the risks may be managed by climbing quickly, by placing only minimal or time-efficient protection, and by seeking safe positions for pauses or belay stances.

In considering alternatives, favor the simplest solution. Rockfall hazard is best managed by avoidance. Falling is best managed by being a better climber and by judicious choices about when to forge ahead and when to back off. The risk of travel on softening snow is best managed by getting up earlier. The simplest solutions may not always be possible or applicable, but when they are, they should always be preferred. It can be tempting to settle for technical solutions alone: belay-protected systems to guard against falling or helmets to protect against rockfall. These are often wise actions to take, but they are not usually the most effective ways to manage these risks.

In 1991 we made an ascent together of the South Face of Aconcagua in the Andes of Argentina. In our planning, we had to consider several risks: the notoriously violent and changeable weather of the region, the technical challenge and looseness of the rock climbing, the difficulty of finding anchors, the high altitude, and the cold. We knew that the heavier our packs were, the more likely we would be to fall, the slower we would go, and the more quickly we would tire. However, we also knew that we would have to spend at least one night out on the route, so we had to carry enough to do that safely, if not comfortably.

We decided to take an aggressive approach and to carry very little bivy gear, enough for just one night. We were very well acclimatized from just having guided the Polish Glacier route on the same mountain the previous week, and we figured this fact would allow us to move quickly. We resigned ourselves to one uncomfortable night out with minimal gear, in exchange for light packs that would increase our chances of finishing in two days. We brought no tent, only one sleeping bag with an insert to allow us to squeeze in together, a bivy sack, a stove, fuel, and food. The cold, breezy night we spent in a shallow snow trench we had dug on the glacier was not fun, but we did finish the route the following day. We didn't get much sleep, but this was one of our more satisfying and memorable climbs.

This example illustrates a somewhat delicate balancing act. On the one hand, by bringing so little bivy gear, we increased our risk of exposure to the cold and to bad weather if it had come in. On the other hand, our light packs, together with our acclimatization, allowed us to move very quickly. Every ounce saved reduced the risk of being caught by weather, and reduced our exposure to many other risks as well.

Remember that "speed is safety." This old truism of alpinists expresses a central notion of risk management. By going faster, you reduce your exposure to such things as unstable ice cliffs or climber-generated rockfall. You avoid hazards that change or develop over time, such as softening snow conditions or afternoon thunderstorms. You reduce fatigue—even standing around takes some energy, and the climb will tire you more the longer it goes on. These are just a few of the hazards that are reduced if you go faster. There are many ways of managing different risks, and these are discussed in more detail throughout the book, but this one notion is so important that it is especially emphasized.

Consider boldness, recklessness, and the role of luck. Climbing challenging mountains often requires a certain amount of boldness. However, the line dividing boldness and recklessness can be a fine one. One concept we have often used to express this distinction and keep ourselves out of trouble can be summed up in two simple rules:

1. Put yourself in a position to be lucky.
2. Don't put yourself in a position where you rely on luck.

For example, occasionally you wake up in the morning to poor weather and have to decide, do I get up and go or roll over and go back to sleep? Resist the pull of the bed for long enough to ask a couple of questions. First, what are the odds that the weather or conditions could improve enough to enable you to do the climb? Second, how far up the route can you safely go and descend in poor weather? Many climbs have an easy approach that can reasonably be climbed and retreated from, even in bad weather. If there is no chance for improvement, then perhaps the sleep-in is the best choice, but if there is even a small chance that the weather might improve while you are on this easier ground, then you might do better going for it, "putting yourself in a position to be lucky." After all, as long as you

adhere to rule number 2, all you lose is a couple of hours of sleep; whereas it's very frustrating to roll over and go back to bed, only to wake up to beautiful weather later in the morning.

The trick is to discern those points beyond which luck would be required to keep you safe. Look back frequently. Consider the difficulty of finding your way back in a whiteout or if blowing snow fills in your tracks. Be sure you can overcome any obstacles you might face if you turn back.

Be prepared to work through challenges and to build confidence in yourself, your climbing ability, and your routefinding decisions. Be curious, not fearful, about the unknowns ahead. Discover the mountain's secrets, the weather's fickle personality. But have contingency plans for when things don't go your way.

Personal Approaches to Risk

Your own approach to risk will differ from someone else's. The level of risk each climber accepts is a personal matter, but it is also a shared risk that affects the entire climbing party.

Acceptable levels. With the analysis of risk comes decisions about how much risk you as a climber are willing to accept. The ambition to achieve harder (and potentially more risky) ascents must be balanced with the need to maintain personally acceptable levels of risk. Too great a focus on achievement could lead to risk levels that become hard to justify, while too great a focus on risk avoidance limits achievement. Think about this balance in your own climbing. Recognize also that your tolerance level can change from one climb to the next, some climbs being worth more to you than others. Your acceptable level of risk can change over time, as can your ability to manage risk. Only you know whether or not your abilities and climbing goals are compatible with a level of risk you can accept.

Individual and shared responsibility. As climbers and as adventurers, many of us consider our lives to be our own—to keep or to lose, to protect or to risk. But this highly personal decision inevitably affects other people as well, friends and family especially. The balance here is for

Climbing on the Rimpfischhorn, Switzerland

us climbers to decide individually what risks we are willing to take, but at the very least we must acknowledge some constraint on our independence out of fairness to those who care about us or even depend upon us.

We also are responsible for our climbing partners, whether we share equally in the decision making or not. One of the great rewards of alpine climbing is camaraderie and trust. The rope is a symbol of that trust, but, more than just a symbol, it also connects the fates of climbers in a very real way—what happens to one will likely happen to the other. Climbers earn each other's trust by accepting responsibility for each other, knowing that each person's actions have a huge impact on the safety of both.

LEARNING

While personal experience in the mountains is ultimately the best teacher, you can also benefit from watching other climbers in action. Listen to their stories (with a grain of salt, of course!) and try to imagine what you would do in various situations. Read about accidents and analyze them. When analyzing another party's accident or response to a risky situation, put yourself in their place. Try to see what factors brought on the risk and whether or not they were foreseeable in that situation. Imagine alternative actions they might have taken to better manage the risk.

From Experience

Every climb is a learning opportunity. You can speed up the process and increase your safety by actively and consciously observing and processing what is happening around you. Here are some tips for learning both during and after your ascent.

Work on routefinding. Start by looking ahead and trying to assess the best route. Afterward, gauge how well your routefinding choices worked out, and do a self-critique. As you gain skills, you will find that more often than not the route you chose was indeed the best one.

Assess difficulty from afar. Try to guess how hard the climbing will be and imagine what sort of protective strategy might be appropriate. Later, compare that with the actual difficulty you encounter and the techniques you end up using. Is there a pattern to how your opinions change? That is, do you consistently under- or overestimate difficulty?

Estimate the time needed. Ahead of time, gauge how long you expect various parts of the climb to take, and then note your actual times during the ascent. A digital camera makes a fine recording tool for times, locations, and the distant view.

Review the day. After your ascent, rate the accuracy of your predictions and the effectiveness of your planning. Every climb is a long string of experiences and decisions, both good and bad. Analyze what went well and what went wrong. Where did events follow your predictions and expectations? Where were there surprises? How would you have acted differently, knowing what you know now? You must sort out the difference between good choices and lucky guesses. Since you rely so much on your own judgment, you need to know how well you did, both so that you can do better next time and so that you can determine the necessary margin for error. Self-critique helps you gauge your progress and build confidence. At the end of the day, ask yourself the following questions. Go through this process with your partner, or compare notes.

- Where was my party most at risk?
- What did I do to address or manage that risk? Was my response adequate?
- Knowing what I know now, what could I have done differently to better manage the risk?
- Did I make mistakes? For example, did I misjudge the difficulty or get off route? If so, why did I make that mistake?
- Did the route take a lot longer than I expected? If so, why? Did I have a good margin for unforeseen problems, or was I pressed for time? Should I have gotten up earlier or moved more quickly?

Keep a log or journal of your climbs. Record weather and time spent on various parts of the climb or approach. Make a sketch or topo of the route, especially if you found inaccuracies in a guidebook's information. Make gear notes. Record any conclusions you draw as a result of asking the above questions at the end of your climb.

Measure your improvement; celebrate your success! Pat yourself on the back for a job well done, while recognizing and learning from your errors. It is very rare that a day in the mountains goes just as expected. If you think you did a flawless job, look harder! Do not expect absolute perfection; instead, strive for a day in which you kept to "guidebook time," when everything felt in control and you were never trusting to luck for your safe return. You will find that you take as much satisfaction in your own progress as a mountaineer as you do in reaching the summit or enjoying the beauty of the mountains.

From Others

There are many resources to help you learn the art of mountaineering.

Guides and instructors. Professional instruction and guides can be extremely helpful. Early in your career, guides can manage risk as you learn basic movement skills and protective systems. They can also identify areas of strength and weakness and focus on activities to speed improvement.

As you progress, your best use of a guide or instructor will be to take a personalized approach for help with specific objectives. If you want to learn decision making, for example, you need to be in a position where you make decisions. You are less likely to have that opportunity in a group setting and more likely on a one-on-one outing.

In most developed countries with mountains, guides are required to pass difficult certification exams in order to practice their trade. Learn the local and national laws governing the profession. At the time of this writing, most U.S. guide services and land managers do not require guides to be certified, though many U.S. guides are. If you are considering hiring a guide for alpine climbing, find out whether your guide is certified in this discipline. Each country has its own guides association responsible for guides training and certification. For a list of these, see Appendix A.

Climbing partners. A good climbing partner can be as hard to find and as precious as a good spouse! Seek opportunities to climb with lots of people, and when you find a good friend and partner, take excellent care of that person.

In many climbing centers around the world, climbers find partners by asking around or posting messages on local bulletin boards. This can be a fine way to meet new friends. A word of caution, however: for your first outing together, build in a large margin for the unexpected by choosing an objective that will be quite easy for both of you.

Clubs and organized groups. One time-honored way to meet other climbers is through clubs and organized groups. Many towns and cities have some kind of climbing club. On club outings, be especially careful to take personal responsibility for your safety; do not relinquish it into the hands of people whose skills you do not know and cannot assess beforehand. There are a lot of self-proclaimed experts out there!

CHAPTER 2

Climber on the west ridge of Mount Earnslaw,
New Zealand

The Alpine Environment

Mountains exert a mysterious power over the human imagination. They can fascinate, terrify, invite, or repel us. They are among the most visually exciting and dramatic geological features of our planet—and, at the same time, the most inhospitable. To climb a mountain is to enter a world where one's own insignificance and vulnerability are painfully obvious—a world that is as indifferent to our desire to overcome its obstacles as it is to our survival. The beauty of mountains is equally obvious. They seem to have changing moods, churning out their own unique and often-violent weather and altering with the seasons. This changeability, along with sheer enormity and complex topography, creates the impression of a moving, living, overwhelmingly powerful being. Avalanches, storms, and rockfall reinforce this impression, resembling deliberate acts of a malevolent consciousness—it's no wonder that beliefs in mountain deities are so common throughout the world.

Our ability to explore this territory and come home safely depends on setting aside both superstition and awe and acquiring a more hard-boiled understanding of the nature of the mountain environment. Alpine terrain is big, steep, broken, varied, and unstable. Travel over this terrain involves dealing with snow, ice, loose or sheer rock, great distances, and often dizzying exposure. We also have to deal with threatening and often violent weather: sleet, rain, snow, freezing fog, lightning, and hammering winds. Cold temperatures and thin air threaten our survival. What the heck are we thinking of, exposing ourselves to all this?

The fact is, we can survive in this environment if we approach it on its own terms, understanding the nature of the potential threats, recognizing them when we see them, and finding ways to avoid or reduce them. We must learn to perceive danger signs and stay out of the way of threatening events such as avalanches and storms. We work around hazards and minimize their impact by means of planning, action, and reaction based on awareness and understanding of the threat.

ALPINE HAZARDS

This section focuses on the mountain environment, particularly its conditions and hazards. Following each hazard, we describe how to manage, avoid, or mitigate its potential to harm us. Hazards can involve either human factors or mountain factors. Danger to the climber usually involves an interaction of both. We address each type of hazard in turn.

HUMAN RISK FACTORS

Our weaknesses and vulnerabilities and/or gaps in our fitness, climbing skill, or knowledge together determine the human factor of risk. These human factors interact and combine with one another. The effect is cumulative. To some extent, strength in one area can make up for weakness in another. Good routefinding ability might help a poor rock climber avoid hard climbing. Good climbing ability may allow a bad routefinder to get away with mistakes. But weakness in both areas is a dangerous combination. Gauge your

abilities honestly, and devote effort to improving them—we all have room for improvement. Training is most productive when directed toward areas of greatest weakness, so for best results, identify and work hardest on areas where your skills, knowledge, or abilities are weakest.

Falling

Falling is the cause of the vast majority of accidents in the mountains and is by far the greatest human risk factor alpine climbers face. The length of alpine routes and the broken, variable nature of the terrain mean that ropes, belays, and other technical protective systems can only occasionally offer any real protection from injury in a fall. More often, climbers simply must rely on their own climbing ability and judgment.

If you can increase your personal climbing skills, you will be much safer than you would be otherwise. You will also be able to take on harder climbs while still keeping the risk of falling to acceptable levels. A skilled and experienced climber is less likely to fall even when the going gets tough.

Travel light. Reducing the weight in your pack greatly reduces the chance of falling, as well as allowing you to travel faster and save energy.

Finally, you must rely on your assessment of your own climbing abilities and of the difficulty of the climbing. Abandoning the attempt is almost always an option, and in some cases it may be the best one.

Whenever you climb on terrain where a

fall is possible, ask yourself these three questions:

1. What is the probability of falling?
2. What is the consequence of falling?
3. How confident am I of the answers to the above questions?

The answers to these questions will lead you to the best protective strategy for your situation: whether to move together roped or unroped, when and where to belay, how much protection to place, or, possibly, whether to back off the climb or find another route.

First, when considering the probability of a fall, consider not only your own climbing ability, but also the quality of the rock, snow, or ice; how much weight you are carrying; how rushed you are; and whatever else might affect your ability.

Second, the consequence of falling may be negligible if you have a good belay and good protection. On the other hand, a fall by either you or your partner could be disastrous if, for example, you are climbing roped but unbelayed on exposed, hard, frozen, 40-degree snow above a crevasse.

Third, your confidence matters a great deal. The more accurate your answers to these questions, the better you can analyze and manage the risk, but self-knowledge and experience are key to accuracy. Beginning climbers find it harder to gauge the probability of a fall and should account for a greater potential for error by doing easier or better-protected climbs or backing off a climb if need be—and if possible.

Climbers also fall into crevasses and through cornices. These risks are best managed by learning to recognize and avoid them. We discuss these in detail in Chapters 6 and 7.

Inadequate Physical Condition, Knowledge, and Training

Fortunately for all of us, there are climbs to suit almost any description of a healthy human, but if you bite off more than you can chew, your risk goes way up. Physical stamina helps you remain alert. Being alert reduces risk, just as inattention increases it. More difficult or lengthier routes require a higher level of fitness.

Fatigue affects every climber at some point. You need a good idea of your body's toughness as well as its limitations. Pushing your limits in controlled situations is helpful—on long, steep hikes, for example—to see just what you can do and what happens when you run out of energy.

Examples abound of how knowledge and understanding influence risk. Knowing how glaciers move leads to good route selection; skill in belay anchor construction speeds up the process; good routefinding reduces the risk of falling. Continue to build your knowledge and understanding of the mountains as well as your technical abilities. Practice movement skills as much as protective systems.

Remember that your partner's level of physical and mental preparedness will also influence your own safety and success.

Discomfort

Climbers have to accept a certain amount of discomfort. Some seem to positively revel in it! In the interests of becoming indestructible, you may even want to seek it out from time to time. But being cold, tired, hungry, or thirsty is distracting, and it is best to avoid discomfort that you cannot control. For example, a late start will force you to rush and allow few if any stops; with better planning, you could take a break now and then.

Stay warm! A warm torso means warm hands, allowing you to wear lighter gloves, which improves dexterity and speeds up your handling of gear. Anticipate clothing changes to avoid sweating. If you expect to move constantly, start out underdressed, knowing you will warm up soon. If you face a long period of inactivity or belaying, put on another layer before you get cold.

Other Climbers

Other climbers on your route or peak are both a blessing and a curse. They can help with routefinding, provide a comforting sense of security, or lend a helping hand when something goes awry (though bear in mind that joining forces can lead to groupthink and less-than-responsible decision making). More often, other climbers pose risks: they can knock down rocks or ice, fall on top of you, or slow you down. This risk can be managed in only two ways: avoid them (do another climb or keep your distance), or be above them by starting earlier or passing them.

MOUNTAIN RISK FACTORS

By this, we mean risks originating in the environment, such as rockfall, icefall,

weather, etc. However, the distinction is not absolute; a climber's behavior still greatly influences the actual hazard that mountain risk factors pose.

Like human risk factors, mountain risk factors vary greatly throughout a climb—most occur on some parts of the mountain but not on others and at some times but not others. Usually the solution is fairly simple: when the risk is active, be somewhere else. An alteration of route or an earlier start might reduce or even completely avoid many risks. For example, if the avalanche danger is high, adjust your travel route if possible to avoid open slopes and stay on ridges. If your route takes you under or across snow slopes with rockfall potential, time your ascent to be off that terrain before the sun rises and the day warms. Learn to recognize the sources of risk, and anticipate where and when hazards are likely to occur.

Rockfall

Of all objective risks, rockfall probably claims the most lives. There are two main causes: climbers above can knock rocks onto those below, or rocks can be released when the warmth of the sun melts the ice that had glued them to the mountain. Falling rocks generally funnel into gullies or rattle down open faces. Anticipate the causes and patterns to avoid the hazard!

- Start early and climb quickly and efficiently to avoid the heat of the day and to be above other parties.

- Where possible, keep to ridges and out of gullies.
- Climb carefully so as not to knock rocks on your partner or others below (if you do inadvertently dislodge a rock, shout loudly and immediately to alert anyone below).
- Keep to solid rock and avoid loose sections.
- Seek protected places to stop, rest, and belay.
- Favor those protective strategies that allow for the fastest travel through exposed areas and/or reduce the likelihood of knocking off loose rocks (see Chapter 5, Alpine Rock).
- Wear a helmet, but realize that this offers only limited protection.

Icefall

Icefall is generally confined to smaller and more specific locations than is rockfall, so it can be somewhat easier to avoid. Icefall has three main causes: climbers knock ice down on each other; ice is naturally released by daily warming; or steep, unstable seracs collapse on a glacier.

Ice knocked off by other climbers is a significant problem, and leading on ice below another party is a risky proposition. If there are others above you, you have three choices: get above them, do another climb, or accept the risk. If you are speedy, you may be able to pass another party, though they understandably will not like it! Move especially carefully when there are climbers below you

(including your belayer). Avoid overdriving your tools, and watch out for brittle bulges that are more likely to fracture around your tools and crampon placements (see Chapter 6, Snow and Ice). If you decide to follow another party up an ice route, position your belays and line of ascent as much out of the line of fire as possible.

Natural icefall released by the sun normally involves only icicles (though some can be quite large!) and plaques of ice that form during a cold night. The best solution is timing—avoid being under this stuff when the sun hits it.

The threat of icefall on steep glaciers and the collapse of the glacier ice features called seracs are covered in Chapter 7, Glaciers.

Cornice Collapse

Cornices form on the lee side of ridges during snowstorms accompanied by wind (as most snowstorms in the mountains are). Cornices can collapse under the weight of climbers walking on them, and when warm weather weakens them enough, they break under their own weight. Falling cornices can injure climbers moving underneath or trigger avalanches on the slopes below.

Avoid climbing under large cornices whenever feasible, especially in warm weather. When approaching a steep, snowy ridge crest, assume it is corniced until you can see that it is not. Investigate to determine the size and extent of the cornice. Take precautions as you do

Cornices on the Breithorn, Switzerland. The angle of the slope below the cornice, projected upward, intersects the windward slope. This is the potential fracture point. Stay below this imaginary line, as these climbers are doing.

this: take a belay or at least keep a taut rope to your partner down the slope, who should stay well down on the windward side below any potential fracture point (see photo above) to provide a counterweight while you investigate. When traveling along a corniced ridge crest, traverse on the windward side below the potential fracture point. Watch out for cracks in the snow on the ridge, which present their own hazards and indicate that the cornice is not well attached.

Avalanche Hazard

A book such as this can at best offer only a small step in gaining wisdom in the mountains, especially in the area of avalanche hazard, which is extraordinarily complex. Our discussion here is limited to the type of avalanche problems most commonly found in the summer months. While there can be big snowfalls even in summer, the warmer temperatures of that season usually cause the snowpack to settle more quickly and behave in more predictable ways than in winter.

A CAUTIONARY TALE: AVALANCHES

I have been caught in one avalanche. It happened about twenty years ago while I was climbing up to the Col du Mont Brulé in Switzerland. As with many such accidents, in retrospect it seems foolish and embarrassing—I should have known better. In the end, I was lucky. After tumbling down the mountainside some 120 meters (400 feet), over two small cliff bands, I ended up lying on top of the snow with one broken ski, two slightly sprained ankles, and a good excuse to spend a bit of time exploring Paris. I frequently think about this incident, hoping I have learned from it and will recognize the chain of events that led to it and that will no doubt appear again. And I'm left wondering just how much such experiences, or lack of them, color our so-called objective analysis—I suspect more than we would like to admit.

—*Mark Houston*

In winter, prolonged cold temperatures make snow stability generally harder to assess—complex processes resulting in long-term instability are more common. Wind slab and persistent weak layers are major concerns in cold, wintry snowpacks. Understanding these types of problems is well beyond the scope of this book and requires taking avalanche courses and spending lots of time poking about in the snow.

These types of cold-snow problems can certainly occur in the summer as well, especially on chilly north faces or at high altitudes. Climbers need to be on the lookout whenever the grain size is small, the snow lacks a distinct crust, or it does not appear to have gone through a melt-freeze cycle (described below).

But the situation is usually better in the warmer temperatures of summer. In the sunny days following a snowfall, if the slope faces the sun, the new snow rapidly becomes denser through an alternating process of daytime warming and nighttime freezing, a process called *melt-freeze metamorphosis*. Crystals grow into small ice grains, packed tightly together. This is the summer-type snow we are all familiar with, called névé.

During the first few days after a summer snowfall, a set of common conditions arises—frequently encountered by alpinists and too often ignored. This particular combination, new snow and sunny weather, can bring stable conditions at night and in the early morning but also produce wet snow avalanches in the afternoon. The obvious appearance of this cycle should appear as a wildly waving red flag. The good news is that even in snowy ranges such as the European Alps, the Cascade Mountains of the northwestern U.S., or the Southern Alps of New Zealand, for much of the summer, avalanche hazard is low to nonexistent and climbers can go wherever they want, at least from the perspective of avalanche hazard. But climbers need to be able to determine when these conditions change.

Below, we discuss ways to judge snow stability in a summer alpine context, ways to use terrain to help keep you safe, and a few special concerns about traveling in avalanche terrain. At the end of this section, we discuss how to go about getting the additional experience and knowledge necessary for building confidence and accuracy in hazard assessment. When assessing avalanche hazard, two main points are particularly important to understand:

- It is absolutely necessary to form an opinion about snow stability. Your opinion can be that it's OK, that it's not OK, or that you simply can't tell. However, if you don't have an opinion, you have no rudder to guide your decision making.
- Daily temperature cycles and varying slope attributes (steepness, aspect, and configuration) can completely change the hazard. What is true for one place or at one moment is not true for another time or place.

The alpine climber has a few unique avalanche concerns that differ from those of the general winter traveler.

- Summer snow is often completely bombproof. Climbers must be able to tell when this is the case and when it is not.
- Climbers frequently face spikes in hazard stemming from rapidly rising temperatures on a warm day. This change frequently catches summer climbers unaware.

- In alpine mountaineering, steep and confined terrain is often unavoidable; whereas in winter ski or snowshoe touring, terrain typically offers more options for where and how to put in a route. The snowshoe or ski tourer may ask, "Where can I safely go, using terrain features to protect me?" whereas the question for the mountaineer is more often simply, "Is it possible to safely do this route?"
- Alpine routes are steep and fraught with such hazards as cliff bands and crevasses—the consequences of getting caught in an avalanche are usually tragic. Unlike winter snowshoe and ski touring, in summer climbing the live recovery of avalanche victims is rare. This fact, combined with the normally excellent stability of summer snow, suggests that winter avalanche safety equipment (beacons, shovels, and probes) is usually not that helpful. More often, the best strategy is to keep your pack light and to be up and down again before the snow softens in the warming day.
- Alpinists seldom have time to perform snow bonding tests such as Rutschblock, shovel shear, or compression tests. These tests are not conclusive, and any additional information they provide is usually of minimal use to the alpinist. If you are highly skilled in the use of these tests, they may occasionally be appropriate in very particular circumstances. If you have less experience with them, they will not help you and will only consume valuable time.

The most important elements in determining avalanche danger are (1) the stability of the snow itself and (2) the terrain features. If you can eliminate doubt about either one of these factors, then you can eliminate the risk of avalanche.

For example, if you are on terrain that cannot be in either the start zone or the path of an avalanche, such as a pronounced ridge, then the stability of the snow does not matter. Similarly, if the snow is so stable that avalanches are virtually impossible, then it doesn't matter what sort of terrain you are on, be it a narrow, snow-filled gully or a wide-open 40-degree slope.

As usual, things are seldom this clear-cut in practice. Since the alpine climber's choice of terrain is so often constrained by the route itself, reducing doubt about the snow stability is usually the best bet. This may be hard, occasionally even impossible; but where it is possible, it can allow you to go anywhere with confidence.

Conversely, if you cannot remove doubt about snow stability, then you must stick to safe terrain. This sounds all very well in theory, but in practice it may not be so easy to avoid every little section of windblown snow, every small loaded slope.

However, persisting despite evidence of instability amounts to relying on luck and is bad policy even if only for a few short moments. To sort all this out, ask yourself the following questions:

1. Can I time my ascent so that I encounter no unstable snow? If the answer is yes, great! If the answer is no, then ask:

2. Can I avoid unstable snow by using terrain features? If the answer is yes, go ahead! If the answer is no, then ask:

3. Is the exposure to avalanche potential worth the rewards of making the ascent? If the answer is yes, go for it! If the answer is no, turn back or choose another route, so long as these options entail less risk than going on.

These questions are seldom easy to answer, and there are usually shades of gray. The last question is particularly difficult. It may be tempting to answer in the absolute ("It is never worth the risk"), but this is unrealistic because for most climbers it is simply not true. It is often the case that risk, though real, is minimal and rewards are high. Only you can decide, but the point is that you must decide. By asking these questions in this order, your thinking leads to the most appropriate decisions: avoiding risk where possible, and where it is not possible, determining what is acceptable.

Snow stability. In summer alpine climbing, your assessment of snow stability should take into account the following factors. (We examine each factor in turn below.)

1. slope angle, shape, and aspect
2. recent snowfall or wind-transported snow
3. current snow temperature and trend
4. temperatures since the last snowfall
5. how the snow feels underfoot

1. Slope angle, shape, and aspect. Most avalanches start on slopes between 30 and 45 degrees in steepness, and about half of the total are on slopes between 35 and 40 degrees. Much steeper slopes tend to slough snow as it falls during storms, limiting buildup. Therefore, steeper, more technical climbs are often much safer from avalanche hazard than are lower-angled moderate climbs. In either case, identify **slope angles** in this critical range. Use the clinometer in your compass to help you learn to accurately judge slope angle.

Convex **shapes** in the slope, such as a bulge or an easing of steepness at the top, are often the fracture point of slab avalanches. The steeper slope below creates tension in the snowpack as it pulls away from the snow on the less-steep area above. A climber's weight can then trigger a fracture at the point of tension. Concave areas, on the other hand, tend to be better supported from below; the weight of the snowpack compresses rather than stretches.

Slope aspect governs the amount of sun a slope receives and, to a large degree, the amount of snow that can be wind-deposited on it as well. We discuss both of these factors below under items (2) and (3). Slopes sharing similar aspects usually have similar characteristics. If you form an opinion about stability on a particular slope, odds are that you will have the same opinion about other slopes of the same aspect, angle, and elevation.

2. Recent snowfall or wind-transported snow. Along with rising temperature, **recent snowfall** is one of the two most important red flags for summer alpinists, especially when accompanied by wind. In general, hazard is highest during or just after a major snow event. The weight of the accumulating new snow overcomes the bonding in the snowpack, and avalanches result. This is pretty obvious, and most climbers tend to stay indoors when the flakes are flying. In addition to the large avalanches that may cover entire slopes, snow falling in steep gullies will continually slough during storms, creating frequent small slides that can knock climbers off their feet.

Once the snowfall stops, the typically warm temperatures of summer gradually help stabilize it. Nighttime freezing and daily warming work to strengthen the snowpack, often within a few days. But watch the snow during the warming part of the cycle, because that is when the snow is the least stable.

Wind governs how snow is deposited. Accumulations on lee slopes can be several times as deep as those on windward slopes. And even after a storm passes, wind can move large amounts of snow, creating large and potentially unstable wind slab. Look for signs of wind transport, such as deep new snow on the lee of ridges, sculpting of snow, as well as plumes blowing from ridge crests.

3. Current snow temperature and trend. In summer, rising temperature usually brings rising instability in the snow. The tiny frozen bonds and necks between snow grains melt, the snow softens, and stability decreases. With falling temperatures, these necks of free water refreeze and the firm frozen snow has great strength, with minimal avalanche hazard. To predict these changes in hazard, you should know a bit about how the temperature of the snowpack can change.

In direct sun, snow soaks up tremendous heat. The more perpendicular to the sun's rays the slope is, the more heat it absorbs. At night, however, snow radiates great quantities of heat to a clear sky, and nighttime snow surface temperature drops precipitously. This explains why after a clear night we can have good freezing conditions with easy cramponing, even if the air temperature never actually got much below 0° C. The same process can continue during the day as well, keeping snow surface temperature below air temperature as long as the snow remains in shade and the sky clear.

Cloud cover, on the other hand, reflects radiated heat back to earth, blocking radiative heat loss and keeping the snow much warmer. Even a thin, high cloud cover has a pronounced effect. Under a cloudy sky, snow that is slushy at sunset will still be slushy at sunrise.

4. Temperatures since the last snowfall. One deadly but common scenario is a summer snowfall followed by clearing and warm sun. Pinned down in camp or town by the bad weather, climbers chomp at the bit to get into the hills. A late start or slow going can put them on or under storm-loaded slopes just as the sun starts to warm things up. As melting increases moisture in the snow and breaks down bonds, stability decreases and wet snow avalanches result.

The solution is to get up (and down) early and stick to safe terrain or, better still, to simply wait a day or two for the snow to stabilize. But how can one know when the snow is stable again? Three main factors are at work (the diagram in Figure 1 illustrates these points):

■ The repetition of day/night cycles, alternately freezing and warming, increases stability with every passing day. The greatest changes are in the first 2 or 3 days after the storm.

■ During each hot, sunny day, snow stability degrades along with the rising temperature, usually reaching its worst state in the late afternoon and then improving again as the evening freeze develops. The greater the daily temperature fluctuations, the more extreme the difference between daytime and nighttime snow stability.

■ If the daytime high temperatures in the days following a snowfall remain fairly constant, stability increases with each passing day, even at its worst point during the peak of afternoon warming, because the snow never gets warmer than it did on the previous days. If, on the other hand, the weather grows ever hotter with each passing day, then stability at the warmest part of the day might not improve much for several days.

The moral of the story is, even if snow stability is increasing over time, avoid those warmer times of the day when the snow softens and hazard increases,

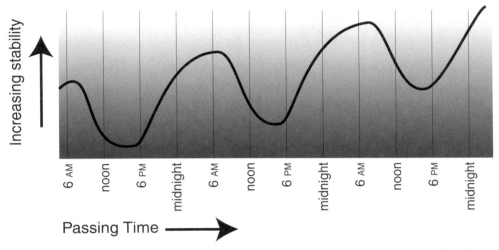

Figure 1. *Stability varies with time of day, but usually increases with each passing sunny day after a storm. Poor stability can be found in the late afternoon soon after the storm, and good stability near 6 AM days later. Slope aspect affects the daily timing, and nighttime cloud cover can keep stability low.*

especially in the first two or three days of warm weather following a storm.

5. *How the snow feels underfoot.* The feel of the snow under your boots is an important source of information about snow stability, as well as something that influences the difficulty and speed of travel. The main things to feel for in terms of stability are: Is there a frozen crust, and how strong is it? Will it bear body weight in its frozen state? How quickly does it break down under body weight as the day warms? How dense is the snow under the crust (measured by "foot penetration")? Let's look at these more closely.

■ **Weak frozen crust:** A fragile crust can be the result of a weak freeze, or maybe soft new snow under the crust is not dense enough to help support it. Either way, snow stability depends partly on the strength of this crust. If it almost holds your body weight, then avalanche hazard is low until the crust melts later in the day. A more fragile crust weakens quickly, however, and the already soft underlying snow may be unstable. The thinner and weaker the crust, the less ability it has to hold the slope together and the more quickly it will break down with daily warming.

■ **Well-frozen surface snow:** Firm frozen summer névé is bombproof, with easy and secure cramponing. This snow will not avalanche as long as it remains frozen, and it can remain frozen well into the day. This is the ideal, something we all hope for, and is one of the main reasons to get up early. But it too eventually softens with the warming sun and can turn to mush by midafternoon. Get up early, be quick, and enjoy the fruits of your good planning.

- **Foot penetration:** If the crust is weak or nonexistent, the density of the snow can help you assess its stability. Foot penetration (a measurement of how far your boot sinks into the snow when you stand on it) is one quick and easy indicator of snow density and strength. In general, a shallower penetration means more stable snow, at least in summer. See Table 1.

Terrain. If you determine that there is some unstable snow out there, use terrain features to avoid hazardous areas. In the simplest sense, this means sticking to ridges as much as possible. Otherwise, try to connect safer areas and string together a functional route. This is not always easy and involves endless trade-offs. For

example, is it better to cross a large slope with moderate hazard or a short one with high hazard? Not surprisingly, simple answers are rare.

Gullies, bowls, faces, and open slopes all have potential problems. In assessing the type and severity of the problem, analyze the feature in question in terms of the following criteria:

1. Is it potentially a start zone of an avalanche?
2. Is it part of an avalanche track?
3. Is it part of the avalanche runout zone?

1. Avalanche start zones. Potential starting zones for avalanches are areas where snow accumulation and angle, shape, and aspect of slopes create special weaknesses, stresses, or loads as discussed above under snow stability. Here are a few pointers for managing these areas:

- **Stay above the potential fracture line.** If you must cross a suspect slope, try to stay high, above the point where avalanche release seems most likely. For example, on convex slopes, visualize

TABLE 1

Foot Penetration	Probable Snow Stability
Less than 5 cm	Generally very strong snow, avalanches very unlikely. You can probably climb anywhere you like.
5 to 10 cm	Strong snow, avalanches not likely. Watch out for changes in the snow or for softer areas above you.
11 to 20 cm	Not bad yet, but be on your guard. Try to stay out of steep gullies.
more than 20 cm	This is pretty soft and gooey snow, without good stability. Stay off and out from under steep slopes, and avoid steep gullies.

where the tension is greatest and hence where a fracture would most readily occur. It is best to stay above this point, but if you cannot cross the slope that high, the alternative is to go as low as possible, preferably at some point where the slope is less steep and the snow compressed.

- **Trigger avalanches intentionally.** When approaching a suspect slope or gully from above or from the side, you might try to deliberately trigger a slide, assuming you can do so without being caught up in it. Once a slope has slid, it will likely be safer to cross, assuming other potential avalanche slopes don't feed into it from above. From a secure location, knock down cornices or throw big snowballs or rocks at the slope. However, be sure nobody else is below, and be very careful about getting on the slope yourself. Being a human trigger might work but is fraught with risk!

- **Belay across slopes.** It may be possible to belay across small areas of unstable snow, but bear in mind that a climber caught in an avalanche puts an incredible amount of force on a belay, often exceeding the breaking strength of climbing ropes. Not only must you be sure your belay is up to the task, but you must also consider the corresponding force that would be applied to the falling climber's body. Snow anchors of any kind are unlikely to be strong enough for this purpose. If you do this, build a good anchor in solid rock or ice, and belay directly off it, not off your harness. If you do not plan to belay, then do not rope up where avalanche is a concern unless you are on a crevassed glacier. If you are caught in a slide without a belay, the rope will only tangle you up and drag you down.

- **Climb straight up and down slopes.** In soft snow, put your track in straight up or down the slope. Cutting across it diagonally usually increases the chance it will release.

2. Avalanche tracks. Avalanche tracks are usually easy to identify either by seeing evidence of previous slides or simply by visualizing the path that sliding snow would take. Climbers spend a lot of time in potential avalanche tracks, because many great climbing routes run straight up them. Gullies, couloirs, and slots can offer fine climbing on firm, compacted snow and ice and are often quick and direct lines both up and down.

Avalanche tracks can go over cliffs, especially on summer alpine routes. When cliffs, climbers, and avalanches mix, climbers do not fare well. Always consider the consequences of getting caught in a slide in your calculation of risk. Consequences are determined by the length and steepness of the track and also by obstacles in its path, such as crevasses, moats, cliff bands, or boulders. Here are some techniques to consider if you must cross or ascend a potential avalanche track:

- **Stick to the edges.** When climbing in an avalanche track, try to guess exactly where the snow would go, and stay off to the side, hugging the rocks on the edge and belaying in sheltered areas.

- **Beware of grooves.** Snowy faces and wide gullies often develop deep, distinct grooves or troughs down the middle of the slope, carved out by small, frequent wet slides in the heat of the day. Because of the pounding and scouring they undergo, these grooves often provide good, firm snow for climbing and may in fact be the fastest route up or down, which makes them tempting. But realize that these are natural funnels for projectiles and slides, and that whatever comes down will probably come very fast. Definitely never place a belay in a trough.
- **Expose one member at a time.** In the unfortunate case that there is no other reasonable option (including turning back) to crossing a suspect slope, have one climber cross at a time. This reduces the total added load on the slope, which might make a difference on particularly ticklish areas. Position other party members to watch whomever is crossing the slope. If there is a slide, they will be able to note the location where the climber disappeared. This helps searchers guess where the victim will end up, limiting the search area.

3. Avalanche runout zones. Terrain traps are the climber's main concern—places where snow could pile up in particularly dangerous ways. Anywhere the snow will deposit deeply, be it in a crevasse, in a gully, or under a small cliff, climbers can be buried deeply, and deep burials have very low survival rates.

Human factors. The influence of human factors in avalanche accidents is increasingly recognized among experienced observers of these too-often tragic events. For the alpine climber, there are two main concerns.

A CAUTIONARY TALE: AVALANCHE TERRAIN TRAPS

Early in our climbing careers, we read a chilling story in *Accidents in North American Mountaineering* that has stuck with us ever since. Climbers glissading a snow gully in the Tetons got caught up in a small, wet-snow avalanche that they triggered themselves. This phenomenon— one's own private, homemade wet-snow avalanche—is not unusual and is not in itself serious; anyone who has butt-slid in soft summer snow has experienced the pleasant ride on a soft cushion of snow down the hillside. However, unfortunately for these climbers, a stream below the snow had thinned it, particularly where it splashed over rock bands. The group broke through the snow in one of these places, and their avalanche followed them into the hole. The cementlike snow partially buried them and also plugged the gap between the snow and the rock. The stream continued to flow, of course, and formed a little lake. The climbers drowned, being unable to dig out quickly enough. This story, although it is particularly pertinent to glissade runouts, points out the fact that not all potential terrain traps are visible or obvious.

The first and most important concern is the groupthink problem mentioned under Common Problems with Decision Making in Chapter 1, The Making of an Alpinist. This is particularly tricky in avalanche terrain, where hazard assessment can sometimes be especially difficult and you are more likely to occasionally lack confidence in your assessments. But even when hazard is predictable—for example, during afternoon warming—climbers in groups tend to be reluctant to assert themselves when concerns arise. In Chapter 1, we emphasize the importance of forming strong opinions about dealing with risk in general. In the case of avalanche hazard, the best way to strengthen your confidence in your opinions is to take avalanche courses and spend time poking around in snowpacks of dubious stability. Become a student of avalanches, and you are less likely to become a victim of one.

The second human factor is other parties and the avalanches they can trigger. Beware of climbers above you on questionable slopes. While having a few "avalanche poodles" ahead of you to assess the slope can add some reassurance, this is only true if you can stay well out of the line of fire while they check out the dubious terrain. Remember, as always, to make your own decisions, based on your own opinion, not theirs.

Avalanche rescue. If you should be so unlucky as to have one of your party caught in a slide, follow the steps below. The scenario we describe here assumes you do not have avalanche beacons, because this is the most usual case in summer alpine climbing.

1. Determine how many of your party are missing.
2. Get a good view of the avalanche path, and try to identify the point where any climber was last seen and likely areas of deposition.
3. If possible, gather other nearby climbers to help with a search, but don't bother if this will take more than a few minutes.
4. If possible, get someone else to call local authorities for help. If you are alone, do a quick search (described next) before trying to seek outside help yourself.
5. Walk downhill through the debris, looking for clues—bits of clothing or equipment. Try to cover the entire deposition zone in less than 5 minutes. If you see nothing the first time around, do it again.
6. If your visual search yields nothing, you will need to probe. Get others to help if possible, as many as you can. Your ice ax or trekking poles with their baskets off can serve as probes. Start in the areas you consider to be most likely to produce results. Be methodical but quick. The more holes you poke in the snow, the better your chances of finding your friend. If you hit something, dig like mad with whatever you have available. Once you figure out the orientation of the victim's body, uncover the head right away.
7. Consider what to do next if you find your friend alive. The victim may be

injured and will almost certainly be hypothermic. If you have lots of helpers, you may have someone prepare shelter or warm drinks, first-aid materials, etc. However, don't let such planning slow the search! Time is your enemy—after about 30 minutes of burial time, the odds of survival are less than 50-50.

Learning more. To learn more about avalanches requires both theoretical study, such as taking courses and reading books, and also actual practice, spending time in snow in all its varied forms and types, looking and poking around. The need to spend more time in the snow presents a dilemma. The most efficient use of time is to get out when stability is poor, presenting the tough-to-assess conditions you want to learn to recognize and deal with. But being out in such conditions is risky! The best approach is to take the courses first, learning how to recognize times and areas of greatest hazard. Armed with this knowledge, get out in the snow but use your understanding of terrain and other factors to keep you off, and out from under, slopes that might actually slide. You can manage risk and still learn a great deal by simply being near areas of danger but not within them.

In recent years, avalanche courses have become more readily available and generally have improved in quality as well. This is good news for the alpinist. Courses are typically offered at varying levels, designed to match both the expertise and the goals of prospective students. For more information about course providers,

contact the following organizations:
American Avalanche Association:
www.avalanche.org
American Institute for Avalanche Research and Education:
www.avtraining.org
Canadian Avalanche Centre:
www.avalanche.ca

INTERACTION OF HUMAN AND MOUNTAIN RISK FACTORS

Many of the risks associated with mountains are best described as an interaction between human- and mountain-generated factors. Humans are designed to survive within a fairly narrow temperature range and at low to moderate elevations. The mountain environment can be ill suited to human health or even survival, with life-threateningly low temperatures and/or oxygen pressure. In this section, we discuss such risks to health and safety as altitude, cold, and sun and discuss strategies for survival and prevention of illness.

Acclimatization and Altitude Illness

Even though most discussion of altitude-related illnesses and acclimatization focuses on expeditions and peaks above 5000 meters (16,000 feet), altitude-related problems may still plague climbers at much lower elevations. In this section, we focus on the challenges posed by climbing at altitude and provide some tips for maximizing acclimatization, improving performance, and avoiding illness. Finally, we briefly describe signs, symptoms, and treatment of acute mountain sickness and the more life-threatening conditions of high-altitude pulmonary edema and high-altitude cerebral edema.

Every climber's performance is reduced at altitude. This is true regardless of fitness, genetics, or acclimatization. Most people do not notice a real change below about 2000 meters (6500 feet), but the higher one climbs, the more performance suffers. The average, poorly acclimated climber is able to climb only about half as quickly at 5000 meters as at sea level. Acclimatization significantly lessens this effect, and it certainly aids enjoyment! It might even dictate whether you reach the summit.

Acclimatization is a complex interaction of changes in our bodies' chemistry and physiology. Some of these changes happen quickly and others take months. Acclimatization is a relative thing. It is a state your body moves toward but seldom achieves unless you take up residence at the target altitude. Most climbers take as little time to acclimate as they think they can get away with for their chosen project.

For example, nonacclimated climbers often devote a mere two days to climbing peaks well over 4000 meters, such as Mount Rainier in the Cascade Range. This is neither easy nor particularly pleasant, but people do it. For many, the cruel work habits of the weekend warrior preclude the luxury of ideal acclimatization. However, comfort, success rates, and risk management are all improved if one takes more time to acclimate.

Each person has a unique pattern of adjusting to altitude. It is important to learn your own pattern and take it into account when making time estimates for a climb at altitude. You can't really learn these things without experiencing them. The trick is to gain this experience in a deliberate and controlled way—one that still allows you to effectively manage risk. For example, as you explore the limits to your performance at altitude, do it on climbs from which you can easily descend (both emotionally and physically) should the problems be worse than you expect.

In order to acclimate to higher altitudes, we need to stress our bodies to induce change. Without enough stress, our bodies are slow to respond. With too much stress, we could succumb to various altitude illnesses, which can range from unpleasant to life-threatening. Below are some general guidelines for acclimating as efficiently as possible.

If you are coming from sea level, light exercise is helpful while you are acclimating, but avoid exerting to the point that your heart really pounds. Climb at a pace that allows conversation.

Most people do not need to worry about acclimatization when climbing peaks below about 4000 meters (13,000 feet) and sleeping no higher than 3000 meters (9800 feet). Although susceptible individuals can have problems at these elevations, they are rare.

For gradual, multiday acclimatization to higher elevations, your sleeping elevation is generally more important than the elevation to which you climb during the day. For most people, an efficient acclimatization strategy is to sleep at about 3000 meters and climb to about 4000 meters during the day. Do this for a couple of days and nights, then increase both sleeping and climbing elevations another 300 to 400 meters (1000 to 1500 feet) and repeat.

Sleeping at modest elevation, below about 2500 meters (8000 feet), doesn't much help with acclimatization, but you should avoid sleeping above about 3700 meters (12,000 feet) until you are at least a little acclimated. Even at this elevation, most nonacclimated climbers will experience altitude-related headache, loss of appetite, or insomnia.

Clinical studies indicate that the prescription drug acetazolamide is helpful to acclimate, and our personal experience supports this finding. It is particularly helpful if you do not have the time to acclimate properly as described above. Acetazolamide increases the rate and depth of respiration, particularly at rest. It seems to be most beneficial during sleep, when a naturally slower breathing rate means that you take in less oxygen, which can increase the likelihood of acute mountain sickness. Check with your physician to see if this drug is for you.

As you become acclimated, continue to climb and sleep at progressively higher elevations as needed. Avoid jumps of more than about 300 to 400 meters in sleeping elevation. If terrain forces a greater jump than this, spend at least a couple of nights at the previous, lower sleeping elevation before moving up. When you go for the summit, you can afford a big jump in elevation knowing you won't be sleeping up there.

Do not move to a higher sleeping elevation if you are experiencing moderate to severe headache, nausea, or periodic breathing during sleep (see below).

Several illnesses are associated with climbing at altitude. These include acute mountain sickness (AMS), high-altitude pulmonary edema (HAPE), and high-altitude cerebral edema (HACE). All are brought on by too rapid ascent to altitude. All can be prevented by thorough acclimatization. Each person is uniquely susceptible. Our genes, more than any other factor, govern our degree of susceptibility. These three illnesses are commonly thought to be related, so if you see or suspect one disease, keep an eye out for the others. For more information, see the bibliography.

Acute mountain sickness. AMS is a group of symptoms that include headache, insomnia, loss of appetite, and sometimes nausea and vomiting. It is more unpleasant than it is dangerous, but it is a critical sign of exceeding the body's ability to acclimate to a given altitude. Many physicians believe AMS is the first manifestation of cerebral edema, which can be fatal. AMS is common among climbers who ascend too quickly to altitude. It is quite common above about 4000 meters. It is much less common below 3000 meters.

A climber with severe AMS symptoms should move to a lower sleeping elevation if possible. With mild AMS, simply remaining at the same sleeping elevation is usually enough to resolve symptoms. A nonprescription analgesic, such as aspirin or ibuprofen, may reduce the headache. Acetazolamide has been shown to be moderately effective in reducing symptoms and helping with acclimatization. A person with symptoms of AMS should not take medications or drugs that might depress respiration. This includes alcohol, sleeping pills, or most strong pain medications. If symptoms are mild during a climb, it may be reasonable to continue on to a summit if you know that significant descent will soon follow.

Periodic breathing. Also called Cheyne-Stokes respiration, this is a frequent phenomenon during sleep at altitude, before you are well acclimated. Typically as you drop off to sleep, you take several deep breaths and then stop breathing for a short time, then resume breathing, often with a gasp and a panicky feeling of asphyxiation. This disrupts sleep, though in itself it is not harmful. Periodic breathing is caused by an imbalance in the relative amounts of oxygen and carbon dioxide in the blood stream. Again, acetazolamide is generally very effective in the treatment of this problem. Even a low dose of 125 mg at bedtime can help.

High-altitude pulmonary edema. HAPE is the leakage of fluid into the alveoli of the lungs. If the condition is untreated, the fluid prevents the transfer of oxygen into the bloodstream and the victim eventually "drowns." Fortunately, HAPE is rarely seen on peaks below about 5000 meters. Less fortunately, its onset can be surprisingly rapid, and immediate action must be taken to treat it. Besides bottled oxygen or a hyperbaric chamber, descent is the only practical treatment. In most cases, as little as 1000 meters is effective. In emergencies, the prescription drug nifedipine may be useful in reducing the severity of the disease and can aid in evacuation. Thorough acclimatization is the best way to reduce the chance of HAPE. Some individuals find that they are more susceptible than others, frequently through a frightening experience with the disease. Signs and symptoms include:

- breathlessness at rest
- markedly reduced ability to walk uphill
- persistent cough, sometimes dry
- greater ease in breathing while sitting up than while lying down
- rales—crackling noises in the lungs—faint at first, becoming louder as HAPE worsens
- increased pulse and respiration rates at rest
- other AMS symptoms combined with suspicion of HAPE

High-altitude cerebral edema. HACE is another altitude-related illness that is usually fatal if left untreated. It is thought to be less common than pulmonary edema but is more difficult to diagnose. With HACE, fluid leaks from the capillaries in the brain into the enclosed space of the skull. Intracranial pressure increases and eventually disrupts brain function. As with HAPE, good acclimatization reduces the chance of HACE, and descent is also the best treatment. The steroid dexamethasone has been shown to be helpful in emergency treatment. Signs and symptoms include:

- severe headache, unrelieved by nonprescription analgesics
- ataxia (loss of balance or coordination)
- nausea or vomiting
- personality changes or combativeness
- changes in level of consciousness
- other AMS or HAPE symptoms combined with suspicion of HACE

ALTITUDE ILLNESS: A LEARNING EXPERIENCE

An example from our own experience may help to illustrate the challenge of decision making and the importance of quick action with altitude illness in general and HAPE in particular. Several years ago, we were guiding two other climbers up a 5800-meter (19,000-foot) peak in the Andes and making successive camps; Camp 1 was at 4300 meters (14,500 feet), Camp 2 at 4900 meters (16,000 feet), and Camp 3 at 5100 meters (17,000 feet). We moved up to sleep at Camp 2, having already made a carry there and having spent a total of three nights at Camp 1. One of our party was moving very slowly, but since he had also moved quite slowly on the previous carry day and seemed well acclimated to Camp 1, we were not overly concerned. He ate dinner with a reasonable appetite, and we all turned in early to sleep, he in a tent with one other person.

At about 10:00 we noticed that he was coughing. By midnight it seemed worse, and we went over to check on him. He was sitting up, reading by his headlight, and we could hear roughness in his breathing from several feet away. He assured us he felt fine as long as he sat upright rather than lying down. This raised our concern still higher. We told him we suspected HAPE and that he should prepare to go down to Camp 1 with us. He seemed surprised, but he complied. As he prepared to leave, he realized that there was in fact something wrong; he was having a great deal of difficulty coping with the task of dressing himself, especially getting his boots on.

We descended through the night, taking several hours to cover terrain that would ordinarily take about 45 minutes. Every few minutes, our friend had to sit down and breathe. Fortunately, he was able to walk under his own power; since the terrain was fairly steep and he was very tall and sturdily built, it would have required a larger team than ours to carry him. Also fortunate was the fact that on the way up, Mark had scouted out and marked an easier route than the one we normally took. This new route avoided terrain on which we surely would have had to belay and lower our friend in the darkness, and this saved us valuable time. Back in Camp 1, our friend recovered quite a bit and continued to improve over the next couple of days of supervised rest.

This experience reinforced for us several points: HAPE and HACE can come on quite quickly, and HAPE in particular often worsens at night. An hour or two of delay can make the difference between a simple evacuation of a patient who can still walk and a complicated and dangerous evacuation of a victim who needs to be dragged or carried. When HAPE or HACE are suspected, rapid and conservative action may be called for, especially on difficult terrain or with a small party. HAPE or HACE sufferers are not reliable in diagnosing or monitoring their condition alone—if HAPE or HACE are suspected or severe AMS symptoms are present, sufferers should never be left unsupervised for long. The group should by no means go on to the summit if it means leaving a suspected victim alone!

Terrain difficulty can influence options for evacuation of a sick person. When moving to higher sleeping elevations, consider the difficulty of descent, and assess your party's state of acclimatization more conservatively when the terrain is more committing.

Frostbite

Frostbite is frozen tissue and results from exposure to subfreezing temperatures. Damage is caused primarily by obstruction to circulation after thawing, which results in oxygen not reaching rewarmed tissue.

By far the most useful advice we can give about frostbite is how to avoid it. First, keep your torso warm to maintain circulation to extremities. When you are chilled, your body shuts down circulation to extremities, greatly increasing the chance of frostbite. Second, pay constant attention to your feet and hands. If they are cold, put on another jacket or a hat, get moving, wiggle your toes strenuously, loosen your boots, keep your hands low to increase circulation (shorten or put away your trekking poles), have a bite to eat, and, if possible, put on warmer gloves. Numbness is a danger sign that calls for immediate action.

Once tissue begins to freeze, it usually looks rather horrendous (hard and white or purple); protect the area from further damage and descend. It is best to have a medical professional rewarm the tissue in carefully controlled conditions, but in most climbing situations the tissue will rewarm by itself during descent. Blisters may develop. Treat these very gently. Avoid popping or draining the blisters at least until you can get to medical help. Infection is a big worry.

Sometimes exposed areas of thin skin, such as the tip of the nose, the outer edge of the ears, or the cheeks may freeze very lightly. They turn chalky or white and numb but still feel soft to the touch. If these are covered up, they almost always rewarm quickly, with little or no lasting effect. In cold, windy weather, partners should check each other's faces for small white patches and warm them by covering.

Hypothermia

Hypothermia occurs when the body's temperature drops below normal range. The first symptoms of mild hypothermia—shivering and fumbling—should never be ignored. As the condition progresses, other symptoms that can be expected include apathy and impaired mental function—clearly undesirable on a hard climb.

One of the things that makes hypothermia so dangerous is that as we get colder, we have more and more difficulty doing the things necessary to reverse the condition: find or build shelter, brew a hot drink, get out of wet clothes and into dry ones, or simply eat some food and keep moving. This is why prevention is so vitally important. Stay dry. Wet clothes are bad news. If you can't keep dry on the climb, be sure you have some dry clothes in your pack, and keep them dry while packed. Avoid sweating, a preventable cause of wet clothing. Eat something. This is especially important if you are not moving. Digesting food takes energy, and this helps to warm you while fueling your internal fires.

Look ahead. Are you moving from sun to shade? From sheltered gully to windy ridge? From moving together to belayed climbing? What changes are coming up in your environment and in your level of activity? Anticipate these changes, and plan necessary clothing changes before you get cold.

Overexposure to Sun

High altitude and bright reflection off snow greatly intensify ultraviolet (UV) radiation. Watch out on days of thin misty cloud cover, when the sky is blue not far above you. A long alpine career includes a tremendous amount of UV exposure, entailing risk of snow blindness and sunburn in the short term and skin cancer over the long term. Fortunately, sunglasses and sunscreens get better and more effective each year.

Use a sunscreen with a high—at least 25—sun protection factor (SPF), and apply it before you become exposed. Be sure to hit those tricky, not-so-obvious spots: the ears, the forehead above the eyebrows but below the helmet, the neck and chin when traveling on snow and ice because the light reflects upward. Use clothing as part of your protective strategy. A light cotton shirt with a collar not only looks natty but is comfortable in hot weather as well. Just be sure you have a noncotton layer to change into if the weather gets worse.

Snowblindness, which is painful and debilitating, can begin within minutes in bright sunlight on snow or even in bright fog or light overcast. Losing your glasses can force you to abandon a climb. See Chapter 3, Preparation and Equipment, for specific advice on eyewear.

MOUNTAIN WEATHER

There are two things a climber needs to know about the weather: what it is going to do and how it will affect the experience of the climb. This section discusses forecasting from an alpinist's perspective—out in the hills based solely on what you see and feel. We then offer some tips about climbing in storms—why and how to do it.

FORECASTING

There are two main sources of information about what the weather is going to do: outside sources, such as weather reports, phone calls to friends, and talking to other climbers; and your own observations. Your final self-made forecast will be a combination of both these sources.

In this age of information, there are innumerable sources of forecasts—the Internet, posted local forecasts, recorded telephone forecasts, National Oceanic and Atmospheric Administration (NOAA) weather radio in the United States—as well as more personal sources such as local officials, hut keepers, and friends. All of these sources have the great advantage of enabling you to analyze weather that is not immediately visible to you. All have the disadvantage of offering forecasts either for a general area or for someplace where you are not. All have varying degrees of reliability and relevance. So how do you balance all this? First, learn what information is available, then decide what you think will be most useful to you. Finally, compare these forecasts to what actually happens on the hill. Only by doing this last step can you really determine the value of your information sources.

Despite its great variability, most

weather tends to follow a few fairly predictable patterns. By understanding the typical evolution of these patterns and their movements through time and space, you can gain an understanding of your geographical position relative to those movements. This helps you to anticipate likely future developments.

Lifting

Precipitation, be it rain or snow, is caused by the condensation of water vapor. Water vapor condenses as air cools, because colder air can support less moisture than warmer air. Air cools largely because it is rising—it is "lifting." There are four main things that cause air to rise: orographic lifting, when air is forced by wind to rise over a mountain; convective lifting, when air rises because it is warmer and hence more buoyant than the surrounding air (like a hot air balloon); cyclonic lifting, when air spiraling into the middle of a low-pressure zone rises into the upper atmosphere; and frontal lifting, when an air mass is pushed up over another heavier (usually colder) air mass. Each of these mechanisms leads to a different precipitation and weather pattern. In order to understand the pattern you are in, you must figure out which of these four causes is the culprit. Just to complicate things, often several causes are acting at once.

Convective lifting. This is the cause of afternoon cloud buildup, thunderstorms, and other usually temporary nasties. Convective lifting is caused by instability in the atmosphere. The atmosphere is more stable when relatively warm, light air lies on top of colder, heavier air. Any parcel of air warmer than the surrounding air will rise, driven by convection. Given enough moisture, clouds will form as this rising air cools, and precipitation will occur. The necessary conditions for convective clouds are differential heating of the atmosphere (usually driven by hot sun on dry ground), adequate moisture, and lack of high winds, which tend to blow apart these rising columns of air.

Convective clouds usually follow a daily cycle. They form in response to warming by the sun, develop during the heat of the day, and usually dissipate in the cool of evening. Typically, such clouds form at moderate altitudes in an otherwise blue sky, appearing as "friendly," puffy cumulus with distinct edges. If you watch them carefully, you can see them rising into the sky. The air around the rising columns of clouds gently subsides, moving down and warming, keeping it free of clouds.

Another common source of convective clouds is the passage of a cold front, as cold air pushes warmer air out of the way. In a cold front, the boundary between the air masses is often very unstable and chaotic, occasionally with relatively warmer air trapped under colder air. As it rises, warmer air finds itself surrounded by colder air above, and it keeps on rising. All this lifting causes clouds and rain. The passage of a cold front is usually quick. The air behind it is drier and colder. Blue skies return, though it can be windy.

In the mountains, the type of solid

precipitation normally associated with convective lifting is **graupel**—small rounded pellets that form as tiny water droplets (rime ice) freeze directly on the snowflake surface. Rising and falling air currents in convective clouds carry snowflakes up and down, giving them lots of opportunity to accumulate ice. Be particularly on the lookout for lightning when you see graupel, as all this vertical movement in the clouds builds up an electrical charge.

Orographic lifting. Moving air must rise whenever it encounters such an unavoidable obstacle as a mountain; this is orographic lifting. In rising, it cools. If the air contains enough moisture, it will condense into clouds and possibly rain.

Orographic lifting is predictable; the mountains are always there, so anytime there is wind, there will be lifting. Whether or not this produces clouds depends on the moisture content of the air. Cloud forma-

Cumulus (convective) clouds building in the Alps. These clouds thickened and produced some rain in the late afternoon but dissipated quickly in the early evening. Solar heating on the east and south sides of the Matterhorn drives the convection forming the large cloud. The perfectly clear blue sky between clouds suggest that tomorrow's weather will be much like today's.

Lenticular clouds in Patagonia. A nasty storm arrived a day later.

tion is therefore a useful clue alerting you to otherwise invisible changes in moisture content and in wind direction and speed—factors that signal weather changes to come. For example, lenticular (lens-shaped) clouds forming over summits tell you several things: first, moisture content is increasing and wetter air is heading your way; second, there is wind aloft, and by carefully examining the forming clouds, you can determine its direction and relative speed, which can help you predict the arrival of cyclonic and frontal lifting. In general, building lenticulars indicate deteriorating weather.

However, though the appearance of lenticulars usually indicates high winds, it does not *always* indicate them, as many climbers mistakenly believe. Often on summits we have been engulfed in lenticulars with only a gentle breeze blowing. Watching the ghostly formation and dissipation of a cloud only a few feet above your head, like a phantom spirit in the sky, is an amazing sight. In very high winds, lenticulars may be distorted and torn apart, especially on the downwind side of the cloud, as turbulence disrupts the normally laminar flow of the air over the summit. We call these "claw clouds," partly because of their shape and partly because the threatening image the name evokes is almost always justified by the weather that rapidly follows.

Orographic lifting creates a rainshadow effect: wetter on the windward side of a mountain range and drier on the leeward side. This effect is most pronounced in mountain ranges oriented north to south, thus perpendicular to the prevailing bad-weather wind direction, such as the Cascades and Sierra Nevada in the United States, the British Columbia Coast Range in Canada, the Patagonian Andes of South America, and the Southern Alps in New Zealand. The European Alps, by contrast, run roughly east to west and therefore are positioned endwise to many approaching storms. As a result, they have much less pronounced dry and wet sides. However, even there, storms often approach from slightly to the north or south. If you can learn a storm's path, you might be able to flee to the lee side in search of better weather. At the very least, your under-standing of orographic lifting can help you predict the intensity of precipitation for your location, should bad weather arrive.

Cyclonic lifting. Both cyclonic and frontal lifting stem from the interaction of areas of high and low air pressure. Under-standing a bit about highs and lows will enable you to predict how these forms of lifting will affect you.

Very large air masses cover the globe, each extending for hundreds of kilometers. They are more or less homogenous in temperature and moisture content. They tend to keep to themselves—those over the equator tend to stay there, and ones in the middle latitudes and polar areas also remain aloof. When an air mass brushes up against a neighboring one with different temperature and moisture characteristics, a storm usually results. This discussion is concerned primarily with the middle latitudes (from about 30° to 60° north or south latitude), where the tropical air masses meet the polar air masses. These are the latitudes most of us live and climb in, and this is where we find most of the type of climbing this book covers.

The line of demarcation between tropical and polar air masses, called the Polar Front (see Figure 2), is the spawning ground for the cyclonic storms that dominate the weather in these latitudes. Areas of low pressure are born as warm air nudges toward the pole (or cold air toward the equator), causing the warm air to rise up over the cooler air. The coriolis force (a product of the rotation of the earth) causes lows to rotate in a counterclockwise direction in the northern hemisphere and clockwise in the southern. Likewise, areas of high pressure rotate clockwise in the north and counterclockwise south of the equator. The gently spiraling lows march eastward along the boundaries between the air masses (generally following the line of the jet stream, which usually defines these boundaries). Each low contains a center of slowly rising air—this is cyclonic lifting. Cyclonic lifting is quite gentle and slow, but it is enough to bring clouds and light precipitation. Usually the moist air of the low being forced over the mountains in orographic lifting causes much more precipitation.

Because lows rotate counterclockwise (in the northern hemisphere) and also travel generally west to east, most of the time there is plenty of warning of their arrival. Look for the following signs to help in your forecasting:

■ Watch for changes in wind direction. When the wind shifts to the southwest in the northern hemisphere (or the northwest in the southern), a change for the worse is afoot. Think of a low as a giant rotating wheel of weather slowly passing overhead, from west to east. Imagine how the apparent direction of motion, when viewed from underneath, will change as it passes your location.

On the other hand, as a low passes on to the east, winds usually swing around

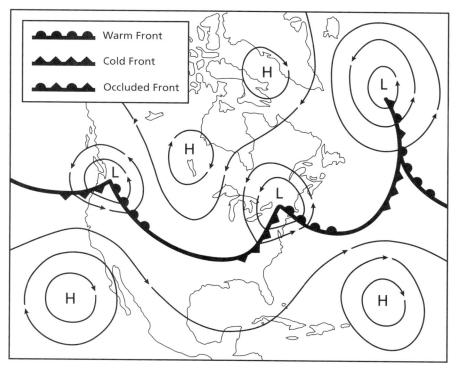

Figure 2. *The Polar Front, dividing the polar air masses to the north and the tropical air masses to the south. The isobars circling the lows and highs closely define the wind direction at altitude. Wind speeds will be highest where isobars are close together. Circulation is opposite in the southern hemisphere.*

to the northwest (or southwest down under). This is a good sign of improving weather. Gauge wind direction from high clouds if you can, not those tucked in among the peaks and valleys. Mountains funnel low-level winds in odd directions, so these are not always a true indicator of wind direction aloft.

- High clouds are a common warning of an approaching low. If the low passes far to the north of you (in the northern hemisphere), you may never see anything more than a few high clouds. Consider yourself lucky. But if high clouds continue to thicken and your barometer drops significantly, the low is probably heading your way.

- Air pressure will drop with the approach of a low. Use your barometer/altimeter (see Tips sidebar) to confirm the arrival of a low and also to sense when it is passing.

TIPS: INTERPRETING BAROMETRIC PRESSURE CHANGES

When tracking weather trends, millibars—also called hectoPascals (hPa)—are more useful as a unit of measurement than inches of mercury. Most people find them mentally simpler to conceptualize and remember, and they are the standard used by meteorologists on weather maps. Average air pressure at sea level is about 1013 millibars. A change of 1 millibar is equivalent to a change of about 10 meters (33 feet) of elevation. Use wind direction aloft to support your barometer-based forecasts.

- Pressure rising (or elevation dropping) more than 6 hPa (60 meters) in 12 hours: the weather is rapidly improving, probably with moderate to high winds and cold temperatures.

- Pressure rising more than 3 hPa (drop in elevation reading of 30 meters) in 12 hours: expect slowly improving weather.

- Pressure steady, not rising or rising to 1 hPa (0 to 10 meters) in 12 hours: expect no change. The weather is likely to keep doing whatever it is currently doing.

- Pressure dropping (or elevation rising) more than 3 hPa (30 meters) in 12 hours: weather is slowly deteriorating. It may be hard to predict how bad it will get, but you will probably know more within a day or two.

- Pressure dropping more than 6 hPa (rise in elevation reading of 60 meters) in 12 hours: weather is rapidly deteriorating. Expect increased winds and precipitation within 12 hours.

Lows, stacked up one behind the other on the Polar Front, often bring storm after storm with only a day or two of respite between bouts of nastiness. The distance between lows on their eastward march is hard to judge from our view on the ground. In order to determine how long a break you will have between lows, look for wind direction up high and the amount of high clouds, as well as the amount of rise in barometric pressure. When the weather begins to clear and you get a few sunny breaks, this is your chance to gauge wind direction aloft and to look for more high clouds. If the sky is clear and blue between the lower clouds, then good weather is coming. If there are still high clouds visible above and they are moving in from the southwest (or the northwest in the southern hemisphere), the clearing will most likely be very brief indeed.

On the lee side of some mountain ranges, such as the Rockies in both Canada and the United States, we occasionally find poor weather coming upslope, from the east. This is caused by the "backward" circulation of a low passing to the south. Though these upslope storms can be intense (and surprising on the normally dry side of the range), they usually pass quickly and are followed by fine weather.

Frontal lifting. This happens when one air mass pushes another out of its way. If the air doing the pushing is warmer than the air being pushed (as in a warm or occluded front, described below), it slides gently over the cooler air, pushed upward as it goes by the wedge of colder air below. The warmer air cools as it rises, condensing into clouds with likely rain or snow. In a cold front, the lifting is much more abrupt and chaotic. The pushing cold air forms a very blunt wedge, bullying and shoving the displaced warmer air as it goes.

Fronts

As you can see in Figure 2 above, fronts extend outward from the center of the areas of low pressure. In the early stages of frontal development, a cold front extends to the west of the center and a warm front to the east. These rotate slowly around the center like spokes on a wheel. The cold front almost always moves much faster than the warm front, usually catching up to it, overriding it, and occluding it. By the time the cold front has rotated about 120 degrees from its original position west of the low, the low begins to become separated from the Polar Front, fills up, and peters out, becoming less of a worry to us.

In truth, your main concern is not so much with the various cold, warm, or occluded fronts associated with the low; it is the presence of the low itself—the combination of cyclonic and orographic lifting creates plenty of bad weather. But understanding and recognizing the characteristics of warm, cold, and occluded fronts gives you a better handle on what is coming next.

Warm fronts. The warm front normally extends southeast from the center of the low in the northern hemisphere and to its northeast in the southern hemisphere. It forms where the warm air of the tropical air mass overrides the cold air of the polar air mass. Because warm air is lighter than cold, and also because these fronts move relatively slowly, the actual line of the front forms a very gentle slope, a shallow wedge of warm air pushing and being lifted over the top of the cold. We normally get plenty of advance warning of the arrival of a warm front; in fact, the approaching warm front is our first visual clue of the coming low, and the early signs are the same as those mentioned for cyclonic lifting, above: wind direction change, high clouds, and falling air pressure.

As the warm front approaches, high

clouds thicken, midlevel clouds increase, and eventually it will start to precipitate. Once precipitation starts, it is fairly continuous, not overly violent—a dull, drizzly sort of day. Cloud cover is usually 100 percent.

Cold fronts. A cold front marks the passage of the low-pressure system, with better weather soon to come. As cold air displaces warmer air, the contact surface dividing the air masses is very steep, close to vertical near the ground—much steeper than in a warm front. This leads to instability in the atmosphere. The instability creates convection and hence the squally weather that accompanies cumulus clouds. With a cold front, expect sometimes intense showers and gusty winds with alternating sunny spells and precipitation. Graupel is common. Gradually the skies will clear, the temperature will drop, and the winds will shift to come more from the direction of the poles—northerlies in the northern hemisphere, southerlies in the southern hemisphere. Even after the passage of the cold front, when the low-pressure zone has moved east of you, temperatures may stay cool for a day or two and winds aloft high, especially in fall and winter.

Occluded fronts. Because the trailing cold front moves faster than the leading warm front, part of the cold front (starting with the section nearest the center of the low) may overtake, or occlude, the warm front. This is a particularly common phenomenon on the west coast of the United States and Canada, from the British Columbia Coast Range to the Sierra Nevada. Here, cyclonic storms brewed in the North Pacific have had good opportunity to mature before they reach land. Occluded fronts usually look and behave much like warm fronts, and it is difficult to tell one from the other. The good news is that you don't need to. Both show similar patterns as they pass, and both result in clearing weather after they have moved east. An occluded front will exhibit less showery or squally weather as it clears, changing from overcast to gradually clearing without going through the chaotic turmoil of a trailing cold front. By the time you figure out that the front happened to be occluded (or not), it will already be clearing; time to head outside again!

Winds

The wind patterns already mentioned above are those associated with the large-scale circulation of highs and lows and the gusty winds of convective lifting. Other breezy events of interest to alpinists are catabatic winds and foehn, or chinook, winds.

Catabatic wind. This descends down slopes and valleys driven by the force of gravity. Cold air is denser and heavier than warm air and will flow downhill by virtue of its relative weight. We commonly find catabatic winds on glacial slopes and large valley glaciers on warm days, where cold ice and snow chill the overlying air. Usually if you can get just a short way above the trough of the valley, such as on a rock outcrop or a bit up on the side of a valley, you will find calmer and warmer air and a better camping spot.

Foehn wind. Also called chinooks in

the Pacific Northwest, foehn winds are strange beasts; they have been accused of causing all sorts of odd, generally antisocial behavior in humans and other species. Whether or not they actually affect our psyches, they are an interesting phenomenon and one worth understanding because they illustrate some characteristic properties of air as it rises and descends. Notably warm and gusty, foehn winds form on the lee side of a mountain range as bad weather pushes over it. The warmth of the foehn is due to the difference between (1) the rate that the air cools as it is pushed up and over the windward, wetter side of the range and (2) the rate at which it warms during its descent on the leeward side.

A rising parcel of dry air cools at about 10°C for every 1000 meters it rises. This is called the dry adiabatic lapse rate. If its moisture content does not change, it will warm at the same rate on descent. However, if the moisture content is high enough, as the air rises water vapor will condense into cloud and rain will fall. The condensation from vapor to the tiny liquid water droplets of clouds releases latent heat—remember your high school physics? This release of heat changes the lapse rate; now it will cool at the wet adiabatic lapse rate of about 5.4°C for every 1000 meters of elevation change. The rain has effectively removed some of the moisture from the air and put it on the ground. As the air begins to descend on the lee side of the range, it contains less moisture. It therefore warms at the dry lapse rate. The result is a descending parcel of air that is considerably warmer than it was when ascending on the windward side.

Foehn winds can melt snow at a prodigious rate, cause streams to rise, and, some claim, make us all rather irritable. The good thing about a foehn wind is that you know that the weather on the lee side will be dry, even if it is still gusty and partly cloudy. The bad news is that foehn winds usually precede worsening weather, even on the lee side.

Note that you can use the adiabatic lapse rates to help predict temperatures at other elevations. If it is cloudy or raining, apply the wet adiabatic lapse rate; apply the dry adiabatic lapse rate if it is not.

CLIMBING IN STORMS

"Why risk going out in a storm?" you might ask. Several reasons come to mind.

First, storms are amazing things, and mountains in their grip are at once beautiful and awesome, full of energy and wildness. Nature shows its formidable power, and taking a moment to feel it gives us some of that energy and strength to bring home with us. Such an experience is a brutal but healthy reminder of where we stand in this great and amazing universe.

A second reason is the concept presented earlier: putting yourself in a position to be lucky. Many times climbers miss a potentially great climbing outing simply because the forecast was uncertain. If you don't go, you'll never know. But remember the other half of this concept: don't put yourself in a position where you need to be lucky. The history of climbing is littered with terrible accidents due in part to bad weather. Go for it, but be smart!

Last, even if we try our hardest to dodge nasty weather, eventually we will be caught out. To avoid becoming a statistic, you must learn what you can and cannot expect to accomplish when the weather goes south. You learn this by going outside.

Adjust Your Objectives

When we dream of climbs, we think of great feats of daring on difficult routes. The smart climber matches route difficulty with abilities in order to get the most out of the sport. When the weather goes bad, we need to change our definition of difficult and not be apologetic about it. We need to let go of those dream climbs and think of challenge in the context of the actual conditions outside.

Whether you find yourself already in the mountains when bad weather arrives and need to choose an alternative objective or you just want to climb something in the weather for the educational experience, keep in mind the following points:

- In evaluating an objective, consider the type of climb. Snow and ice routes are less affected by more snow or rain falling from the sky than are rock routes. On rock routes, rock type makes a difference. Limestone, for example, is less slippery when wet than most other rock types. But all rock routes get exponentially harder when covered with new snow—holds are hidden and, let's face it, snow is slippery stuff.
- In wet weather, simply staying warm can be a challenge, so routes that keep

STORMS: A MATTER OF OPINION

Years ago, we were camped in our tiny tent in a howling blizzard at the foot of Scotland's Ben Nevis, not far from the sturdy stone climbers' hut. Snug in our down bags, we were oh-so-comfortably warm while the storm raged outside. As we snuggled down, happily sipping hot tea and deciding not to go do a route that day, a voice broke through the howling wind: "You're bloody crazy to be campin' out in this shite!" It was a climber from the hut, crampons crunching by as he walked off to do battle on the hill. "Who is the crazy one?" we wondered.

Well, you could say we are all crazy in our own way. Getting a reservation in that particular hut takes years of planning. Our heroic friend was damned if he was going to waste a precious day moping around indoors. He simply adjusted his objective to meet his need to get out. We, on the other hand, were not constrained by such absurdities as hut reservations, and with a whole winter's vacation ahead of us (often one has either time or money), we decided a lie-in was in order.

Everybody was right. We were happy as clams in our tent, and we imagine he had a fine day out, slogging up some snowy gully in the blizzard.

you moving are preferred. If your climb has a technical section requiring belaying (and waiting), it is better if this happens earlier in the day while you are dry, rather than later, when you may be soaked. Beware of unknowns that might force you to stop and get chilled.

■ In clouds, routefinding becomes difficult. How difficult it is will be determined mostly by your memory, your observation skills, and the distinctiveness of the terrain features you can see. Open snowfields or snow-covered glaciers with few crevasses present few features to remember. Choose routes with bits and pieces you can see and remember, connecting the dots as you find your way home.

■ In blowing snow, tracks and even entire trails can become obscured. Judge how much you will be relying on tracks, either your own or previous existing ones, then pay attention to the wind and snowfall intensity. Time your descent so you still have those aids before the window of opportunity slams shut.

Dress for the Conditions

When dressing to head out in the storm, think of this: it is vastly more important to stay dry than to stay warm. At first this may seem ridiculous, but if you are dry it is easy to warm up—eat a snack, add a layer, and get moving. When you're wet, you chill quickly and lose an immense amount of energy to the water in your clothes. In the face of inclement weather, beginning climbers too often layer on the insulation, topping it off with a waterproof shell. This leads to overheating and sweating. Before long, they are as wet as if they had done nothing, with the added disadvantage of now having lots of wet clothes.

Choose clothes that breathe well, and avoid putting on your rain jacket before you are sure it is seriously raining. You may get wetter from condensation and overheating than you would from a few drops of rain or minutes of drizzle. Consider using an umbrella when hiking, if it is not too windy.

PRESERVING THE ALPINE ENVIRONMENT

Many alpine areas might see no other human visitors, apart from us climbers. Our passage leaves a trace, however imperceptible it may seem to us at the time, and our sheer numbers gradually multiply the impact. Higher-elevation environments are fragile—soils are thin and poor and growing seasons are short, so plant growth is extremely slow. Alpine flora is easily destroyed by footfalls and campsites and is slow to recover. Wildlife can be disturbed by our presence or, worse, attracted to our food and garbage. We can't completely eliminate our impact, but we can lessen its severity.

Alpine climbing takes place predominantly on publicly owned lands such as national parks or other preserves. Use may be highly regulated and in many cases severely restricted. It is very much in the self-interest of alpinists to ensure that regulation of mountaineering is as reasonable and minimal as possible. Our own behavior as climbers makes such regulation either more necessary or less. Thoughtless practices on the part of some climbers have subjected the entire community to an often-negative image among land managers and the public, resulting in increasingly burdensome regulations and even prohibitions. We can do much to avoid such restriction to our activity by proactive self-regulation.

Learn and follow all regulations. Environmentally sensitive climbing practices protect the wilderness and our own right to climb on public lands. Climbers increasingly work hard to preserve access rights. Do not threaten that effort! Preservation efforts require both personal awareness and group action; preservation efforts have two goals:

- to protect the value of the resource into the future
- to allow other visitors the best possible experience of the mountains

In this section we focus on minimum impact practices on the route itself and during the off-trail portions of the approach. We assume that the reader will learn and practice minimum impact wilderness practices while traveling and camping in wilderness, but we do not cover these here. For a more thorough and systematic discussion of minimum impact principles, please refer to "Leave No Trace"

publications available through the National Outdoor Leadership School and the U.S. Forest Service (see the bibliography).

MINIMUM-IMPACT CLIMBING

Party size. Keep your party small. Large groups intensify social impacts. Smaller parties spread out over a larger distance and interact less with each other. This reduces noise and overall impact.

Route marking. Climbers like to mark their routes in various ways, nearly all of which are damaging. Do not use temporary route markers such as wands, surveyors tape, or plastic bags. These inevitably are left behind as litter. Blazes damage trees. Cairns tend to proliferate and become less than useful as numerous parties express different opinions about where the best route might be. On snow and glacier routes, use a GPS to mark waypoints, rather than leaving wands behind as route markers (see Chapter 4, Routefinding and Navigation).

Local regulation and practice. Local climbing communities establish certain environmental traditions and ethics in the process of developing routes. Out of respect for them, learn about and follow local practices and standards.

Anchors. On rappel descents, clean up bulky anchors choked with useless old webbing. Carry such waste off the climb. Put slings around trees rather than running your rope around them. This prevents damage to the bark that will ultimately kill the tree. In some areas, new permanent anchors may be prohibited. Follow regulations.

Waste disposal. You've heard this one

since you were three years old: pack out all paper, waste food, and garbage. In some popular areas, garbage is a real eyesore; worse, it can attract critters, which become habituated, influencing their health and behavior in ways that threaten their survival.

HUMAN WASTE

The problem of poop deserves extra discussion because of the especially burdensome regulatory impact it can have on us as climbers. Careful wilderness pooping practices protect water from contamination, speed up decomposition, discourage animals from digging it up, and avoid disgust to other visitors—all extremely important issues not only for us but for land managers as well.

Failure to properly dispose of human waste has such a nasty impact on other visitors that in heavily used areas it has led to rules requiring visitors to carry poop out with them (so-called blue bagging). While arguably the only acceptable method in some extreme cases, blue bagging entails great hardship for climbers, especially on trips longer than a couple of days or on traverses where all gear must be carried up the climb and over the top. It adds a toxic, bulky, potentially delicate load to a pack already full of heavy climbing gear. Therefore it is particularly important to us as climbers to avoid the need for this requirement.

Do your part to delay the day when this is the only solution left to land managers! Think hard about where and how you dispose of your poop, and have a plan! The best method for dealing with our elimination needs depends on the climate, terrain, and season. Always use established backcountry toilets where available.

Cat holes. Digging cat holes is a good method where there is plenty of topsoil and vegetation. Make your hole 6–8 inches. deep. Cover it amply with dirt afterward. Cat holes should be widely dispersed and at least 200 feet away from water sources; walk a few minutes away from camp or take care of your needs during the day when you are elsewhere.

On snow, poop decomposes very slowly, so extra effort is needed to get away from heavily used areas and routes. If possible, avoid defecating on snow at all; search windward slopes or around rocks and trees for patches of dry ground where you can dig cat holes. Otherwise, use tree wells away from popular summer-use areas.

On glaciers, use a crevasse if you can access it safely. If you have no access to dirt or crevasses, dig a pit or trench at least 45 cm (18 inches) deep if possible, and bury it.

Smearing. In hot, dry climates or where topsoil is too limited for cat holes, you can smear fecal matter on flat rocks. Exposure to sun and wind decomposes it quickly. Smears must be even more carefully dispersed for social reasons and are appropriate only in very isolated, rarely visited areas. You may be able to find flat rocks to poop on and throw them off cliffs or down steep slopes to help disperse the smear, so long as you are absolutely sure that no person, route, or used area lies below.

Toilet paper. Do not bury toilet paper or feminine hygiene products anywhere in the wilderness: animals love to dig these up. Do not bury toilet paper in snow or chuck it into crevasses. The covering snow will melt or the toilet paper will blow out. On snow and glaciers, bagging and carrying toilet paper out is the only reasonable option.

Burning toilet paper is fine on rocky terrain, but pack out any bits that will not burn. Toilet paper burning tip: The key to complete combustion is to open it out and prod it with a stick to expose it all to air. Do not burn toilet paper in areas of wildfire potential; pack it out instead—it's small and doesn't weigh much. Double-bag it if necessary to contain odors. Bottom line: Do not leave toilet paper in the mountains.

SOCIAL IMPACTS

In popular climbing areas, consider the quality of your interactions with other climbers. You never know when you might need a friend in the mountains; climbers have a long-standing tradition of helping each other out. In any case, other climbers have as much right as you do to be there.

PASSING OTHER PARTIES

Passing another party in the mountains can be perfectly justifiable. If you are moving significantly faster, there is no good reason why you must wait. A slower pace could keep you out late, expose you to hazards, and eat up your margin for unforeseen . problems. Being first on an alpine route does not give anyone a right to keep others waiting, much less to keep others off a climb. As more people wish to enjoy the mountains, the need to coexist and share routes becomes all the more important.

When passing another party, take steps to avoid inconveniencing, endangering, or further slowing them down. On many routes, passing may be a simple matter of walking on by. However, on technical ground, especially on rock, where a route necessarily follows a specific line, a bit of strategy may be needed. Here are a few common-sense rules for passing in technical, belayed situations:

- Talk to the other party! Be polite and tactful and seek their cooperation, permission, or at least acquiescence. If you are moving a great deal faster than they are, they should understand your wish to pass.
- Be especially careful! No matter how skillful you are in passing, merely placing yourself above another party increases their risk. Any rocks or ice you knock down or objects you drop could hurt or even kill them.
- Interfere as little as possible with the other party. (1) Look for good passing opportunities. Take a slightly different line, pass as they take a break, or wait for easier terrain where you can shorten the rope and, moving together, quickly get around them. (2) Belay short of the usual anchor, if possible. Using a different belay stance gets you out of other climbers' station and sequence. If you are really efficient, you may be able to

make your transition to the next pitch and get above the other party before they have even completed their pitch.

BEING PASSED BY ANOTHER PARTY

If yours is the slower party, recognize the increased risk of having another party above you. There may not be much you can do about it, but look for opportunities to increase your security. Take another line if possible, find sheltered places for breaks and stances, consider belaying even if you otherwise might not, and put in extra protection when leading on ice.

When you are being passed, it is in your interest that the passing party get out above you as soon as possible. Do what you can to help: make room for others at your stance, allow them to clip in to your protection, help them with rope management.

PASSING AND BEING PASSED: FOCUS ON THE PROCESS

While climbing a bolted multipitch rock route in France once, I was overtaken by a French guide, obviously familiar and comfortable with the route, moving very quickly. He led the pitch I had just finished, unclipping my quickdraws from the bolts temporarily, clipping his quickdraws in to the bolts, and then clipping mine back in to the top carabiner of his. This allowed my second to clean the pitch easily with no confusion or crossing of ropes. Intrigued and impressed by this technique that was new to me, I took advantage of the situation to get a free lesson in seamless overtaking. It was a friendly and positive encounter.

—*Kathy Cosley*

CHAPTER 3

Alpamayo's southwest face, Cordillera Blanca, Peru

Preparation and Equipment

The focus of this chapter is on movement and what it takes to go as fast, as far, and as sure-footedly as is humanly possible. Our suggestions here fall into three areas: physical training and movement skills, planning, and equipment selection—and are all aimed at helping you move, move, move!

First of all, movement skills are at least as important as fitness. And among movement skills, scrambling ability is arguably even more important than technical climbing ability. In training for the mountains, it is tempting to focus on only steep, belayed rock and ice climbing, but in fact alpine climbing is typically only about 20 percent technical climbing on steep terrain.

Therefore, high-angle technical climbing ability is not enough. An alpinist must also be able to move gracefully and efficiently over the boulders, talus, scree, and technically easy but exposed rock or snow that make up about 80 percent of a typical alpine climb. When done well, this looks like mere walking, but in fact the skills involved are quite complex and require effort to develop. Small inefficiencies of movement add up to a great deal of wasted energy, which can cause even the fittest athletes to achieve below their potential. More important, lack of scrambling skill can cause missteps or require more belaying than would otherwise be necessary. These nontechnical movement skills seem so simple and mundane that most people underestimate the importance of working hard on them, but they are the foundation of success and safety. Fortunately, they improve quickly with practice. In the physical training section of this chapter, we offer tips and suggestions and point out some common problems.

Second, the right kind of research and

planning can help speed you along. Although mountains can be full of surprises, careful planning helps to avoid much wasted time and effort. In the route selection and planning sections of this chapter, we discuss choices and strategies to maximize success and learning.

Third, equipment and packing choices make a big difference. The best gear selection not only best matches the type of climb you are contemplating, it also reduces the weight of your load as much as possible while still fulfilling its intended purpose. For better or for worse, this means that the serious mountaineer will spend a significant amount of money on equipment! In the equipment section of this chapter, we discuss gear selectively, with special emphasis on features desirable for the alpinist.

PHYSICAL TRAINING

Training is most effective when it closely resembles the activity you're training for; obviously, the best training for climbing is to climb. Unfortunately, most of us can't get to the mountains every day or even every weekend. We need to design a training program that mimics the demands of climbing and incorporates the necessary movement skills as much as possible. Here we provide a few tips and an idea of where your emphasis should lie. For more detailed advice on developing a structured training regimen, see the bibliography. In general, you need to decide what your

areas of strength are regarding the requirements of the climbs you want to do, and work on your areas of weakness. It is much easier to bring up areas of weakness than to improve already good skills.

AEROBIC FITNESS

Even a very fit person unfamiliar with mountains can have trouble accurately imagining the nature of the difficulty and just what makes mountains so strenuous. The terrain is off-trail, rough, and often at high elevation. The level of exertion, though usually moderate at any given moment, is sustained for long hours on end. Add to this the weight of a pack, and it's clear that aerobic fitness, endurance, and leg strength are extremely important. In your aerobic training, emphasize activities that include balance and agility challenges and elevation gain, as much as possible. Brisk hiking or running on rough trails or off-trail, cross-country skiing, and ski touring are a few excellent examples. If you don't have access to hilly terrain near your home, climbing stairs or using a stairclimber in a gym can help with leg strength and aerobic fitness if you do it long and hard enough. Unfortunately, this does little for movement skills.

Some people like to climb hills or stairs with added weight in a pack. We advise caution with this strategy. Carrying more weight slows you down. The slower you walk, the less you challenge your balance and agility. Faster walking over rough ground trains these movement skills far more effectively. Also, the more weight you carry, the greater the stress on your joints and the more damage is done by a misstep, ankle twist, or fall. Go lighter; you will travel farther and faster for the same amount of time and have more fun! If you are one of those who really enjoy adding a bit of weight in the name of training, keep it to less than 30 pounds, and carry the weight as water so you can dump it on descent or at the first sign of strain.

MOVEMENT SKILLS

In our modern societies, most of us grow up and live the majority of our lives walking around on level or engineered surfaces such as floors, roads, ramps, and sidewalks. Our bodies don't learn to deal with the unstable and chaotic footing that is typical in the mountains. The following discussion focuses on training and movement issues specifically for scrambling, talus, scree, and rock climbing. Movement skills on snow, ice, and mixed terrain are discussed in greater detail in Chapter 6, Snow and Ice.

Scrambling

Skilled scramblers move fluidly and surely. They travel faster and cover more ground with less expenditure of energy. They have the confidence to face out while descending, which is faster and more efficient than facing in. Skilled scramblers are less afraid of falling, and for very good reason: they are less likely to fall. Poor scramblers spend so much effort on the approach that by the time they get to the steeper climbing, they have much less left energy to give to the endeavor.

Scrambling involves many different components: terrain evaluation, balance, confidence, agility (particularly in the ankles as they learn to be quicker and more sensitive in response to changes underfoot), muscular strength, and aerobic endurance. All of these improve quickly with practice and experience. But how can the average person, with a typical work schedule, family obligations, and varied interests in life, find opportunities to practice scrambling?

Start by spending daily workout time doing things that will help you improve balance, flexibility, and agility along with aerobic capacity. Trail running is particularly helpful. Depending on the terrain available to you, use a bit of imagination and a sense of adventure to vary your regimen: clamber up and down boulders; leave the trail; go the steep way; follow the ridge crest; try to go faster and farther. Hike up and down talus fields or dry rocky streambeds. Ski.

If you live in a truly flat city with no rough ground at all accessible to you, you can still choose activities that challenge your reflexes and balance: take up ice skating; play tennis, soccer, or racquetball instead of using a stationary bicycle or stair-climber—and use weekends and days off to get to more challenging terrain.

Although scrambling mileage and experience will develop this skill almost automatically, those of us who lack easy access to mountains must take a more conscious approach. Many of the suggestions below may seem obvious or mundane when described in such detail, but they address a handful of widespread and stubborn movement problems we commonly see people struggle with.

Take small steps. Smaller steps allows a smoother and more controlled weight transfer that improves traction on small footholds and makes loose rocks less likely to shift underfoot. Short steps decrease strain on the back and hamstrings and allow you to stand more upright and in balance. On descent, long steps can cause your trailing foot to hang up and pitch you forward.

Practice one-footed balance. When you lack faith in your balance, you tend to rush between foot placements. You are more likely to trip, miscalculate, or miss your target foothold; it is harder for you to control the force of your footfall or the distribution of your weight on loose or slippery ground. Develop the ability to stand on one foot for a long time (seconds!) between steps. Practice extreme slow-motion walking on the flats, on rough ground, on slopes, and especially on boulders (see **Improve boulder-walking skills,** below). Practice on a railroad track or a low balance beam; stretch or perform various exercises while standing on one foot—have a little fun.

Use trekking poles. Trekking poles are extremely helpful on off-trail approaches. This may seem to contradict our previous point about building balance, but it doesn't really. Even if your balance is very good, poles bring your arms into the act, enabling you to go faster with less struggle because you don't have to try as hard or be as precise. Poles help especially on rough ground, talus, small boulders, stream crossings, and chopped-up or sloppy snow.

Vary walking to match the terrain. The texture, steepness, and difficulty of the terrain will determine the most efficient approach at any given time. Experiment a bit to get a feel for what works best in different situations.

- Clean, dry rock provides good friction. Flatten your foot to put more rubber on the rock for the best grip. Use boots with flexible uppers to allow freedom of ankle movement.
- On hard but slippery surfaces—lichen- or snow-covered rock, wet or icy slabs, or wet grass—it may be best to spread weight evenly over the entire sole of the foot. Shift weight delicately and take tiny steps. Look for and step onto islands of security such as rougher textures, snow patches, roots, rocks, or dry spots.
- On hard or compacted dirt, frozen mud, or firm snow, aggressively kicking an edge can often provide the best security. When kicking an edge on steep, hard ground, get your foot level across the slope rather than pointing your toes upward, and sidestep up the hill (more on this in Chapter 6, Snow and Ice). This allows you to use the entire edge of your boot and to put some weight on your heel. Centering weight over your heel allows you to stand upright and in balance, which reduces strain on your calves and back.

Watch your step on talus, scree, and hard dirt. Plunging downhill in loose sand, gravel, scree, or even small talus can be a delight, much like plunge-stepping in soft snow. But a hard underlying surface may create a treacherous "ball bearing on a slate roof" effect.

- Take pains to avoid sand, dirt, gravel, or pebbles lying on any hard surface such as rock slabs or firm or frozen dirt and mud. Wherever possible, seek alternative routes and foot placements on clean rock, especially on descent. Because of the much better friction and security it provides, clean rock is usually preferable even if the "dirty" way looks easier or more tracked.
- Rocks poking up out of the dirt, sand, or gravel can serve as an anchor. On the way up, try to step on or just above these anchoring rocks, and balance your heel on them if you can. Going down, aim your footfalls to land so that the ball of your foot rests on or just above the rock.

Improve boulder-walking skills. For many aspiring alpinists, few things are more disconcerting or exhausting than working through a boulder field with a pack on, wearing stiff-soled mountaineering boots. If this describes your feelings, take heart; as skills improve, moving on boulders actually can become enjoyable, like a sort of daring dance. Many years ago, Sierra alpinist and legend Doug Robinson wrote a wonderful piece about the joys and benefits of running talus—one of the best pieces of mountaineering advice we have ever read and yet another reason why we have always so admired his insight and philosophy! Here are some tips for improving boulder-walking skill:

- Assess the stability of the boulder you are about to step on. With each step to a new boulder, look at how it sits on the ground, how many points of contact it has with its neighbors, etc. With just a little practice, your assessments will improve a lot. Some talus and boulder fields are more stable than others. Usually the more stable slopes are not very steep and have a bit of lichen growing on the rocks. Lichen grows slowly and it is usually a good indicator that the rock has not moved in a long time.
- If boulders are big and stable, consider stepping into the trough between neighboring ones rather than on top of a boulder itself for easier balance.
- Keep your boot soles dry and watch out for spots of water, dirt, gravel, or snow.
- Be wary of using trekking poles on boulders—they slip easily on the hard, angled surfaces. The temptation to weight them causes catastrophic loss of control when they do slip.

Rock Climbing

When it comes to high-angle rock climbing, nothing can duplicate the effectiveness of climbing itself for developing strength, kinesthetic knowledge, and experience. Weight training helps in some respects, but it is not enough. Rock climbing, even indoor on plastic holds, is much more effective. It develops balance, agility, flexibility, and strength, but even more important, it builds a repertoire of body positions and movements that allow you to quickly recognize possibilities and make fast decisions. Climbing gyms are increasingly common; most cities have at least one. Join, go two to three times a week, make friends, have a blast.

Be sure to give yourself adequate recovery time between sessions. Climbing hard every day can eventually lead to tendon injuries that could keep you off the rock for a long time. For more advice on how to develop rock-climbing skill, see the bibliography.

MENTAL PREPARATION AND PLANNING

Climbing is an adventure, and adventure is defined by unpredictability. Preparing for an ascent entails imagining what might possibly happen, both good and bad, and readying yourself and your equipment to face a range of possible futures. Despite the unknowns, you must gather information and make certain decisions before the climb in order to avoid unnecessary risks and mistakes.

ATTITUDE AND CONFIDENCE

Most climbers like a challenge. Though this is not necessarily the motivation for every climb—some we expect to be relatively easy, and we enjoy other aspects of that experience—still, most of us feel the need to occasionally choose climbs that we know will push us into new territory of mental or physical challenge and test our abilities to meet new demands. When you contemplate notching up the difficulty, do so with forethought and a deliberate, confident attitude. Your confidence needs to be based on reality—a realistic assessment of the skills you have systematically built.

Preparation enhances psychological well-being. We perform best when we are confident. We are confident when we feel equal to a challenge, when we know more or less what to expect, and when we have made reasonable provision for the unexpected. But climbers also must accept a degree of uncertainty and relish the process of discovery. The only preparation for this is to cultivate an attitude of trust in yourself and openness to the unknown.

ROUTE SELECTION

Your choice of objective is the first decision you face in planning a climb. Most of us choose our climbs based more on emotion and less on logic—a good thing! Climbing is, after all, a personal journey. Recommended climbs may be known for a variety of qualities—a unique combination of challenges, purity of line, fantastic views, or aesthetic appearance. However, you must also consider such factors as conditions, appropriate season, difficulty, and matching the route to your party size and abilities.

Season and Condition

Seasonal and current conditions greatly affect the difficulty, hazards, and remoteness of a climb (see Chapter 6, Snow and Ice, and Chapter 7, Glaciers, for more on this topic). If a particular climb would be a challenge for you under perfect conditions, it may be unacceptably risky otherwise. For example, new snow on rock routes makes the climbing many times harder, so most alpine rock routes are best done in the season of relatively warm and stable weather. Many ice face routes are in good shape in early summer or late spring, under the mantle of firm snow typical of that season, but become hard, gray ice sheets by mid- to late summer. Rockfall hazard can be negligible in cold weather or when snow covers a route, but horrendous once a warmer season or a hot day removes this protection.

Consider other climbers on your route to be an element of current conditions. Tracks in the snow can make things easier, but climber-induced rockfall is a serious hazard. Both season and weather affect the crowd factor.

Route Difficulty

All of us have our own unique set of skills, areas of strength, and weaknesses. Take these personal variations into account and select climbs whose challenges match your climbing and risk management abilities. Length, technical difficulty, routefinding complexity, objective hazard, commitment, remoteness—all these factors differ from one route to another. The variations are endless, and there is a climb for everyone.

Rating Systems

The Naming of Cats is a difficult matter,
It isn't just one of your holiday games;

You may think at first I'm as mad as a
*   hatter*
When I tell you, a cat must have THREE
DIFFERENT NAMES.

—*T. S. Eliot,*
Old Possum's Book of Practical Cats

Substitute "Rating of Climbs" for "Naming of Cats" and you'll get a good idea of the complexity of this messy subject! Actually, the situation is far worse than even the above excerpt might suggest. Many different mountain areas have their own unique system—the continental United States, Alaska Range, Canadian Rockies, and Eastern, Western, and Southern Alps are all different. Some of these systems, particularly the U.S. system as it has been used in the Lower 48, focus on technical rating and length alone and do not adequately describe important aspects of alpine difficulty. Other systems work fairly well, particularly those developed in the Western Alps (French), the Southern Alps (New Zealand), and the Canadian Rockies. When traveling from one area to another, you'll need to spend a bit of time acquainting yourself with the local rating system in use. In Appendix C, we describe some of these systems in greater detail.

Because of the variability and sometimes paucity of ratings information given by some systems and guidebooks, it is important to identify the type of information you need to accurately predict the difficulty of a climb and then to go out and find it. Below we list the type of information currently supplied with the latest generation of French guidebooks, because we feel that this system does a good job of adequately describing the difficulty of an alpine climb (see Appendix C).

- Overall level of seriousness, commitment, and hazards, including difficulty of getting protection, remoteness, difficulty of retreat, etc.
- Difficulty of hardest rock move (or sustained series of moves).
- Overall technical difficulty of the entire route. For example, a short, relatively simple climb containing a single very difficult pitch is easier, globally, than a longer, more complex route with less-difficult but more-numerous crux pitches.
- Steepness of ice or snow (expressed in degrees), or the ice grade if it is water-fall-like.
- Time required for a typical competent party (in hours).

Party Makeup and Size

Make sure the climb matches the abilities of the whole climbing party. The level of difficulty and hazards a group can successfully manage are governed by the individual attributes of its members. If the various skills needed for the ascent are spread among the group, then be sure the group sticks together!

For routes involving much technical or belayed climbing, a team of two moves faster than a larger team and can be safer on belayed terrain. If greater numbers are desired for additional security or rescue power, the best solution is to have two or more independent parties of two on each rope. For some very difficult climbs with many technically hard pitches, a team of three can work well, but this is the exception and requires a much higher skill level to be efficient. (See Mark Twight's *Extreme Alpinism* for more discussion of this technique.)

Other considerations for team size and composition in glacier travel are discussed in Chapter 7, Glaciers.

FORETHOUGHT AND RESEARCH

In preparing for an ascent, you must develop an image in your mind of the climb and the descent and how you will manage risk in its various parts. Start at the very beginning and walk through your trip in your imagination, considering every part in detail. If you are unsure about some aspects of the route, try to get more information. Think about where routefinding will be hard or what time you hope to be on the summit or back down again. Visualize changes in the snow as the day warms and how this might impact your pace or security. If you do a thorough job of preparation, the actual climb should more or less reflect what you visualized beforehand.

Study the guidebook. Good photos are particularly useful. Make copies of photos, topos, or complex information you want to remember. Talk to others who have done the route. Read accounts of the climb. Gather maps and identify the approach as well as your return route if it's not the same. Make sure you know the descent, and try to identify possible escape routes or bailout options.

If possible, find alternative climbs nearby in case your original choice turns out to be a bad idea at the last minute (weather, conditions, crowding, etc.). Find out as much as possible about the character of the climbing, and select your gear accordingly. Know the emergency response system available in the area and the appropriate procedures for contacting it. Decide what emergency communications or first-aid equipment you will bring with you and note any appropriate phone numbers or radio frequencies. Contact local land management authorities to learn whether or not you need a backcountry use permit or a hut reservation. Make a route plan.

THE ROUTE PLAN

A route plan is essentially a cheat sheet that helps you to make decisions beforehand and keep track of your progress once you're in the mountains. It is an extremely useful tool. First, plot out your line of travel in detail on a map (see Chapter 4, Routefinding and Navigation, for more detail on creating a whiteout travel plan). Divide your route into distinct stages between points such as key elevations, trail or stream junctions, or distinctive terrain features. Estimate distances between these points and the amount of time you will likely take to cover them. Once you are underway, this will help you to stay oriented, check your progress, and make timely changes to your plan if needed. Some very simple route plans can be committed to memory, but more often you will want to write things down on your map or carry photos, notes, drawings, or diagrams.

We often carry a small notebook with us in which we put our plan, photos, and route descriptions. During the climb, we keep this notebook handy to check on our progress. Afterward we use it to check the accuracy of our plan, to correct errors, and to fill in missing information. We draw pictures, write down gear needs, and take notes. This is an indispensable learning device as well as an invaluable future reference.

TIME PLANNING

One of the main purposes of a route plan is to estimate how long things will take. This information is needed to avoid time-sensitive hazards or difficulties: softening snow, rockfall, afternoon cloud buildup, or nightfall. A good time plan also helps you to manage your energy levels and determine how much food and water you should carry. The accompanying sidebar gives a general guide to average rates of travel on differing types of terrain, assuming a typical climber's day pack and appropriate levels of acclimatization.

With a good estimate of the total amount of time the route and descent should take, you can determine what time to start. First, identify the time you ideally want to be off the peak, then work backward through your route plan, establishing various times you expect to arrive at various points along the way. Any time-critical passages on your route, such as snow that you want to hit while it's frozen or climbing you need daylight for, could shift your whole time

TIPS: AVERAGE RATES OF TRAVEL

Typical ascent rates:

- 2.5 miles per hour on good trails of moderate grade.
- 1.5 miles per hour off trail in easy terrain or on glaciers with firm snow and minimal crevasse problems.
- 0.5 mile per hour off trail in bad conditions, i.e., dense forest, rough ground such as boulders or talus, trail breaking in deep snow, crevassed glaciers.
- Less than 0.5 mile per hour in thick brush or on rough terrain in poor visibility such as fog or darkness.
- Add about a half hour for every 350 meters (1000 feet) of elevation gain.

Typical descent rates:

- Descending snow or scree takes about a third as long as coming up.
- A steep trail or easy scrambling takes about half as long to go down as up.
- On technical terrain where you belayed on ascent, the ratio of time up to time down varies: where climbing up was difficult, rappelling down will take much less time, especially where rappel anchors already exist. Where climbing was easy and fast on the way up, downclimbing will be your quickest option for descent and will take about the same amount of time.

For example, on long, moderate alpine rock routes such as the Northwest Arete of Mount Sir Donald in British Columbia or the Hörnli ridge on the Matterhorn, descent time is normally about the same as the ascent time.

frame forward or back—and that's fine. At the end of this process, you will have a preliminary start time. Add in a little extra time to accommodate error or a summit nap, and you arrive at your recommended start time. It is almost impossible to start too early, except maybe in extremely cold temperatures—in all the years we have been climbing, we can recall only a couple of instances in which we really were too early.

During the climb, be aware of whether you're behind or ahead of schedule, and change your pace or your plans as neces-sary. As you climb, you may learn more about conditions and difficulties that might lead you to refine your descent plan, especially if the descent route is the same as the way up. Think about how long the route will take to reverse. Going down is usually faster than coming up, even if you follow the same route. Gravity is on your side, rappelling a blank section of rock is easier than climbing it, and going down steep sand, gravel, or soft snow can feel more like flying than walking. Revise your time plan after your trip to learn from mistakes and do better on your next trip or to help other climbers seeking information about your route. Work on improving the accuracy of your planning.

"Guidebook time." The "guidebook time" is an estimate of the average time required by a party of two, competent for the route, climbing in good conditions, and making few if any routefinding errors. A good guidebook with realistic and accurate time estimates can help you assess your abilities. To keep to time, you need to make good decisions and choose the most efficient protective strategies. Beating guidebook time is a sign that you were competent for that route. Taking longer than guidebook time may indicate otherwise, though there may be other factors as well. A guidebook author will usually indicate where the "clock" starts, normally at the hut or trailhead but sometimes the base of the technical climbing. Some guidebook authors seem to fear committing themselves and state such useless information as "6 to 10 hours" or may say nothing at all. When very specific times are given for a route, they are usually reasonably accurate; when vague or broad, they aren't much help.

BEFORE YOU LEAVE HOME

Call a reliable source for updated road and trail information and conditions on your climb. If possible, contact people who have been in the area or on the climb recently. Guide services, climbing gyms, mountaineering equipment stores, park rangers, and other land management personnel can be good sources of information or referrals if you do not know anyone locally. Evaluate the reliability of all information sources. Get the best and latest weather forecast possible and snow stability evaluation if applicable.

Finally, notify someone about where you are going, where you will park your car, and when you are due back. Make sure that person knows what to do and who to call if you are late. Do not forget to let the person know when you are back!

EQUIPMENT

In this section, we focus on those qualities most useful for alpine climbing—light weight, simplicity and ease of use, versatility, and reliability—as well as certain features designed specifically for alpine climbing.

Some of the most helpful recent design developments have involved new materials and manufacturing methods shaving weight off everything from clothing to ropes to ice axes. This is an especially important factor in our discipline because so much of alpine climbing consists of the simple act of steep scrambling where weight has enormous impact.

PACK FOR SUCCESS!

Statistics show that the greatest risk factor in mountaineering is falling. The heavier your pack, the higher that risk. Technical gear such as racks and ropes weigh quite a bit, so unless you plan to free solo, there is no avoiding a somewhat burdensome load. The trick is to pack as little as you can

GEAR: KEEPING IT IN PERSPECTIVE

A few years ago, we attempted a climb of Kang Tengri on the Kyrgyzstan-China border. We came equipped with all of our modern, high-tech clothing and gear, a marked contrast to the relatively primitive clothing and equipment of several Russian climbers who shared our base camp. We saw former national champions, professional climbers, and heroes wearing oven mitts for gloves, climbing with no sunscreen, and using homemade crampons. They were doing at least as well as us Westerners and, in fact, had energy and generosity to spare, making us tea, warming us in their tent with their enthusiasm, hospitality, and vodka. They proved to us that if you want to climb, you can make do with surprisingly little. We need not look far back in history to find examples of incredible mountaineering feats done with what now looks like very crude equipment. In the insane world of marketing hype and consumerist frenzy, we often lose sight of the experience of climbing, which has remained essentially the same despite amazing technological evolution. While gear is important, it is attitude that sets your limits in alpine climbing.

reasonably get away with by carefully considering every item, balancing your need for gear, food, water, and clothing with your need to go light.

The harder the climbing, the more important weight will be. Consider the difficulty of your route in estimating an ideal total weight budget, and limit yourself strictly to this budget as you select your gear and clothing. Include in your total all the clothing and climbing gear you wear on your body, not just what you carry in your pack. Everything weighs something; bringing one item means leaving behind another. A hard climb entails hard choices.

Select Gear Appropriate to the Climb and the Climber

It can be hard to know when you've got the right balance between minimizing weight and leaving out something essential. Gear and clothing needs depend on the diffi-

culty of the climb (and remember that changing conditions may require different equipment from one day to the next) and the skill of the climber. A highly skilled climber will take less time on a given route than a less skilled one, which influences the amount of emergency gear needed. In your efforts to decide what is essential and what is optional, consider the following:

- What is the terrain like? Rock, snow, ice, glacier? How much time will you spend on each medium? On which will the hardest climbing occur?
- Is there reliable fixed gear on the route?
- What are descent or escape options like? Would aborting the climb require extra gear for a technical descent?
- What do the guidebooks or other climbers suggest for gear?
- To what extent will the weight of your pack affect your safety? In other words, how hard is the climbing and for how

long will the difficulty last? Consider not only the risk of falling but also time management, since a heavy pack slows you down. How much will that matter on this climb?

■ What are the weather conditions? What is the forecast, and how reliable is it?

■ How well do you know the route? What are your chances of getting lost?

■ What is the local rescue capability? How might you contact a rescue party?

■ How long will the route take? Will it be easy for you to finish before nightfall, or is a bivouac a significant possibility?

Climbing Packs

When it comes to pack design, features desirable for climbing and those best for multiday backpacking are mutually exclusive. Multiday backpacking involves carrying more weight, for greater distances, on easier ground than that on technical climbs, so elaborate suspension systems and padded waist belts greatly improve comfort with little downside for backpackers. The demands of technical climbing, on the other hand, require that a pack be as simple, small, and lightweight as possible. A small pack, carefully packed, holds weight close to your center of gravity so you can climb better. The lighter load renders unnecessary all the elaborate suspension systems and padded waist belts with their extra weight and bulk.

For trips on which you bring a single pack for both the approach and the climb, climbing features should take precedence over backpacking features. Even if your climb involves an overnight, it is better to put up with discomfort during the approach than with a big, awkward pack on the climb. If you do a lot of overnight trail hiking, you will want a different pack for that purpose. When choosing a climbing pack, consider size, features, weight, and fit.

Size. For summer day climbs such as the Grand Teton, the North Face of Athabasca, or the Eiger's Mittellegi Ridge route, carry a simple 30- to 35-liter pack (1800–2100 cubic inches). For overnight trips, keep it as small as possible and learn to cram until the seams are ready to burst (see Packing Your Pack, below). A good maximum size is 45 to 50 liters (3000 cubic inches).

Features. The fewer the better. Avoid shovel/crampon panels or pouches, external pockets, separate compartments, and frames. A simple top-loading pack with minimal or no waist-belt padding is best. Side compression straps are useful for expanding the carrying capacity of a small pack and can make it possible to use your climbing pack to also carry your overnight gear on the approach. Gear loops on the waist belt are a useful feature, as is an extendable top pocket.

Weight. A simple 30-liter pack weighs about 1 kilogram (2.2 pounds). For overnight trips, a 45- to 50-liter pack should weigh about 1.5 kilos (3.3 pounds).

Fit. Getting a comfortable fit is extremely important but hard to do. Try on a variety of packs with weight in them (bring full water bottles or ropes), and spend a lot of time in the shop.

Packing Your Pack

Packing with skill will improve your balance and efficiency on the climb. Pack as much as you can on the inside, including crampons and water bottles, even ropes and helmets where possible. This isn't just some natty Euro-fashion statement; there are sound reasons: better visibility, better weight distribution, less snagging and less chance of losing things off your pack.

Use forethought and planning about what you will need when, keeping the things you will need first near the top of the pack. Fill the spaces between large or bulky items with clothing and smaller items, and cram tightly: empty spaces form loose hinges that waste capacity and make the pack carry poorly. Heavy items should be low and near your back. If you must carry something heavy outside the pack, such as the rope or crampons, try to lay it under the top lid or lash it on the sides, rather than off the back where it will pull your center of gravity backward. If you must carry your helmet on the outside, avoid just clipping it in to a carabiner. Tie it down to prevent it from rattling around.

TECHNICAL EQUIPMENT

Of all the contents of a climber's pack, technical gear tends to be the most bewildering and tricky to select. Technical features vary widely and should fit the nature and requirements of the chosen climb. For example, most serious alpinists own more than one type of rope, because different lengths and diameters best suit different climbing applications. Different boot and crampon designs work better in different environments and on different climbing media; this must be considered both in purchasing gear and in selecting what gear to bring on a given climb. The following sections attempt to make sense out of the rather dizzying choices facing the modern alpine shopper.

A word about standards: The Union Internationale des Associations d'Alpinisme (UIAA) is an international body that tests and approves equipment for use in technical climbing applications. UIAA approval is recognized worldwide as a minimum requirement for technical climbing gear. Virtually all such gear sold in the U.S. market conforms to UIAA standards. Look for the UIAA logo on the gear or label to be sure.

Rope

Length. In the mountains, the ideal length for a rope is as short as you can possibly get away with—shorter ropes are easier both to manage and to cart around. The difficult terrain in the mountains is often much shorter and less sustained than at climbing crags. On climbs we have guided frequently enough to know intimately, we bring a rope of the exact maximum length needed for the longest pitch or rappel, in some cases as little as 25-meters. One exception to this general rule is on long alpine ice faces. Here, the leader can often run out a very long pitch very fast, and a longer rope facilitates traveling a greater distance for each belay anchor built.

Climbing ropes today are growing longer and longer—not a good development for the typical alpine climber. Lengths of 60 meters are common, and although this is longer than usually needed in the mountains, you might have a hard time finding the rope you like in a 50-meter length. We keep waiting for popular rope lengths to eventually reach 90 or 100 meters, at which point we will cut them in half to get two of our preferred length!

Type. Climbing ropes are classified according to their intended use. The three basic types are single, half, and twin (we discuss the particulars of belay methods with different rope types in Chapter 5, Alpine Rock).

Single ropes range from about 9.2 mm to 10.5 mm in diameter. They are designed for technical climbing where there is a real chance of a leader fall on steep terrain. They can be used for all types of climbing, though lighter ropes are recommended for glacier travel and moderate snow.

Half ropes are typically 8 mm to 9 mm in diameter. Two strands are used together for steep technical climbing, or a single strand may be used for glacier travel and moderate snow climbs. A half rope used singly can also be adequate for short sections of easy rock or for belaying a second, but where a leader fall is possible, double strands are recommended (one half rope can be doubled to belay a leader if crux pitches are short enough).

Twin ropes are thinner still, usually between 7.5 mm to 8 mm in diameter.

They are typically used doubled for technical climbing. A single strand of a twin rope does not inspire much confidence on rock with its potentially sharp edges, but on snow or easy glacier travel it is usually fine (though the narrow diameter can complicate some aspects of crevasse rescue).

"Hand" or stiffness. Alpine climbing ropes should not be too stiff. Common alpine techniques such as belaying off the anchor with a Münter hitch and shortening the rope with over-the-shoulder coils (see Chapter 5, Alpine Rock) have a tendency to twist the rope. Soft ropes absorb these twists with less kinking. In the alpine environment, this advantage more than offsets the fact that soft ropes tend to wear out a little more quickly than stiff ropes.

Weight and waterproofing. Light weight is, as always, desirable; a single rope for alpine use should weigh less than 60 grams per meter (remember too that another effective way to reduce weight is simply to take a shorter rope). For alpine climbing, buy treated ropes—waterproof treatment helps keep the rope dry longer and saves a lot of weight in wet conditions.

Slings (Runners)

For alpine climbing, sewn slings are preferable to tied slings. Sewn slings are stronger, lighter, and less bulky, and they do not come untied during use. Slings combining nylon and Spectra are strong and durable. Single slings are about 60 cm (24 inches) when pulled in a line. Double slings are twice that. These two sizes are by far the most useful lengths. We usually each carry one double runner and vary the number of single slings to match the climb.

Cordelettes

Most rock climbers these days are familiar with the cordelette: a length of cord used mainly for building anchors and for self-rescue. It is typically made from 5 meters of 7-mm nylon cord. Despite several modern ultralight alternatives, 7-mm nylon is still the most versatile and reliable cord to use. In the name of lightness and ease of handling, consider 5 meters a maximum length. Typically you will carry two to three cordelettes per party.

Quickdraws

Quickdraws are well known to the modern rock climber. If your climb entails much steep belayed climbing, you may want a few quickdraws in addition to several single slings. On less technical routes, more versatile single slings (see Figure 3) are all you need.

Prusik Loop

A small 25-cm (10-inch) loop of 6-mm nylon cord tied with a double fishermans knot is handy for backing up rappels and for rescue purposes. Slings or a cordelette can serve the same function if necessary.

Carabiners

An alpine rack contains a combination of locking and nonlocking carabiners. The number of nonlocking carabiners you should bring depends on the amount of technical gear you need. The combined weight of carabiners on a rack becomes significant, so

Figure 3. *Turning single runners into quickdraws.*

when shopping for nonlocking carabiners, compare weights carefully. Small wire-gate carabiners are a good choice. The number of locking carabiners you should carry also depends on the climb, but for most routes you will want one light locking D carabiner and two pear-shaped lockers suitable for use with the Münter hitch.

Belay and Rappel Device

Plate- or tube-type devices function well for both rappelling and belaying and are lightweight and simple to use. Models that allow an autoblocking function for belaying a second directly off the anchor, such as the Petzl Reverso (Reversino for narrow-diameter ropes), are particularly useful.

Another excellent belay "device" is the Münter hitch (see Chapter 5, Alpine Rock). Requiring only a pear-shaped locking carabiner and the climbing rope, it can be used for belaying off your harness or for belaying a second directly off the anchor (though it is not good for rappels, unless perhaps they are very short!). If you expect very little belaying or rappelling, you can plan on using a Münter hitch and leave the belay plate at home.

For rappelling, the plate- or tube-style device you normally use for belaying is your best choice. There is no need to bring a separate rappel gizmo such as a figure eight, especially since the figure eight twists the rope.

Mechanical Prusik and Ascenders

Ascenders are traditionally used for aid climbing; due to their weight and bulk, they have virtually no place on an alpine free climb. Recently, small mechanical prusik devices such as the Ropeman or Tibloc have been developed for prusiking or creating a haul system in a rescue. Though these do speed things up, you can accomplish the same tasks using the tools you nearly always have with you: carabiners, cordelettes, slings, and a prusik loop. The need for a rescue is rare—carefully assess on a case-by-case basis whether or not you really want to carry items only for this eventuality.

Harness

Desirable alpine features in a harness include:

- Adjustable leg loops to accommodate various clothing levels.
- Buckles in the back of the leg loop risers, so you can drop them easily should nature call.
- A belay loop—handy for belaying off your harness and for shortening the rope.
- Buckles that are quick and easy to manipulate.
- Gear loops that come out the bottom of the waist belt so that they extend below your pack waist belt.

Helmet

When you are alpine climbing, your helmet stays on for hours, so it must fit well and be comfortable and lightweight. Modern helmets incorporate lightweight materials and various fit-adjustment systems. For fit, test various helmets with a hat on underneath. Consider how a headlamp would be attached; some systems are more secure than others. Helmets designed for other sports and multisport helmets are not appropriate. Use a UIAA-approved helmet designed specifically for climbing.

Boots

When you are buying boots, the most important features to consider are climbing performance, warmth, and fit. Which of these features takes precedence depends on the type of climbing you will do; for example, extreme warmth and high performance are somewhat mutually exclusive, so you have to prioritize accordingly. It is also necessary to spend some money. Technical mountaineering boots are expensive, and a single boot model will not fulfill all the requirements of the typical mountaineer.

Your best choice of boot is the one that best matches the terrain on which you will climb. Obviously, a boot must be warm enough for the temperatures you will encounter, but in the vast majority of alpine climbing, those temperatures are not extreme. This means that technical performance is usually far more important than warmth.

The wrong boots can slow you down or significantly increase your danger of falling, while proper footwear stacks the odds in your favor by making you as nimble and efficient as possible. Because more accidents result from falls or slips on rock than from any other cause, your choice of boot design is a genuine safety issue when climbing on that medium.

For nearly all alpine climbing, a good leather or leather-synthetic boot is preferable to plastic. Though design improvements have been significant, plastic boots still perform relatively poorly on rock, especially on easy, scrambly ground. Plastic boots are a better choice only in very cold temperatures, such as in winter mountaineering or high-altitude ascents.

For alpine rock climbing. Choose leather or leather-textile boots for climbs with any significant amount of rock scrambling, and look for the following additional features:

- A narrow sole, cropped close to the toe and edges of the boot for precision and control. The thicker the sole, the farther your foot is from the rock, which compromises sensitivity and precision. For the same reason, avoid molded grooves for front crampon bails (see Crampons, below), which also place more rubber between you and the rock.
- A fairly stiff sole for staying on small holds.
- Flexibility in the uppers and ankles for good agility.
- Light weight. Some boots combine fabric with the leather in the uppers, which saves substantial weight. These boots are less waterproof, but this should not be an issue on alpine rock routes.
- A snug fit in the heel prevents it from creeping up when you are edging on your toes.
- For cold conditions, choose insulated leather.

For snow and ice climbing. Desirable boot features for snow and ice climbing are similar to those for alpine rock, with the following differences:

- Boots with or without grooves for front bail–style crampons work equally well in these mediums.

- Insulated leather boots are warm enough for most midlatitude ice climbing, even in winter. Modern design and materials have resulted in insulated leather boots combining excellent performance on snow and ice with sufficient warmth for most winter conditions. If you do choose plastic double boots, fit them snugly (more on fitting boots below).

- While boots suitable for alpine rock might have a fairly low ankle, on snow and ice a higher ankle is needed to provide good support for French-technique cramponing. This is particularly important for climbs involving a lot of moderate-angle terrain where this technique is the normal mode (see Chapter 6, Snow and Ice).

For each type of climbing. Unfortunately, no boot is versatile enough to work adequately for every kind of climb. Buy boots designed for the type of climbing you will do most often. As you progress in the sport, your boot collection will inevitably grow—Imelda Marcos was onto something. The collection in our closet includes:

- Plastic boots for extreme cold and high-altitude expeditions, such as Denali, Aconcagua, the Himalaya, or the highest peaks of Peru, Ecuador, and Bolivia.

- Insulated leather boots for technical ice and mixed climbing, such as waterfalls in Colorado or New England and mixed or glacier climbs in the Cascades, Canada, European Alps, or Southern Alps of New Zealand.

- Lightweight boots with leather or mixed leather-textile uppers and lug soles for moderate rock ascents that might involve some snow or easy ice, such as many summer routes in the Cascades, Tetons, Sierra, Rockies, or European Alps.

- "Sticky" approach shoes for approaching an alpine ascent and for easy rock ascents with no snow or ice, such as many Sierra or Tetons routes in late summer and early autumn.

- Rock shoes that will be comfortable all day long for technical rock climbs.

Keeping your feet warm. Generally speaking, the warmer the boot, the less good its technical performance, so avoid buying boots any warmer than you really need. Loose-fitting boots feel warmer and more comfortable for walking but perform poorly on both rock and ice, so don't try to increase the warmth range of your climbing boots by means of a looser fit and more socks. Supergaiters—gaiters with rubber rands covering the entire boot upper—make boots much warmer. Some supergaiters are insulated, extending the warmth range of any boot still further.

Getting the fit right. Alpine routes are long and demanding. Try front-pointing for hours on end on a big alpine ice face with a pair of ill-fitting boots, and you'll be sure never to make that mistake again. Also on rock, where much time is spent standing on the front or inside edge of the boot, heel-lift can be a big problem, causing blisters and sapping performance.

Try on leather boots with a single midweight sock. With the boot unlaced and your toes touching the front, insert a finger behind your heel. If you can just fit your finger in, you have a good length. Be picky about pressure points, rubbing, or pinching. If you can feel these in the shop or when the boot is new, you will definitely suffer after a few hours in the mountains. Some ski shops can punch boots out to accommodate trouble spots such as bunions. Take your time in the shop, and wear each boot around the floor for as long as you can stand.

Custom-molded foot beds or insoles can provide extra support, help fill in excessive volume (a little), and mitigate some fit problems. They can help stabilize more serious foot problems such as low arches and bunions. For climbers with problem feet, these are a very worthwhile investment.

When fitting plastic boots, a snug fit is still important for technical climbing, but less so if you will use them primarily for glacier travel, easy climbs on snow or in winter, or extreme cold weather. For a snug fit, remove the inner boot and fit your foot in the shell alone. Touch your toes to the front of the boot, and you should have 1.25 to 2 cm ($\frac{1}{2}$ to $\frac{3}{4}$ inches) behind your heel (two fingers stacked together just fit). Keep in mind that plastic boots will feel significantly more snug in the shop than they

will after a couple of trips, since the liner insulation compacts with use.

Selecting boots for a particular climb. It can be quite difficult to decide which boots, or how many pairs of boots, to bring when you are selecting footwear for a particular climb. The selection is most complicated on climbs that include a variety of terrain: snow, ice, and rock. Your selection will depend on the season and conditions, on the comparative and absolute difficulty of the climbing in the various media, and also on your climbing skill. To illustrate this rather complex decision, let's consider a climb of Mount Whitney in the Sierra Nevada of California via two different routes: the Mountaineers Route and the East Buttress Route.

Example 1. First imagine planning an early summer climb of the Mountaineers Route. The approach hike is fairly long with steep slabs, hot weather (usually), lots of boulder hopping, and possibly some snow. The route itself involves 3rd- and 4th-class rock, and up until mid-June there is usually a 30-degree snow couloir requiring crampons and extending for nearly 330 meters (1000 feet) of elevation. Your range of footwear options includes the following:

- **Option 1:** bring approach shoes only, with strap-on crampons for the couloir. This solution has the advantage that you bring only one light, comfortable pair of shoes that will work very well on the slabs of the approach and the easy rock climbing on the route. Disadvantages are that snow sections will be quite hard, tenuous, and uncomfortable. It may be tricky to get crampons to fit securely.

- **Option 2:** bring lightweight mountaineering boots for the climb and more comfortable approach shoes for the hike in. The mountaineering boots will be much more secure and comfortable on the snow but will be heavy and bulky in your pack.
- **Option 3:** bring only lightweight mountaineering boots. They will be stiff, too warm, and uncomfortable during the hike but will be better on any boulders or snow you encounter on the approach, and they will allow you to carry a smaller, lighter pack.

Option 1 is quite committing and a bit risky. You will probably regret not having beefier footwear if there is much snow on the approach or if the snow on the route itself proves to be very firm. The risk is not outweighed by any performance advantages, since the rock portions will be very easy and you do not need the superior performance of approach shoes. In fact, you can handle easy rock in clunky boots far better than you can snow in light shoes. This option could work out fine, but only if you know for certain that there will be little or no snow on the approach and in the couloir.

Choosing between options 2 and 3 is a bit trickier. Option 3 will involve a long, hot approach hike in mountaineering boots and possible foot abuse. Option 2 will allow you to save your feet during the marching, while still having the boots

where you need them. Generally we prefer option 3, sacrificing hiking comfort but keeping life simpler and packs smaller and lighter by bringing only the mountaineering boots. Tough feet, careful fitting, thorough breaking in, and a well-stocked blister kit (see below) all make option 3 more feasible.

Example 2. Our second example is a climb of the East Buttress of Whitney, descending by the Mountaineers Route. The East Buttress involves between 10 and 15 pitches of moderate rock climbing, ranging in difficulty from stiff 4th class to about 5.8. At least eight pitches are rated 5.6 or harder. The descent is via the Mountaineers Route, so snow conditions have to be considered. The approach is exactly the same as for the Mountaineers Route.

- **Option 1:** use approach shoes for the entire approach, climb, and descent (bringing compatible strap-on crampons), similarly to option 1 above.
- **Option 2:** use lightweight technical mountaineering boots for the approach hike and for the descent of the Mountaineers Route and rock shoes for the route itself.
- **Option 3:** use lightweight technical mountaineering boots for the entire route, similar to option 3 above.

In this case, your choice will be governed mostly by your skill as a rock climber. You may take it as given that the lighter the pack, the more enjoyable the climbing, especially on technical rock. Therefore option 2 might look the least attractive at first glance, because it forces you to carry your mountaineering boots in your pack during the technical part of the climb. However, option 2 is the only one that allows you to climb in rock shoes. The 5th-class climbing will be much more difficult in either approach shoes or mountaineering boots. So if you are skilled enough to handle the hardest rock climbing in approach shoes, and if there is no snow or if it is not too hard or frozen, option 1 may be preferable. If you can

handle 5.8 in mountaineering boots, option 3 could be preferable if there is significant snow in the couloir.

Crampons

Alpine climbing involves all kinds of conditions, from hard-frozen snow to sloppy-sticky glop warmed by the sun, from soft glacier ice to hard water ice. The best crampon design to handle this diversity has a flat, horizontal frame to

Figure 4. *Grivel G12 and Charlet Moser Super12 crampons with antibottes. These versatile crampons will fit most alpine climbing boots.*

prevent snow from balling up on the bottom in gooey snow, and horizontal front points which hold better in soft ice than vertical ones.

Crampons specially designed for waterfall ice have a number of severe disadvantages in the mountains. They are heavy; their complex, often vertical frame encourages ball-up problems in gooey snow; and their vertical front points shear through snow. Superlightweight aluminum crampons save weight and are great for snow-only ascents but are not durable enough for technical climbing, mixed climbing, or very hard ice.

Crampon-boot attachment system. Crampons popping off at the wrong moment have been the cause of some disastrous accidents. Be sure they stay on your feet! Designs with a front toe bail and a snap-on back lever require that the boots with which they will be worn have a deep front groove for the bail and that the curve of the boot toe matches that of the bail. A front groove requires that the sole of the boot be fairly thick and extend out in front of the boot, which is not so good for rock climbing. Hybrid-style crampons (see Figure 4) with a snap-on lever in the back and a strap attachment for the front can accommodate a wider range of boot types and are just as quick to put on as the bail type, so they are a good choice for mountaineering.

Few crampon models will provide an adequate fit with every mountaineering boot. Make sure when you buy either boots or crampons that your choices will work well together. Very soft boots typically fit poorly with most crampons, while a stiffer boot with a good heel shelf provides a more secure fit.

Antibottes. These are rubber or plastic plates fitted to your crampons that prevent snow from balling up underfoot, an annoying and often dangerous problem. Most crampon manufacturers make models to fit their particular crampons. Consider these an integral part of your crampon setup.

Crampon bags. Carry crampons inside your pack when possible. Wrap them in a simple nylon bag to prevent them from putting holes in your gear or spreading mud over your clothes. Avoid crampon bags with zippers, pack strap slots, and hard plastic panels, which just add unnecessary weight.

Rock Gear

Nuts and cams. As you know, cams rely on friction to work, so any dirt, water, ice, snow, or moss in a crack will compromise the placement. In the mountains, it may take more searching than usual to find clean cracks in solid rock. Nut placements, which rely on wedging rather than friction, may be a better choice than cams in some situations. Also, mountains are full of loose blocks, and the tremendous outward pressure exerted by a cam under load can displace even huge flakes and boulders.

Some folks like to bring hexes in place of cams in an effort to save weight. We prefer to stick with cams, because they fit in many more places and are generally much faster and easier to place and remove.

Tri-cams. Depending on the rock type, a few Lowe Tri-cams on your rack may prove useful. They are particularly well suited to holes, pockets, and irregular cracks where cams and nuts won't easily fit. The downside is that placements are trickier to establish and evaluate, and the smaller sizes can be hard to remove when solidly placed.

Pitons. Though pitons are not commonly used these days, you still find many fixed pitons on classic routes, especially in the Alps. Assess the quality of piton placements that you encounter. Pitons loosen over time in any freeze-thaw environment. On a very difficult climb, it may be appropriate to carry a few pitons, especially if rock quality is poor. Knife blades and small Z-section sizes up to about 1.25 cm (½ inch) are the most useful in these cases. Remember that you will need a hammer (your ice hammer will do).

Match the rack to the route. Choosing the right rack is a balance between carrying the minimum you absolutely need and having enough to get the job done. Research your route in order to match your rack to the nature of the climbing and the characteristics of the rock. If you know there will be almost no 5th-class climbing, bring slings and carabiners but leave the quickdraws, cams, and nuts behind. If your route includes several pitches of moderate 5th-class rock climbing, you'll want a small alpine rack. How small is small? As always the answer is, "it depends," but think of a small general alpine rock rack as consisting of five or six wired nuts ranging in size from about 0.6 to 2.5 cm (¼ to 1 inch); two or three cams from 2.5 to 5 cm (1 to 2 inches), a half dozen slings, and a couple of quickdraws. Plan on using horns and other natural anchors as much as possible.

You can further reduce the size and weight of your rack if you can determine beforehand that your route is equipped with a lot of fixed protection. Guides in the Alps often bring virtually no rack on a familiar route, knowing every hold and being very skilled and experienced climbers. Someone else's idea of adequate protection may differ markedly from yours, however, so take that into account when you hear that a route is completely fixed and no rack is needed.

Many classic alpine routes involve no 5th-class climbing and require little more than a rope and a harness. Using a minimum of equipment keeps things simple and fast, exercises your imagination, and gives you a sense of freedom from the complexities of modern life. See how little you can get by with.

Match the rack to the rock. Different rock types tend to favor different kinds of protection. Granite is usually hard and monolithic; it fractures in very big pieces, creating wide and clean cracks. Larger cracks suggest bigger gear, so adjust your rack accordingly; large cams may be more useful than small wedges. Granite ridges often fracture into horns and spikes of rock, ideal for slinging.

Limestone is less weather-resistant than granite and tends to fracture into smaller blocks. It usually has fewer wide cracks and more small ones, and solution pockets are common. Your choice of gear should reflect this; emphasize smaller pro and Tri-cams. Ridges tend to be very stepped, with lots of large ledges favoring quick stances and terrain belays (see Chapter 5, Alpine Rock).

Snow and Ice Protection

Ice screws. Modern improvements in ice screws have been dramatic, especially in the machining of threads and the incorporation of various sorts of handles for speedy placement and removal. A hanger large enough to accommodate two carabiners is desirable, because it makes belay construction easier. Machined steel is the material of choice. While titanium screws are lighter in weight, they are usually much harder to place.

Ice screws come in various lengths. In our experience, a 17-cm screw offers a good compromise between holding power and weight and bulk for the relatively thick ice typical of most alpine climbing. However, at least one longer 22-cm screw is helpful for building an Abalakov anchor (see Chapter 6, Snow and Ice).

Abalakov hook. An Abalakov anchor entails drilling two intersecting holes in the ice in the shape of a V and then threading webbing or cord through the hole. The hook is used to pull the webbing or cord through. Commercial hooks are available, or you can make your own from a metal coat hanger.

Pickets or snow stakes. Pickets are long aluminum stakes, usually in a T- or V-shaped cross section, driven into the snow or buried sideways as an anchor. The longer the picket, the greater its holding power, but 60 cm (2 feet) is the maximum reasonable length for racking and carrying. Permanently tie a short loop of webbing or cord to the top hole for racking your pickets and for clipping in to them. Sharpen the end you put into the snow and always hammer on the other end (see Chapter 6, Snow and Ice).

Ice Tools

Of the wide variety of specialized ice tools available today, no single tool is equally well suited to all types of alpine climbing. Match your tool to the type of climbing you plan to do: the best design features for traveling on moderately angled snow and ice differ from those best for technical or steep water ice, as follows.

For moderate terrain. When you are traveling on moderately angled snow and glaciers, the ice ax serves mostly as a balance support on steeper slopes and as a potential snow anchor or self-arrest tool. For this application, look for the following features:

- **Weight:** light—some modern models weigh as little as 336 grams (12 ounces).
- **Length:** 55 to 60 cm—to provide support on steeper slope angles.
- **Shaft:** mostly straight—for driving in as an anchor in soft snow.
- **Adze:** traditionally shaped—for comfort on the hand, ease of grip, and chopping steps or platforms in frozen snow.

For steeper ice or water ice. For these applications, look for the following features:

- **Weight:** a heavier head—gives more

secure placements; very light weight is not so advantageous.

- **Length:** 50 cm—a short shaft is best, standard for waterfall climbing.
- **Shaft:** curved—performs better on very steep ice and provides a nice handle when used in piolet manche (see Chapter 6, Snow and Ice).
- **Pick:** narrow and steeply drooped (usually replaceable)—holds better in hard ice.

For versatility. Some models provide a mix of features well suited to routes with occasional but limited sections of technical ice. Desirable features of this type of tool are medium weight, a traditional fixed adze, a steeply drooped and narrow pick, and a smooth, mostly straight shaft no longer than 55 cm.

Ice hammers. These are needed on alpine climbs that will involve driving pickets in firm snow or for steep, two-tool climbing. Hammers are by definition technical climbing tools, so look for a narrow, removable, drooped pick; a curved shaft; and 50 cm length.

Ice-ax leashes. On easy to moderate snow and glacier climbs, we don't bring leashes (see Chapter 6, Snow and Ice). On more difficult climbs with some belayed climbing on steep snow or low-angled ice, leashes are desirable, but choose designs that are easy to attach or remove from the tools.

OTHER EQUIPMENT

Our development as alpinists in the late 1970s and early 1980s was greatly influenced by a seminal book of the time: *Climbing Ice* by Yvon Chouinard. The book was revolutionary in its emphasis on climbing technique and on the importance of going fast and light. It is not as widely read these days, which is unfortunate, because much of its information is as current and helpful today as it was 25 years ago. One particularly useful and still widely quoted idea is: "Leave most of the 'ten essentials' and other impedimenta behind. Remember: if you take bivouac equipment along, you will bivouac."

Chouinard's point was that you simply cannot carry enough on a technical climb to guard against every possible mistake and that trying to do so will make some problems more likely. For example, rather than carrying gear to help survive an unplanned bivouac, keep your pack light to help you avoid the night out. Hone your routefinding and navigation skills to prevent getting lost; move quickly and keep to your time plan.

Every climb is different and has its own unique equipment needs. Consider every item individually, ask yourself whether you really need it and under what circumstances you would need it, and weigh the probability of those circumstances arising. Bring only those items that address your assessment of more likely problems, omit those geared toward more remote or preventable possibilities, and then take great pains to prevent the preventable!

The Ten Essentials
The Ten Essentials has evolved from a list of individual items to a list of functional

systems, as follows:

1. Navigation: map and compass
2. Sun protection: sunglasses and sunscreen
3. Insulation: extra clothing (see Bivouac Gear, below)
4. Illumination: headlamp or flashlight
5. First-aid supplies
6. Fire: firestarter and matches or a lighter
7. Repair kit and tools
8. Nutrition: extra food (see Bivouac Gear, below)
9. Hydration: extra water
10. Emergency shelter (see Bivouac Gear, below)

This list helps climbers with limited experience to avoid forgetting important items. However, the actual mental process that more advanced climbers go through should be more than simply checking off items on a list. Instead, imagine the climb and all the possible events that could happen during the course of the day. Then assess the likelihood of each of these possible events. The final decision about whether to bring or leave behind equipment to deal with any given event or problem follows that assessment. The number and type of "essentials" therefore can vary greatly from one climb to another. Do not fall into the trap of thinking that all ten essentials must be brought on every climb or that other items not on the list need not be considered. In the mountains, all decisions should be situational. Avoid blindly following rules and protocols.

Navigation

On most alpine climbs, you will want the following items: photos of the route and/or a copy of the route description or topo; your route planning notes; and a map, compass, and altimeter. A waterproof map case is handy if the weather is wet (a sturdy resealable plastic bag can work well). Also carry a notebook and pencil to update your route plan and for emergencies.

Watch

A watch is a necessary piece of equipment, both for waking you up for your "alpine start" and for keeping you to your time plan. A watch is often your altimeter. If navigation might be tricky, make sure the battery is fresh or bring a spare.

Hydration

There is a trade-off between staying hydrated and limiting the weight of your pack. Depending on conditions, the length of your climbing day, and your sustained level of exertion, you will typically sweat and/or breathe away much more liquid than you would want to carry. You have to draw the line somewhere and accept the inevitability of some level of dehydration. Guard against its worst effects by hydrating as well as you can before and after your climb, taking advantage of refilling opportunities along the way, such as running streams or snow patches where you can often find meltwater. Equally important is to avoid excessive sweating due to overdressing.

We commonly go all day carrying $1/2$ liter

of water or less. But if you watch carefully, you'll see that we stop to drink or refill at every stream, and we will make up for it by drinking a great deal once we are back in the hut or tent. When deciding how much water to carry, consider the following:

If you know you will come across sources of water, carry little and refill when you have the opportunity. Use water purification tablets in areas where water quality is a concern. Filters are too heavy and bulky for technical outings, though they may be useful in camp.

Consider 2 liters a maximum to carry. Carrying water up and down again is clearly a waste of energy. If you find you consistently descend from your climbs with water left over, either make an effort to stop and drink more or carry less.

Water containers. Thermoses offer a hot drink just when you want it most and are wonderful on very cold climbs or at altitude, but they are heavy and bulky for their carrying capacity, so we tend to bring them on only nontechnical climbs. In freezing temperatures, the traditional old bottle still works well, but carry it inside your pack and wrap it in clothing or other insulation.

Bladders are great for warm temperatures and for technical climbs on which you may have little time or opportunity to stop and get into your pack. Bladders must be packed carefully, and the tubes have a tendency to freeze in very cold temperatures, even when insulated. Preventive strategies such as clearing the tube by blowing water back into the bladder can help, but they are not infallible. One manufacturer solves this problem by incorporating the tube into the pack shoulder strap, allowing body heat to keep it warm. With all bladder systems, there's no good way to know when you are about to run out, so rationing is difficult.

Sunglasses

Use sunglasses that block 100 percent of UVA and UVB radiation and that block peripheral light while preserving peripheral vision, which is important for balance and agility, as much as possible. Modern wraparound or shaped-lens sport sunglasses do both of these jobs well. In contrast, old-fashioned side shields impair vision quite a bit, which is a real handicap when you are scrambling on rock or rough ground. Sunglasses with interchangeable lenses are versatile and last a long time, because scratched lenses can be replaced.

Consider the nature of the climb and the weather forecast when you decide which eyewear or lenses to pack. For snow or high altitude, use very dark brown or neutral lenses that block 90 percent or more of visible light, and bring a backup pair. On alpine rock, lighter-colored lenses give better visibility (about 85 percent light transmission is adequate). Yellow or light rose lenses are best for fog, high overcast, or flat light on snow.

If you need corrective lenses, use contacts or prescription sunglasses, and be sure to bring your regular prescription glasses as a backup. Clip-on shades over your prescription glasses are not adequate. Ski goggles worn over regular glasses may seem like a great idea for use in blowing snow, but in practice they are not recommended: they tend to steam up and are too warm for most climbing. Investigate corrective laser surgery.

Headlamp

Light-emitting diode (LED) headlamps are lightweight with long battery life and are by far the preferred choice for emergency use. Headlamps with incandescent or halogen bulbs cast a more powerful beam but go through batteries faster and weigh more. You may want an incandescent light if your climb involves significant difficult routefinding in the dark. But choose an LED headlamp when carrying it "just in case" and also for less demanding situations, such as brief night travel or an alpine start on a glacier with an existing track.

Cell Phone or Radio

In an accident, getting help from the outside world can be lifesaving. Cell phones and radios are increasingly practical to carry in the wilderness as they get smaller and as coverage expands to more remote areas. Which you choose depends on where you climb. In the Eastern Sierra Nevada of California, for example, there are currently more radio repeaters accessible from the mountains than there are phone cells. This is also the case in the Southern Alps of New Zealand and, arguably, in the Canadian Rockies. However, in the European Alps, cell coverage reaches into more mountain-ous areas, and it is simpler to use a telephone than a radio.

As guides, we nearly always carry one or the other, depending on the relative usefulness in the area where we will climb. Where we carry radios, they have proven very useful for keeping track of each other when guiding separate teams and also for calling for assistance of various kinds. The most useful type are two-meter VHF radios, designed for amateur operators. Radio communications are strictly regulated, however, so if you carry a radio, it is worthwhile to acquire an amateur radio (ham) license. In a true emergency, you may not be punished for an illegal broadcast, but it is still better to be licensed because of the ease and familiarity you gain from frequent practice. It also earns you a more friendly reception from the folks you may call upon to help you; ham radio operators are very helpful folks. Be sure to note down any useful frequencies of repeaters, rescue services, government agencies, etc., before you head into the hills. For more information on ham radios and their use, see Appendix B.

Trekking Poles

In addition to saving energy and helping you to move quickly on snow, trekking poles are also helpful when you are carrying a heavy pack on a rough approach or descent. Choose collapsible poles that are as compact as possible, especially if you will rock climb with them lashed to your pack. Ours are only 53 cm long collapsed, from top of handle to the tip.

First-aid Kit

First-aid kits can expand infinitely if you think about all the bad things that can happen. Rein in your morbid imagination. On short alpine climbs, you can afford to carry a kit for only two purposes: to deal with minor irritations such as cuts, headaches, and blisters and to address the very small number of life-threatening situations for which your intervention could actually effect survival. These include:

- **Bleeding:** treated by direct pressure, no equipment is required.
- **Anaphylactic shock:** injectable epinephrine is required.
- **Severe high-altitude illness:** prescription medications can buy valuable time and aid in your descent.
- **Severe pain:** strong prescription pain medication can make a patient with a severe injury more comfortable and help you manage the situation.

Most injuries in the mountains are traumatic and there is little that can be done beyond stabilizing fractures and controlling pain and bleeding. At a minimum, carry athletic tape and some kind of pain medication.

For longer trips involving a base camp, you may choose to carry a larger kit. What you bring depends on the remoteness of the area, the nature of the illnesses or injuries you or someone in your party might sustain, the availability of rescue services, and your own training. Wilderness First Responder–level training is highly recommended as a relevant standard for serious recreational climbers. Prepare yourself to improvise with limited materials. Devote thought and creativity to planning for likely scenarios.

Repair Kit and Tools

Repair kits, like first-aid kits, tend to expand out of control as you consider all the things that could possibly go wrong. Strive for prevention and simplification rather than preparation for every contingency. The best overall strategy is to bring reliable gear, in good repair, designed for the use you will put it to; if you have gear that could break, match your repair kit to that gear.

For most routes, our repair kit is usually limited to a pocketknife sporting a minimum of bells and whistles. Our favorite model includes large and small blades, can and bottle openers integrating broad and narrow screwdriver blades, an awl, and a corkscrew (for the bivouac wine). You can buy a tiny screwdriver designed to fit inside the corkscrew of such a knife. It is very handy for repairing eyeglasses and setting compass declination and weighs next to nothing. Buy crampons that can be adjusted without special tools.

On expeditions or long trips, we have found that we most often use repair items for the following: tent poles, tent fabric, tent zippers, inflatable sleeping pads, and crampons. Our typical expedition repair kit therefore includes tent pole repair sleeves, a small file, duct tape, self-adhesive repair fabric for tents and sleeping pads, and miniature vise grips or multitools.

Bivouac Gear

Earlier in this chapter, we emphasize the importance of avoiding a bivouac. However, bivouacs, though uncomfortable, are rarely life threatening even when they are unplanned and can be among the most remarkably satisfying parts of mountaineering. The memory of a night out under the stars, high on a big peak, stays with you for years.

There are, in fact, two types of bivouacs: those you expect and those you don't. The first type is generally more comfortable, because your expectation of the need for a bivouac makes you pack certain gear that you might otherwise have left behind. The question of how much, if any, bivouac gear you bring depends on the following:

- the probability of bivouacking
- weather forecast and conditions: temperature, precipitation, wind
- how important it is that you sleep well
- the impact that the weight of the extra gear will have on your climbing

These factors vary with each climb. Each factor must be assessed individually and reconciled with the others. For example, the equipment needed for a good sleep conflicts with going light; the effect of added weight on your climbing will vary with the difficulty of the climb. The best balance is different in every case.

A bivouac can teach you how little you truly need in order to survive; make a point of bivouacking intentionally at least once or twice in your life. However, when you hope not to bivouac, do everything you can to avoid it. Get up early, be efficient, do not dawdle, go light, and bring a headlamp. If you do bivouac, make sure that you do not bivouac in restricted areas, and visualize potential impacts when selecting even an emergency campsite.

Extra clothing. You'll need less clothing than you might think, but when you curl up for the night, it needs to be dry! A dry change of socks, an extra hat, and an extra layer for the legs help a lot with warmth and comfort.

Extra food. While quick energy foods are great for the climb itself, on a bivouac it may be better to have some high-calorie, fat- and protein-intensive food. Pack a bit of both if you think you will need to bivouac.

Stove, fuel, pot, and lighter. Generally you will not bring a stove unless you really plan to bivouac and the only possibility for water is melted snow or ice. Make sure that your stove will operate adequately out in the wind; some will not, even with a windscreen. Bring a minimal amount of fuel and the lightest stove that will do the job. Your pot can serve as a bowl or cup. Lexan spoons are light, but it is even lighter to bring no spoon. If you might be bivying down in the woods where you can build a small fire, a single cigarette lighter can substitute for the stove, fuel, and sleeping bag. Build fires only where safe and legally permitted; build only in existing fire rings, if available; and use only dead and down wood from outside of the camp area.

Bivouac sack. These should be compact and as lightweight as possible. A one-person sack should weigh no more than 224 grams (8 ounces). Our own favorite is a simple

BIVOUAC FOOD STOKES THE FIRE!

At the end of a summer's guiding time in the Alps, we took advantage of fine mid-September weather to do a quick traverse of the Chamonix Aiguilles. It was getting colder, with shorter days and longer nights, but conditions in the mountains were still good and the forecast was superb. We started early from the Cosmiques Hut, and before dawn we were up and over the Aiguille du Plan. It was an ideal climb: a wild ride over and around clean granite spires, with fantastic exposure and a sense of remoteness, even with Chamonix so close in the valley below. It was a perfect calm and clear fall day.

Happy and tired, we descended the Glacier des Nantillons as the daylight faded and stars emerged. We had traveled light, bringing only a double bivy sack and the clothes and gear we would normally want on a day climb. At the edge of the glacier, the environment changed from ice and alpine rock to grassy meadows with narrow, winding trails among the boulders—and fine bivouac spots. Too tired to hike on to the Plan des Aiguilles hut, we decided to make our bed on the moraine. We spread out ropes and packs, laid out the bivy sack on top of them, put on all of our clothes, and crawled in.

Sleep came quickly, but before long we both woke up shivering; our bodies had run out of fuel. Kathy had had the foresight to pack extra chocolate and some baguette sandwiches with chèvre cheese. We found that a few bites of chocolate warmed us up quickly; we dozed off, only to wake up maybe 10 or 15 minutes later, shivering again. The goat cheese sandwiches, on the other hand, warmed us up just as fast and gave us three or four times as much sleep before the cold woke us up. After several eat-and-sleep cycles, gradually nibbling away all our supplies, we concluded that the cheese was the critical ingredient that made the difference.

At last dawn came, rising red behind the Grands Charmoz, and we could hear the cable car starting up, beckoning us. We rode it back into Chamonix for a proper breakfast: café au lait and a croissant. Watching the morning light move across the peaks above, we traced the route we had taken over one improbable-looking tower after another, all the way to the bivouac. One thought came to mind: cheese. While high-energy bars and candies may be the choice for quick energy, we concluded that cheese was the ideal food for cold bivouacs. We are still testing the effectiveness of different varieties: Gruyère, perhaps Compté, chèvre is a favorite still; maybe a selection of several works best. Our next project is to find the perfect bivouac wine. Red, of course.

—*Mark Houston*

sack with a drawstring and no zipper, made of fluorescent orange fabric; it is large enough for both of us to lie side by side. In a pinch, three can squeeze in, and it weighs only 336 grams (12 ounces). It is possible to rig such a bag to close up between two people's heads, using Velcro or adding another drawstring. A large, simple bag like this is probably the lightest per-person alternative, and the shared body heat makes it warmer for the weight.

For a truly emergency shelter, you can buy single-use aluminized Mylar sacks (emergency "space blanket" material) that weigh only an ounce or so and are about as big as a pack of cigarettes.

Insulation. You may need a sleeping bag and possibly a ground insulating system when it's really cold, you truly need to sleep, or you will spend more than one night on the climb. Two climbers can share a single sleeping bag: make a zip-in triangular insert to turn a one-person bag into a double. In dry conditions, or for a single night out, a down insulated bag is a good choice. For multiple nights in wet environments or snow caves, consider synthetic. If your rope and pack are part of your insulating system (for under your feet and head), you can make do with only a short pad.

THREE BIVOUACS COMPARED

On each of the following bivouacs, we got the equipment just about right. Were we to do these routes again, we would bring the same gear.

October 1978, Northeast Face of Forbidden Peak, North Cascades of Washington State. This bivy was completely unplanned. Mark and his climbing partner, Bruce Pratt, were simply going too slowly. Rather than risk complex routefinding down an unknown route (they climbed the North Ridge and were descending the Northeast Face), they sat on their packs on a small ledge, waiting for the morning light. They had no "extra" gear save for some figs and chocolate, which turned out to be sufficient to stay warm enough for fitful sleep. Once the sun and movement finally warmed them up the next morning, they already looked back on their night out as a great experience.

January 1992, South Face of Aconcagua, Andes of Argentina. For this planned bivouac (referred to in Chapter 1, The Making of an Alpinist), we brought a simple two-person bivy sack, one sleeping bag (which we shared), light foam sleeping pads, a tiny pot and stove, and enough food and fuel for two nights and three days. Though it was a bit tough to cook in the wind at the bivy, we managed just fine. Traveling light allowed us to summit the second evening, and we spent that second night walking the trail down to the Plaza de Mulas base camp. Our light and fast tactic was reasonably comfy.

September 1999, Chamonix Aiguilles Traverse, European Alps of France. This is the same incident referred to under "extra food," above. On this climb, we thought a bivy was somewhat likely but hoped to avoid it by going as light and fast as we could. Our minimal concession to the possibility was to bring more extra food than usual, our light two-person bivy sack, and one extra hat each. We figured we could get water off the glacier, so did not bring a stove. We also knew that we could use packs and ropes to insulate against the cold and to soften our bed of rock and dirt—no sleeping bags or pads needed. As described above, it worked out reasonably well.

—Kathy Cosley

CHAPTER 4

Climbing on the South Ridge of the Weissmies,
Switzerland

Routefinding and Navigation

A guide is never lost until he (or she) admits it.

> —an old saying of guides

Some of our most satisfying moments in the mountains have happened when we were nearly, but not quite, lost. These involved either routefinding, when our theory about the best way to go proved right, or navigation, when we managed to arrive at a hidden destination in fog or storm. In both planning and the field, routefinding and navigation create a sense of discovery and intimacy with the mountain's deepest secrets, its nooks and crannies, its shapes at varying scales. Both of these skills require scientific precision and attention to detail, married to a holistic sense of your surroundings.

In this chapter, and particularly in the discussion of routefinding, we begin to get at the heart of alpine climbing's rewards and complexities. Identifying the best route to the top is a creative act, even on an established route. With no road signs or rules to follow, you make it up as you go along, creating your climb step by step. Your routefinding decisions influence both the degree of hazard and the difficulty and quality of the climbing you encounter, which is what makes this skill so vitally important.

Routefinding and navigation are related but separate skills. Routefinding uses eyes, brain, and sometimes a map to determine the best or easiest line. Navigation is something we rely on when visibility is so poor that our eyes alone are no longer enough. It uses instruments— map, compass, altimeter, and possibly global positioning systems (GPS)—to help us re-create some "view" of the terrain around us.

Our goals with this chapter are two-fold—and ambitious. For routefinding, our goal is to build habits of observation, analysis, and memory necessary for this highly complex and intuitive skill. For navigation, our goal is to cover the skills and techniques needed to navigate in a whiteout. This means a thorough understanding of the various instruments—map, compass, altimeter, and GPS. It also means having a plan, knowing how to accomplish all the necessary steps to carry it out, and knowing how to perceive and correct mistakes as you go along.

We assume that the reader understands how contour lines depict landforms on topographic maps. You should be able to identify the shapes of individual ridges, valleys, and summits; to read elevations; to determine slope aspect and estimate slope angle by means of contour lines. We also assume familiarity with compasses, including an understanding of declination and how to set it on an adjustable-declination compass. Finally, we assume an understanding of how altimeters express elevation by measuring relative air pressure. See the bibliography for good sources of further information or review of these concepts.

ROUTEFINDING

Because good routefinding allows you to avoid hazards and find the best climbing, it is arguably the most important among all the decision-making skills needed in the mountains. Alpine climbers with superb technical skills but marginal routefinding ability are probably more at risk than mediocre climbers with good routefinding sense.

Routefinding is not a single skill but, rather, a whole group of skills that allow you to find and follow the best route, using only the simplest of tools—your brain and eyes. When done well, it can look almost like magic. Good routefinders seem to know where the route will go and can follow it like a bloodhound. They appear almost to have some sort of psychic connection with others who have climbed the route before. Behind such appearances, however, are specific skills and techniques that can be learned and improved with practice. These take time to master, but the more you get out in the mountains, the more skilled you will become. In this section we focus on the two main elements of routefinding:

- "Routefinding" skills allow you to identify the best line on the mountain and to know where you are relative to that line.
- "Route following" skills help you to follow an established route by recognizing signs of passage of previous climbers.

AT HOME

Your task begins with research to gain an understanding of the mountain and the nature of the climb and to identify key features and where your route goes in relation to these. You continue this process on the approach and on the climb, adding increasingly detailed information on an ever-smaller scale to identify and choose the best line.

Study the peak in a good photograph to identify your route as accurately as possible. Try to understand how the line of your route takes advantage of the mountain's structure, such as following major ridges or ledge systems. Realize that routes do not necessarily follow obvious lines of weakness such as rock gullies. More often, they go where there is more solid, safer, or better-quality climbing. Copy any photographs you have and bring them with you on the climb.

Study the route description in a guidebook, if one exists. Written route descriptions and topo drawings can give much useful information, though they can also be quite difficult to follow. Photos with the route drawn over them can be particularly helpful, but beware that there could be errors in the drawing. Keep in mind that some guidebooks are better than others. Try to get a sense of the quality of the descriptions in the guidebook you are using, and decide how much stock you can put in the information you get from it. As you study your route, also check out any adjacent routes. Identifying where your route goes is easier if you understand the terrain to either side of it. As with photos, copy guidebook information and keep it handy on the route.

Finally, talk to locals or others familiar with your route for further information or to get answers to any specific questions that you might have.

ON THE APPROACH

Each time you get a good view of your route, study it and commit the details to memory. Draw pictures in your notebook or take photos with your digital camera during breaks, but also learn to look around and make mental notes while you walk. Try to identify places where the route may become difficult to follow. For example, the route ahead may be hidden behind other features or through foreshortening, or the terrain may be complicated and nondescript, with many smaller features that all look the same (towers, parallel gullies, crevasses, etc.). Look for options for getting through these tricky bits, as well as landmarks that will be visible to you once you get there and that will help you situate yourself. Note anything you can see of the descent route, if it is different from the ascent route.

We cannot count the number of times we have taken a route based on information seen previously but no longer visible, and have heard our guests ask in wonder how we knew where to go. The answer is usually, "We saw it earlier, and we remembered."

ON THE CLIMB

Routefinding is an ongoing process of constantly gathering and incorporating new data to revise and refine your opinion. Learn to continue this process as you move along, avoiding unnecessary stops. A brief exploration around a corner to check out alternative possibilities or a detour for a better view can help you find the best line or answer some question in your mind. This is often worth the time it takes, but keep it as quick as you can.

Locate the features you identified at home or on the approach, and continually track your position in relation to them. Take full advantage of easy ground, and try to connect together easy passages that allow relatively quick and safe travel. On rock, look for features such as continuous ledge systems or featured parts of slabs, and avoid loose sections. Seek out the lowest-angle slabs, the roughest texture, the greatest concentration of holds, or a continuous crack line. On snow, try to assess the angle and firmness of the slope. Keep in mind that snowy couloirs when viewed straight on appear steeper than they really are.

Wherever possible, gravitate toward ridges, buttresses, and high ground rather than gullies or faces, unless you know that the route follows the latter. Your perception of difficulty is often wrong when you are comparing ridges and gullies—the ridge usually looks harder than it turns out to be, while the gully looks, but is not, easier. Sticking to high ground helps you to maintain the greatest possible visibility of surrounding terrain. It also preserves options; it's often easy to move from the ridge to a flank, ledge system, or gully, whereas the reverse can be more difficult than expected. Finally, ridges are less exposed to rockfall, rock quality tends to be better, and they are simply more enjoyable to climb.

"ROUTE FOLLOWING"

Route following is the ability to follow clues left by other climbers. The vast majority of alpine routes that people climb these days have been done by hundreds, if not thousands, of other climbers. Most (though certainly not all) of these previous climbers were on route. All of these people have had an impact on the mountain. Some effects are temporary, such as tracks in the snow; some are more permanent, such as scratched or polished rock. With practice, you can see increasingly subtle clues to help you sniff out the trail and stay on route.

Amount of traffic. Consider the popularity of the route when you look for signs of passage. Would you expect to see a climbers' trail, given how often the route is climbed? If you do not see one, is it conceivable that it doesn't exist, or is it more likely that you just haven't found it yet? Signs can be quite subtle; always compare the amount and type of plants and lichen in off-route areas with the route line itself.

Consistency of evidence. The evidence of traffic on your trail should ideally remain more or less constant; notice any changes. For example, if your track starts to look ever fainter, you might have strayed off route somewhere earlier.

Forks in the road. Keep track of places where you come to a fork or choice between two apparent trails. If your choice turns out to be a dead-end, your ability to remember what the other alternative looked like, where it seemed to lead, whether it was to the right or to the left, and how far back it was will be a tremendous help.

Rock. On rock, the "trail" created by the passage of thousands of hands and feet is almost always the best line to take. Signs of this trail can be very faint and hard to make out, but you can learn to see them easily by being alert. Note areas of clean rock where lichen has been scuffed and killed or where sand and loose rock have been swept away. Look for crampon scratch marks and worn or polished holds. These are especially common in high-use areas on popular climbs.

Tracks in snow. We all tend to gravitate to tracks in the snow. They make walking easier and almost always bring some sense of security. But their helpfulness depends on who made them and what they knew. On a glacier, for example, you won't learn much from the tracks of a single party who may very well have been lost. On the other hand, several dozen climbers with a guide in the lead create a more reliable track. When you are climbing at night or in the fog, consider whether the maker of the track had any better visibility than you currently do.

Downhill tracks are usually more reliable than uphill tracks if the descent route returns the same way. On the way down, climbers have the advantage of what they found out on the way up: where the crevasses were, how large they were, what lay beyond that knoll, etc.

Also, their course back down will take advantage of information gained from better view points above.

As the summer season progresses, tracks on a glacier that once took a good line may now be dangerously close to open crevasses or may cross bad snow bridges. Alter the route to avoid these hazards. More than once, we have followed tracks up to a wide, yawning hole, where clearly the last party to pass through had encountered a different situation.

Other climbers. Other climbers ahead of you can indicate the route by giving you a target to aim for. Try to remember the terrain features marking the route at their location, so that you can identify these features when you get there. Of course, there is always the chance that they are off route; you have to assess that for yourself.

Cairns. Rock cairns often—but not always—mark the best route. Treat cairns with healthy skepticism. Many climbers build them as temporary markers to help them retrace their steps if necessary in poor visibility. If they do not retrace their steps but instead take a different or better route back, the off-route cairn remains in place. Avoid building cairns unless you are 100 percent sure you are on the best line.

Fixed gear and rappel anchors. Many technical rock routes have some fixed protection or anchors left by other climbers. Usually this gear is on route, but not always. If it looks as though many other climbers have used it—for example, if it contains bolts and chains or well-maintained webbing that is not too old and faded—then odds are good that you are on the right line.

In the Alps there can be quite a lot of fixed gear, especially on popular routes and those that are guided regularly. Local guides often establish permanent anchors to aid them in quickly belaying their clients up or down the mountain. However, guides tend not to fix much intermediate protection. The result is great belay anchors with minimal fixed gear between.

There also will be fixed anchors on a route that is commonly rappelled. Multiple rappel anchors on any given route are usually fairly consistent in quality. If you encounter an anchor that is significantly poorer in quality than others you have been using, it may be an off-route anchor. Look a bit harder for the correct one.

Back-off gear. Sometimes parties who believe they are off route will retreat and leave gear behind in order to rappel or lower off difficult sections. Such gear tends to be minimal, usually consisting of slings on horns or single protection pieces. Often a piton or nut will be left behind with a small piece of webbing tied through it, or a carabiner will be left in place. Back-off gear is almost always a sign that the correct route is elsewhere.

COMMON ERRORS IN ROUTEFINDING

You can save a lot of time and improve your routefinding significantly simply by avoiding some very common errors.

Misinterpreting route descriptions. A common error is to put too much emphasis on a written description in a guidebook or a verbal description from an acquaintance or friend. We all describe things differently and interpret someone else's verbal description differently. Your own observations on the climb should take precedence over what you think you understand from other sources.

Gravitating toward gullies. As noted above in "On the Climb," ridges more often provide better routes than gullies for many reasons: deceptive difficulty of climbing in gullies, loss of visibility in gullies, difficulty of exit from gullies, etc. Beginning alpinists tend to be strongly attracted to gullies because they look easy. This is such a common error that we feel it cannot be overemphasized.

Inaccurately assessing terrain. Misjudging the difficulty of climbing or the quality of rock or snow can lead you off route or into dangerous terrain. Terrain assessment can be quite difficult. To improve your skill in doing this, always compare your opinions developed from afar with what you find on the actual route. Note, and learn from mistakes.

Failing to recognize or correct mistakes. A very common error is either not recognizing evidence that you are off route or not giving appropriate weight to such evidence. Sometimes being slightly off route is okay, if you are heading in the right direction generally. But on technical rock, being off route means you know little about the difficulty of the climbing ahead or whether your "new" route will go.

TIPS: LEARNING TO ROUTEFIND

- Lead the group. Putting yourself in the lead forces you to routefind. Most of us are less observant when we follow others.
- Go out with good routefinders and have them follow you. Their comments can help you learn what you need to look for.
- When you make a routefinding error, try to figure out why. Did you put yourself in a place where you couldn't see? Did you forget or miss some piece of evidence?
- On easy and obvious ground with little routefinding complexity, challenge yourself to find the absolute best way through the terrain. Imagine you're injured, exhausted, or just plain lazy, and you can't afford to expend the slightest unnecessary effort. This "micro" routefinding skill—finding the path of very least resistance—forces you to carefully assess the difficulty of each move and is a good practice in general. In fact, we do this all the time when guiding, to reduce risk and to help our guests (and ourselves) save energy.

NAVIGATION

Navigation uses various instruments and aids—maps, compass, altimeter, and sometimes GPS—to give us information beyond what our eyes can tell us. However, our instruments can give us only a general sense of the location of the route. While navigating, we still must continue to routefind on the smaller scale. Even in a whiteout—perhaps especially then—we must continue to observe and remember the terrain, using all of our senses. For example, with limited visibility we can still discern important things such as the angle or shape of a slope.

The effort required to master the art of navigation and the exactitude navigation demands in poor visibility are more than rewarded by the satisfaction that comes from finding your way safely home no matter what the weather. In this section we focus on:

- Improving map-reading skills, visualizing terrain from map data, recognizing terrain in the field, and identifying features.
- Making a whiteout navigation plan using map, compass, altimeter, and GPS, and following the plan in the field. This includes taking bearings both from sightings and from the map; following a bearing in the field; using techniques such as handrails, elevation, the contour tangent method, and aiming off; and dealing with obstacles and measuring distance.
- How the global positioning system (GPS) works; how to use it in your whiteout navigation plan and in the field.
- Tips on equipment selection.

FINDING THE HUT

Once while skiing the Chamonix to Zermatt Haute Route in Switzerland, we were engulfed in thick clouds as we descended from the Pigne d'Arolla, a 3800-meter glaciated peak. We did not have far to go to reach the Vignettes Hut, our destination for the night. It was late February, an unusual time for the tour, so we were alone with no tracks to follow.

We had two concerns. One was to avoid a large and messy icefall just above the ridge where the hut sits. The other was that we might easily descend too low or veer slightly and miss the fairly small entrance to a traverse leading into the ridge.

We had just reset our altimeter on the summit of the peak, so we had confidence in our elevation reading. We used compass bearings, supported by a periodic assessment of slope angle and aspect, to stay to the right of the icefall area and the altimeter reading to tell us when to begin traversing and find our little entryway to the ridge.

After an hour or so of painstaking work, the narrow ridge and the sheltering hut appeared amazingly close in the thick fog; we felt almost as if we had conjured them ourselves by magic. We slept well that night.

MAP READING

The single most important skill needed for map reading is terrain recognition: recognizing features from the map when you see them in real life, and vice versa. There are three components to this. You must understand what the map tells you; you must convert that information into a mental image; and you must compare that image to the terrain you see or travel over.

Understand the Map

We assume the reader knows how contour lines express landforms. Remember, however, that different maps have different scales and contour intervals. If you go to a new area or country to climb, you may need to "recalibrate" your brain to correctly interpret a new scale or interval. Your goal is to be able to look at a slope on the map and have a good sense of its steepness and size.

In the United States, the best maps of most areas are at a scale of 1:24,000 with a contour interval of 40 feet (about 12 meters). France and Switzerland are similar, with scales of 1:25,000 and 20-meter (about 65-foot) contours. New Zealand and Canada tend to have 1:50,000 scale maps with contour intervals of 20 and 40 meters (about 130 feet), respectively.

Many maps have a superimposed grid, which is very useful both for taking bearings from the map and for transferring bearings from field to map. Different maps use different grid systems, but the easiest to use are set on 1-kilometer (0.6-mile) squares. We talk more about grids in the section on GPS, below.

Create a Mental Image of the Terrain

Study the map before a trip, and notice as much as you can about the features of the terrain. Your goal is to be able to see in your mind's eye exactly what the map represents. Notice shapes and relative heights of peaks or other important spots; distances between these points and their position relative to each other; slope angle and aspect (orientation), as well as the aspect and steepness of faces, ridges, and drainages.

Memorize as much of this information as you can. Mentally follow your route of travel. Try to imagine the visual effect of foreshortening. Anticipate where nearer features may hide more distant ones and at what point particular features will come into view.

Compare the Image to Reality

Once on the trail, compare your image from the map to what you actually see en route. This comparison tells you where you are and confirms where your route lies. It is mentally and visually simpler to do this if you physically orient the map to the terrain, with north on the map pointing to north in reality. Do this quickly, using the shape of the surrounding terrain to aid you.

Once the map is oriented to north, locate yourself simply by identifying some distinctive features around you, noting their relative direction and distance from you and comparing this with the same relationships on the map. Assuming you know your general vicinity and are able to mentally correlate terrain to its map representation, locating yourself is easy; with practice, you should be able to do it at a glance. This skill is extremely important when navigating in poor visibility.

As you get better at interpreting map information and forming an accurate mental image, strive to place more trust in your memory and in your eyes and to use the map more sparingly. The ability to get by with only the occasional quick glimpse at a map rather than frequent and lengthy study sessions will pay off on long approaches when you need to move quickly and maintain momentum. The better your visualization ability and memory, the more likely you are to stay oriented to begin with. A sketch, some notes, or a written travel plan will help you retain highlights and remind you of key facts and landmarks.

PRACTICE: CORRELATING THE MAP WITH VISIBLE TERRAIN FEATURES

With a map and compass, go to a high point where you can see a lot of terrain. Look at the main features around you, and see if you can find them on the map: peaks, major drainages, cliffs, etc. Once you've done this, find smaller features around you and again locate them on the map. Challenge yourself to identify ever-smaller features, up to the limit of the map's ability to depict them. Then go the other direction: find a distinctive-looking feature on the map and try to identify it in the view around you. Strive for accuracy and speed.

COMPASS

For alpine climbing, look for the following compass features (see Figure 5):

- **Adjustable declination**
- **Sighting mirror:** helps you to shoot accurate bearings more easily.
- **Nondigital:** although some watches and GPS units have built-in digital compasses, it is much harder to take, shoot, or follow a bearing using these. Such compasses might work in a pinch, but we'd hate to have to rely on them.
- **Global technology:** most compass needles are weighted to function well within only a limited range of latitudes. Compasses designed for use in the northern hemisphere do not function well in the southern hemisphere, and vice versa. "Global" compasses use clever technology that solves this problem. Buy a global compass if you like to travel.

ALTIMETER

Altimeters use barometric pressure to indicate altitude by measuring the weight of the air above you. As you climb higher and less air lies overhead, the decreasing weight of that air results in lower barometric pressure. Because the alpine world is three-dimensional, an altimeter is equal to a compass in usefulness; in fact, if we had to choose between them, we would also need a coin to flip!

Altimeter technology gets better all the time, and there are many good options to choose from. For alpine climbing, electronic models are best because of their lighter weight, more useful features, and higher resolution (smaller increment of measurement). Select an altimeter with a resolution of 1 meter (3 feet) or less and one that is easy to switch between meters and feet. A log feature can be useful, allowing you to record elevations reached at specific times and dates. Most climbers use altimeters that are incorporated into a watch, and this is quite handy—after all, you need an alarm for those alpine starts anyway.

If you will use your watch's altimeter for navigation, be sure it has a fresh battery or carry a spare, if it can be changed in the field.

Altimeters are accurate to the extent that the relationship between elevation and air pressure is normal. However, several factors can alter this relationship, including weather changes and sea-level air temperature, and this is why altimeters need to be reset at known elevations frequently. Reset your altimeter often, whenever you think that it may become an important navigation tool. Reset where you can be sure of your location on the map and can determine your altitude using contour lines or marked spot heights.

Weather-related air pressure changes. As discussed in Chapter 2, Alpine Environment, changes in air pressure accompany changes in the weather. If you see the weather changing as you climb, expect a corresponding change in altitude reading. For example, if the weather is deteriorating, your altimeter will read a bit too high as you climb. You can compensate for this by adjusting the altimeter 1.5 to 3 meters (5 to 10 feet) lower per hour. Remember that at

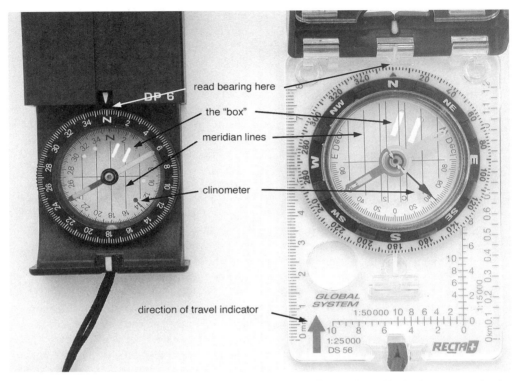

Figure 5. *Compasses suitable for mountain navigation. Both have adjustable declination, on both set to about 22° east in this example—the "box" is offset 22° east of the meridian lines. Declination is adjusted by means of a small screw in the back of the compass. Both have sighting mirrors. The compass on the right (b) has a "global" needle system that functions in both northern and southern hemispheres.*

some point in the middle of the storm, the pressure will level out and eventually begin to rise.

Variation in air pressure gradient at different latitudes. The air-pressure gradient—the rate at which pressure changes as you change elevation—is what altimeter manufacturers use to calibrate altimeters. Unfortunately, this gradient is different at the poles than it is at the equator. The warmth of the equatorial regions makes the overlying air less dense than it is at the poles. Another way of saying this is that the gradient is steep at the poles and flat at the equator. The exact amount of error this problem introduces depends on your altitude and your latitude. Altimeter manufacturers design their units to be most accurate in the middle latitudes, about 30° to 60°. The closer you approach either of the poles or the equator, the greater the error. For example, air pressure at 7300 meters at the equator is about 400 millibars. At the poles, 400 millibars of pressure occurs at 6700 meters.

In addition to setting your altimeter frequently at known elevations, you can also anticipate and compensate for this error. As you ascend, expect your altimeter to read too low near the equator and too high at the poles.

Unusual temperature gradients. Manufacturers also calibrate altimeters for a normal temperature gradient, typically 0.65°C for every 100 meters of elevation change (about 3.6°F for every 1000 feet). Because temperature influences air density, the temperature gradient in turn influences the pressure gradient. An abnormal temperature gradient, such as during an inversion, when warmer air lies above colder air, will cause altimeter error.

GLOBAL POSITIONING SYSTEM (GPS)

GPS uses satellite signals to determine location with amazing accuracy. In optimum conditions, a GPS reading will tell you your location to within a margin of error of about 3–4 meters horizontally and about 10 meters in altitude. A detailed discussion of the specifics of GPS use, as well as its strengths and limitations, is found at the end of this chapter.

WHITEOUT NAVIGATION WITH INSTRUMENTS

Whiteout travel is a dance between doubt and certainty, confusion and confidence. As you proceed, you will occasionally encounter features that confirm your exact location, but there will be times when you know only that you are somewhere along a line between these points.

Navigation in a whiteout is very difficult once you have lost track of where you are. When you travel by instruments, you head toward and look for a specific set of features that can confirm your location. Once you are lost, any features that you glimpse are less able to either confirm or contradict your theories about where you are. Rather than looking in a small area for something that correlates to a specific part of the map, you end up searching in a large area containing too many possibilities. You must keep track of where you are as you go, before you lose visibility, as well as afterward.

Even in very poor visibility where you must rely on instruments, your eyes and other senses are still essential. The briefest of glimpses between the clouds or through the fog may tell you much more of what you need to know than your map, compass, altimeter, or even GPS can possibly tell you by themselves.

Making a Whiteout Navigation Plan

A whiteout navigation plan describes the route you will follow and the techniques you will use to follow it. Your plan may be an elaborate strategy for moving between dozens of known points covering miles of terrain, or it may be a single compass bearing from your current location to a nearby snowy col; in either case, trying to travel in a whiteout without any plan is chancy indeed.

The use of compass, altimeter, or GPS all require obtaining data from the map, determining strategies, and making notes. This is best done in advance of your trip, in the warm comfort of home. You don't want to find yourself stuck in a ripping wind and pouring rain, trying to figure out which feature on the map to choose as your next destination point and how to get there, while holding on for dear life to a drenched map with gloved hands, struggling to take bearings from it while your friends wait freezing or, worse yet, argue with you about how to proceed.

Establishing "Known Points" and Lines of Travel

Your first step is to study the map and lay out the general outlines of your whiteout navigation plan. This plan consists of establishing known points—locations with identifiable features that you will be able to recognize in the field—and lines of travel between them. The easiest features to use as known points are visually recognizable and unique, such as a col, a summit, a cliff band, the end of a ridge, a rock outcrop with a distinctive shape, etc.—but a known point can also be something measurable only by instrument, such as an elevation as measured by an altimeter or a GPS waypoint (note that we use the term "known point"

here as distinct from "waypoint," which we use specifically to refer to a data point entered on a GPS; more on that in the GPS section below).

Judgment and experience both help in selecting the most useful known points and the most practical travel lines. Choosing good known points requires excellent map-reading skill as well as a complete knowledge of the use of instruments and the limits to their accuracy. In plotting known points and drawing up your travel lines, keep the following goals in mind:

Identifiability. In order to confirm your arrival at a known point, it must be identifiable and recognizable even in poor visibility. Besides distinctive shapes or unique features, you can also use less-tangible things such as the intersection of a specific elevation with changes in slope angle or aspect or with linear features such as a ridge crest, gully, or drainage.

Line-of-travel considerations. In a whiteout, you will travel between known points either by instruments alone or by following features that can be easily recognized in poor visibility, such as an obvious ridge crest or drainage. Your line of travel should be as short and easy to follow as you can make it, and obviously it should avoid hazards as much as possible. Nothing is quite so unnerving as encountering unexpected seracs or rockfall in a whiteout. Your choice of known points will influence your line of travel, so you have to consider both of these together.

Traveling Between Known Points

Between each known point, you will establish a line of travel that you can follow in poor visibility. A number of tactics can be used to follow that line. Normally you will use several of these at once, each reinforcing and confirming the other. Keep your overall strategy as simple as possible.

Taking a compass bearing. Lacking useful linear features, you can follow a compass bearing between known points. Your study of the map should indicate places where this may be your necessary tactic. To take a bearing from the map, follow these steps:

1. On your map, identify the two known points in question. Make sure that travel between these will actually be possible by following a straight line.

2. With a pencil, use your compass base plate or a straight edge to draw a line on the map between your two points. This is your line of travel.

3. Place your compass on the map, lining up the baseplate along the line of travel. Remember to orient the compass so that the "read bearing" indicator is in the direction you will travel (to avoid going 180 degrees in the wrong direction!).

4. Turn the circular compass housing until the meridian lines in the compass are parallel to the grid lines on your map—north on the circular housing must be oriented to north on the map.

5. Read the bearing at the "read bearing" indicator on the baseplate.

With this technique, it does not matter if the map is oriented or which direction the compass needle points. You are simply using the compass to measure the angle between the map grid and your proposed direction of travel. Study the example in Figure 6.

Following handrails. Handrails are linear features that you can follow in poor visibility. Many things can serve this function: a ridge, a line of cliffs, a narrow valley or river, etc. Following handrails is usually vastly superior to following compass bearings, because the feature you follow continually confirms you are on route. This is one of the few easy ways to keep track of your location as you go, which allows you to move quickly. Include this tactic in your whiteout plans whenever possible.

Aiming off. Following a compass bearing is difficult to do accurately in poor visibility. Some degree of error is practically inevitable, and even slight error is often enough to miss small or indistinct features in the blizzard. Aiming off introduces deliberate error in order to intercept a handrail that can lead you to your target. For example, imagine that your next known point is a broad, snowy col, and that a long rock ridge leads into the col from the right. Rather than heading toward the center of the col, you can aim off slightly to the right of it to intercept the ridge. No matter where you meet the rock, you know that by turning left you will eventually reach the col.

Figure 6. *Here, we are taking the bearing from the Mönchsjoch Hut (next to the Mönch) to the Walcherhorn. The compass baseplate is lined up between the two points (we have omitted the step of drawing a line on the map) with the direction of travel arrow (out of the photo, but toward the mirror on this compass) pointing from the Mönchsjoch Hut toward our objective, the Walcherhorn. Holding the baseplate steady, we have rotated the housing until the meridian lines are parallel to the grid lines on the map (darkened here for clarity). We can now read the bearing—76° in this case—at the "read bearing here" mark, which is located at the base of the mirror. In Switzerland the declination is 0° and you can see that the compass is set to this. Notice also that we are completely ignoring the compass needle and the black clinometer needle.*

Following a contour line. Using your altimeter, you can follow a contour line as you would follow a compass bearing or as a form of "handrail" to your next known point. Of course, the potential for altimeter inaccuracy can be a problem with this technique. Know the typical margin of error for your altimeter and, as always, reset often at known elevations. You can also deal with error by aiming off, much as you would with a compass bearing. For example, imagine you are following a contour to a notch in a ridge. To compensate for possible altimeter error, follow a contour slightly below the elevation of the notch. When you intersect the ridge, go uphill to find your notch.

Using the contour tangent method.
With the contour tangent method, the shape of the land helps you figure out where you are. This method is one of the very few ways you can confirm your location with no visible recognizable features, using only the map, compass, and altimeter. Even in zero visibility, you can determine the angle of the slope you are on and the compass direction of the fall line (slope aspect). As you travel, note changes in these measurements, and also note your elevation as determined by your altimeter. By correlating this information with matching terrain on the map, you should be able to determine your location.

For a simple example, imagine yourself on the flanks of a smooth, conical mountain, Mount Fuji–like in shape. You don't know where you are, but you do know that your tent is located at 2100 meters (about 7000 feet), due north of the summit. To find your way there, first measure the slope aspect where you are, by aiming your compass straight down the fall line and taking the bearing. If the slope aspect is due west, then you are on the west side of the peak and need to traverse to the north to find your camp. Continue traversing until slope aspect becomes north. Then go up or down, using your altimeter, to reach the 2100-meter camp—very easy.

Of course, mountains do not always oblige us with as regular a shape as in our example. But parts of them usually are unique and identifiable. Use these bits and pieces to stay on track or to confirm data gathered from other methods.

THE CONTOUR TANGENT METHOD IN ACTION

Many years ago, we climbed the Yocum Ridge on Mount Hood in the Oregon Cascades. We had a great climb on a lovely winter day. Winter nights come early and, being a bit slow, we ended up descending the Leuthold Couloir at sunset. As the sun went down, the fog came up and we found ourselves fumbling around, unable to see more than about 2 meters ahead.

The Leuthold Couloir empties into the upper cirque of the Reid Glacier, a half-mile-wide basin between the Yocum Ridge to the north and Illumination Rock to the south. The route back to our camp on the opposite side of the mountain lay over Illumination Saddle, the gap between Illumination Rock and the main mass of Mount Hood. Our challenge was to find the correct gully leading to Illumination Saddle, when it was virtually indistinguishable from the many gullies that climb up into no-man's-land on the west face of Mount Hood. Ice from a recent warm rain had made the snow very hard and we had no tracks to follow. The only distinguishing characteristic of the correct gully was its aspect.

We carefully traversed the upper part of the glacier, tracking the changes in slope aspect as we went, until our compass indicated that we should be just below the saddle. Climbing straight up in zero visibility, we hit it dead on.

Finishing Touches to Your Plan

After determining all the necessary known points and planning your strategies for travel between them, take a moment to review your plan as a whole. For each leg of your trip, consider noting down as much as is relevant or helpful of the following information:

■ Altitudes of your known points

■ Grid references of features, if using a GPS (see below)

■ Approximate slope aspect and angle at a known point, if you anticipate that the contour tangent method will be useful

■ Compass bearing to the next known point, if that will be your line of travel

■ Distance to next known point

■ Altitude gain or loss to next known point

Figure 7. *A small whiteout route plan for part of Denali's West Buttress route. The notebook and map could both be used in the field, along with compass and altimeter. A few descriptive notes help you key into information that is not readily gleaned from a glance at the map, such as elevations of known points, fall line bearings, or estimated travel times.*

- Estimated time of travel to next known point
- Any helpful comments or reminders about your strategy for reaching or finding the next known point. Most of the time this is fairly obvious, but write it down if you need reminding.

Your plan can be depicted in different ways. In practice, it will almost always include the map, with selected notes to give critical information at a glance. Additional notes in the form of a sketch, diagram, or table in your notebook (see Figure 7) can also be helpful, especially for recalling details, such as elevations or time estimates, that can be hard to discern quickly from the map.

IN THE FIELD

When navigating in a whiteout, try to remember all of the terrain you pass through. In poor visibility, the area you are able to observe is too small to distinguish between similar-looking places. For example, any spot you pass through may correspond to countless other locations on the map having the same elevation, aspect, and angle. However, by remembering as you move along changes in these and the sequence of those changes, you begin to form a mental image of a shape, not just an isolated point. This narrows down the possibilities, because there are fewer similar shapes on the map.

Maintaining your confidence is very important when traveling in a whiteout, despite the stress inherent in the task. Confidence helps to keep you moving, and

moving keeps you warm. Also, simply covering more ground adds more detail and information to your mental map. Whiteout navigation is like solving a puzzle, which can be quite enjoyable in a twisted sort of way. We both enjoy the challenge and reward of finding our way in the fog, and often find ourselves competing for the lead when the weather shuts down. When faced with a whiteout, enjoy the energy that blows in with bad weather, and embrace the challenge you are about to face.

When the clouds begin to threaten, it is time to haul out your map, review your whiteout navigation plan, and implement it. Prepare yourself mentally and physically. Be determined and observant, and stay calm and warm. The following section describes techniques you may use and concerns that may arise as you navigate in a storm.

Anticipating Unseen Hazards

Stay out from under areas of avalanche, rockfall, or icefall hazard. Rope up on snow if there is a chance you could walk off cornices or steep edges or into crevasses. Use trekking poles to help with balance and to help alert you to unseen changes in the slope.

Keeping Your Tools Handy

In poor visibility, keep your route plan and your instruments handy. Fold your map up small to display only the relevant section, for quick and easy reference. Carry it in a plastic map case or other waterproof, transparent bag. Good map cases have a cord to go around your neck or attach to your coat. Compasses have cords to prevent loss. Girth-hitch the cord through a zipper slider or other attachment point on the front of your jacket.

Following a Compass Bearing in the Field

As discussed in the preceding section, your whiteout navigation plan may involve various tactics for traveling between known points. One of the more common is to follow a compass bearing you took from the map. Here's how to do it:

1. Set your compass to the bearing you took off the map when you created your plan.
2. Turn the compass until the magnetic needle lies inside the box (make sure it's not 180 degrees wrong!).
3. Follow the direction-of-travel arrow.

A small error over a long distance will take you far away from your goal. Accuracy is possible but requires effort and attention to detail. With care, it is possible to effectively follow a compass bearing solo; however, it is generally more accurate with a partner. Walk in a line, some 15–30 meters apart, with each of your party following the bearing using separate compasses. The climber behind can shout adjustments to the leader if necessary. If deep snow or rough ground makes it hard to walk a straight line, the leader may be better off walking without a compass and relying completely on the second for direction.

Dealing with Obstacles and Measuring Distance

You may have to deviate from your line of travel at some point in order to get around an obstacle. If the obstacle is small, the solution is easy. One of you goes ahead, and the one left behind stops the leader once he or she has passed the obstacle and is back in line with the desired heading.

Obstacles too large for this tactic require a more complicated procedure. You need to make four 90-degree turns to walk around the obstacle. If you travel the same number of paces between the first two turns and the last two turns, you will be back on your original bearing. Measure the distance by counting paces or rope lengths. For the more mathematically inclined, this can be done with three turns instead of four or with varying angles. Whatever fancy geometry you use, be sure to write down turn angles and distance walked.

Measuring Slope Aspect

When using the contour tangent method, you must frequently measure the compass direction of the slope. Face downhill and shoot a bearing directly down the fall line. Be sure the spot where you take your measurement really indicates the general aspect of the slope and is not just some small terrain feature that doesn't show up on your map; repeated measurements should sort this out. Check your accuracy by practicing occasionally in known locations.

Shooting Bearings in the Field

Imagine you have been following your travel line for some time, then the clouds clear and you get a brief view of your next destination point. You shoot a bearing off it in order to improve the accuracy of your travel line, correcting any errors in either the bearing or the path you were previously following. This technique is particu-larly useful when you can see a known point along the route you want to follow but anticipate that clouds will soon come in and visibility will become difficult.

1. With your compass at eye level, point the baseplate at your destina-tion or at the known point you want to sight off (see Figure 8).
2. Using the mirror to view the housing while keeping the compass level, rotate the housing until the magnetic needle is aligned with the box. Make sure you are not 180 degrees off.
3. Read the bearing at the "read bearing" indicator.

Resection

Resection—also known as triangulation—is a technique whereby you can pinpoint your location in the field by shooting bearings of at least two visible known features around you. Although it is helpful for learning and practicing map-reading skills, as a practical matter it is not very useful for whiteout navigation in alpine terrain, since it requires some visibility in order to identify the features and shoot your bearings. Given such visibility, you should be able to locate your position more quickly and accurately simply by correlat-ing the shapes you see with those depicted on the map.

Revising Your Plan

As you travel along in a whiteout, occa-sional views may allow you to change parts of your original plan. Be alert to these and take advantage of them when they occur.

Figure 8. *Shooting a bearing toward the Minarets, New Zealand. With the compass pointing to the peak, rotate the housing so the needle lines up with the box. Read the bearing—in this example, 22°. In order to get an accurate bearing, the center line inscribed on the mirror must pass through the center of the mirrored reflection of the circular housing.*

For example, a brief clearing may allow you to see some of your route ahead. You may be able to abandon a more difficult technique such as a compass bearing or contour line and simply routefind through the terrain you see. If you alter your original plan, be sure to have a way to find your next known point if the weather closes in again. For example, memorize the terrain you must cross or shoot a new bearing of your next destination point before the clouds roll back in.

In general, whenever you get a glimpse of some feature, try to identify it by its shape and any surrounding terrain you can see. Take a moment to study the map. Does your glimpse support or contradict your theory about where you are?

Reducing Risk

Traveling in a whiteout is inherently risky for several reasons. It's easy to walk into or off unseen hazards such as crevasses or cornices; poor weather can bring on hypothermia; stress or discomfort can lead to hasty or poor decision making; prediction of further weather changes is difficult when a view of the sky is lost. However, you can often go a long way in poor weather without excessive risk, so long as retreat is feasible. As you proceed, imagine how you will get back if the weather worsens or if new or windblown snow hides your tracks. There may come a point beyond which retreat in worsening conditions becomes unacceptably risky. Try to avoid being taken by surprise by anticipating and recognizing these times or places.

Avoiding Common Errors

Traveling by instruments is not easy. Seemingly little mistakes can have big consequences. We have seen climbers traveling 180 degrees in the wrong direction as a result of misaligning their compass. GPS units use long strings of numbers to define locations—a single incorrect digit can put you in the wrong valley or even the wrong country. Whether reading elevations off topographic maps or accounting for compass declination, use of instruments carries the potential for great confusion. Beware of the following common problems:

Having tunnel vision. It can be tempting to rely too much on one source of information and to ignore others. Concentrating exclusively on either your compass bearing, altimeter reading, or GPS can distract you and cause you to miss useful visual clues or miss or forget details of the terrain you pass through.

Failing to notice and resolve conflicting data. Everything you observe must add up to a consistent and plausible picture. Your theories about where you are on the map must be consistent with all measured data, especially elevation, slope steepness, and aspect, as well as any visual glimpses of terrain.

Jumping to conclusions. Misinterpretation of glimpsed terrain features is one of the most difficult errors to avoid. Wishful thinking often encourages us to see correlations that don't exist. Again, the solution is to use multiple information sources to confirm your theories.

Stalling out. When in doubt, there is a temptation to stop or slow to a crawl. You don't want to rush, but try to keep moving. The more ground you cover, the more terrain you see, giving you more data. When doubts arise, go a little farther. You can always come back, as long as you pay attention and remember what you've done.

Miscalculating distance traveled. In a whiteout, you usually have not traveled as far as you think you have.

Misperceiving size and distance. Objects seen in the fog are usually closer and smaller than they appear.

Mistrusting instruments. Your innate sense of direction is not reliable in a whiteout. When following a bearing, check your compass frequently.

LEARNING NAVIGATION

Now we come to truth-telling time. We have devoted much discussion to the creation of a detailed, written whiteout navigation plan and to following it scrupulously in the field. But in reality, this process is mostly a necessary stage in a learning progression. Our own whiteout navigation plans rarely entail anything approaching the written detail described here, and we suspect the same is true of most highly skilled and experienced alpinists. Although we do have a plan and it usually includes some written notes, these are highly selective and abbreviated. Our process starts with studying the map carefully, as described above, and assessing the need for partial or miniplans. We identify potential problem areas and, if

necessary, take selective notes on the map itself of details such as key elevations, terrain features, and bearings.

We can omit much of the written planning because, through a great deal of whiteout navigation experience, we know several things: we know that we are capable of quick decision making and fast, accurate instrument reading in the field. We also are very confident in our interpretation of map data, so we can reliably identify places where travel lines will be obvious and easy and others where trickier tactics such as compass bearings might be necessary. This allows us to plan more globally in our heads and to prioritize the notes we do take. Our map-reading ability also means fewer sketches or diagrams are necessary, because we can glean information in the field very quickly from the map itself. Finally, we trust our observation and memory and, hence, our ability to keep track of where we are as we go and to be sparing in our recourse to the map. All of these things make seat-of-the-pants navigation more feasible. This can be advantageous because many things are better assessed and decided on site than from home, and it is easier to accommodate changes of route if necessary.

It is very important to note that we began omitting parts of our written plans only after we had many actual real-life experiences in many instrument-critical situations and had built the necessary skills and confidence. It is also important to note that this is not the absence of planning. We very carefully inspect every piece of the approach, the route, and the descent on the map, and we make sure that we have a strategy for every part of the route—a written strategy, if necessary, or one that relies on only visual clues from the map if that seems adequate.

This approach requires a very high level of confidence and fluency in navigation, which should be an aspiring alpinist's ultimate goal. However, reaching this point requires a lot of practice, and opportunities are rare. The need to truly depend on instruments is fairly unusual, especially in clement climates such as the Sierra Nevada of California and the Rockies of Colorado. If possible, take climbing holidays in varying climates and continents. Notoriously stormy ranges such as the North Cascades of Washington State, the Canadian Coast and Interior Ranges, and the Southern Alps of New Zealand are particularly good teachers!

A realistic learning progression starts with the deliberate and thorough process discussed above, moving on to more abbreviated notes and on-site planning once you have had good success with your navigation plans in several real-life whiteout situations in which you truly depended on your instruments.

NAVIGATING WITH GLOBAL POSITIONING SYSTEM

More and more climbers are carrying GPS receivers into the mountains. Despite the power of this technology and its tremendous potential, most people use the GPS only as a fancy recording device, capturing all sorts of data about a trip as it progresses. While reviewing, plotting, and logging past movements may be fun, it is not the best use of the GPS. Even the "bread crumb" application of the GPS (recording waypoints on the way up, to be followed back in poor visibility) is usually of limited value—keen observation, memory, and perhaps a bit of traditional navigation are all that are really needed to retrace your steps, and you need to develop these skills in any case.

GPS is most helpful to alpinists when it is used to plan whiteout navigation on a route they have never done before. This higher-level skill is the focus of the following discussion. For this discussion, we assume that the reader knows how the GPS unit works, the limits to its accuracy, how to mark waypoints and create a route by stringing together the waypoints, and how to determine and set map datum, map projection, and position format (see the bibliography for more information). We also assume the reader has the ability to use the GPS with a computer, the ability to use digitized maps for marking waypoints and creating routes, and the knowledge of how to upload these into the GPS. Using the GPS with a computer is not strictly necessary—and we do show you how to take waypoint coordinates directly from a paper map—but the use of a computer makes the whole process so much easier that it is worth the effort to learn. Using a GPS in this way requires a high level of map reading and terrain recognition skills; there is no shortcut for this.

The challenge begins with looking at the map and deciding exactly where you want to go. As with any whiteout plan, your route must avoid hazards and follow easy lines of travel via an efficient route. This can be quite difficult, and you are still subject to the limited detail inherent in any map. Serious problems can hide between 20- to 40-meter contour lines! We know this from a personal experience of trying to travel in a heavy snowfall and being led onto an unstable snow slope too small to appear on the map. Once a route is identified, waypoints must be chosen and entered into your GPS for use in the field.

There are some significant limits to the usefulness of the GPS and certain problems you need to avoid; we discuss these a little bit later. But in its proper application, the GPS can be almost as good as a timely parting of the clouds.

Alpine Applications of GPS

To the alpine climber, GPS is most useful on wide-open snow or glacier routes where it allows waypoints to be placed in locations that would not be identifiable using traditional navigational tools. For example,

USING GPS ON A SKI MOUNTAINEERING TOUR: A PERSONAL EXPERIENCE

On a recent hut-to-hut ski tour in the Swiss Alps, a multiday storm with persistent fog and clouds threatened to pin us down at our first hut. We could identify a safe route to the next hut, following the curve of a fairly flat glacier with few open crevasses for several kilometers. As long as we could stay near the middle of the glacier and away from the steep slopes on either side, we could avoid avalanche hazard and the crevassed glacier margin. At a particular point, however, we would need to work our way to the glacier's edge to avoid a crevassed icefall.

With traditional tools, such a route would have been very difficult to follow, entailing hours of exacting and slow travel following compass bearings, guessing how far we had come, and having no reliable way to verify our arrival near the top of the icefall. Finding the place to exit the glacier would have also been quite tricky given the potential for altimeter error on such gently sloping terrain. Alternatively, a route bringing us close enough to see and identify visible features would have exposed us to avalanche and other hazards, since those features were all on the slopes above the glacier's margin.

In this circumstance, the GPS was a perfect solution. Knowing that crevasse hazard was low so long as we stayed on the middle of the glacier, we were able to ski at a slow and comfortable glide, roped together, following the GPS display indicators quickly and easily from waypoint to waypoint. We found our exit with very little hassle. We saved many hours of hard work and worry.

One important note: If there had been significant crevasse hazard on our route, the GPS would not have helped us to avoid it. In fact, it might even have tempted us to travel under unsafe conditions. Do not get caught in the trap of thinking that navigation is your only problem!

any spot on a featureless, level snowfield can be designated a waypoint and located extremely quickly with the GPS. This can save hours of time and much mental anguish, as well as allowing an easier and sometimes safer route.

The GPS can also be helpful in expeditionary situations where the same terrain must be covered a number of times—for example, ferrying loads on a glacier between camps on a high-altitude peak such as Denali in Alaska. In these situations, GPS waypoints can function much the same as route-marking wands but without the litter problem. A route recorded on a day with good visibility, skirting hazards and pinpointing cache locations, can be followed again if hazards do not change; this may allow safe travel even in bad visibility.

Despite the impressive power of GPS technology, it has some serious limitations for use in alpine climbing. It is not useful for rock climbing or scrambling because the scale of the terrain features that will determine your best way to go are too small to appear on the map, so you cannot effectively plot your route using waypoints gathered from a map. Even if you could, the number of waypoints needed to cover the complexity of a rock route would make this impractical. This very complexity of features means that you should be able to figure out where you are even without the GPS. In addition, the margin of error of the technology, though only a few meters, could be serious on rock, where typically the best line is very narrowly defined and

being just a few feet off route means much harder climbing.

Creating a Whiteout Navigation Plan with GPS

Just as with traditional instruments, create your GPS whiteout navigation plan in advance. As mentioned above, this is easiest on a computer, but it is also possible in the field as long as you have a warm, sheltered place to do it. We have had many an evening session in huts and tents, plotting the next day's route and entering the data into our receiver by hand. The key is to create your route before you need it. On-the-fly GPS navigation—trying to take waypoints off the map in the field while out in the nasty weather, then entering them into your GPS—is an invitation to disaster: slow, cumbersome, and prone to error.

Choose your route. The first step is to decide where you want to go. Look carefully at your map (either on paper or on a computer) and plot your route. Give any hazards a wide berth. Crevasses, for example, are very hard to see in a whiteout, even if they are only a meter or two in front of you. Too often we don't see them until we are nearly in them. Crevasses do not show up individually on a map, of course, so whenever possible your whiteout navigation plan should stick to areas of the glacier with minimal crevasse hazard (see Chapter 8, Glaciers, for information on how underlying landforms influence crevasse formation). Also avoid potentially corniced ridge crests, where paying close attention to your GPS may put you too close to the exposed edge or on the wrong side of the potential fracture line. If your route runs closely underneath large, steep cliffs or into deep canyons, consider how the GPS's view of the sky (and necessary satellites) will be blocked, greatly decreasing accuracy in the field.

Draw a faint line on your map to show your proposed route. Be as accurate as you can. Imagine what it will be like traveling that line in zero visibility. As you plot your route, think about what sections of the route can easily be followed with traditional tools, and for what sections you will be dependent on the GPS. Be prepared to switch back and forth between GPS and compass and altimeter. Using all tools helps you stay alert, cross-check data, and avoid mistakes.

Choose, name, mark, and list your waypoints. Once you have identified the best route to follow, mark dots on your map to indicate where you want to place your waypoints. In general, it is better to put in more waypoints than you might think you need, using enough, for example, to create rounded corners where cutting corners would take you close to problems. Long, straight sections are fine as long as they are the best route. Be picky and exacting. Have good reasons for your choices. Make your first waypoint some known location, like your camp, the trailhead, or a hut, to allow you to confirm that your GPS is set correctly before you go out in the mists. If your GPS says you are somewhere anomalous, you will know not to trust it.

After you have marked all the waypoints you want on your map, name each of them. Different GPS units allow for names of varying length, but many allow only six letters or numbers. You can use any names you want, but some sort of sequential system is best. Mark the names on your map, next to the dot indicating the exact waypoint location. If you are using a computer, print out that part of the map that shows your route and carry it with you in the field. Be sure the map you print has the waypoint names indicated.

In your notebook, write down all the names of your waypoints in column form. After the waypoint name, enter the coordinates of the waypoint (we get to that next). Leave a space for this (usually about 12 numbers), then write down a very short description of the waypoint location. Just a few words is usually all you need; for example, "glacier turns" or "middle of flat 3420m."

Determine waypoint coordinates. Determining coordinates on a computer is very easy. Simply clicking on any location on a digital map allows you to mark the waypoint, determine its coordinates, and name it.

To determine waypoint coordinates by hand, you need grid lines on your map. Most maps have such grid lines on them, usually indicating square kilometers, and this is best. Some countries, such as Switzerland and New Zealand, have their own grid system. Most other countries, including France, the United States, and Canada, use the Universal Transverse Mercator (UTM) system. All of these use a kilometer-square grid, and the process for measuring waypoint coordinates is similar (see Figure 9). Do not use latitude and longitude unless absolutely necessary, because they are complicated and encourages mistakes. If your map does not have grid lines printed on it, draw them in yourself, using the UTM tick marks provided along the margins (**Note:** If there are no such tick marks, you may have no choice but to use latitude and longitude). Draw your lines using a straight edge and a very fine pen or pencil.

You will also need a clear plastic map ruler with marks graduated to conform to the scale of your map, in order to measure the location of any point within a given kilometer square. If you are unable to find a commercially available map ruler, you can make one yourself.

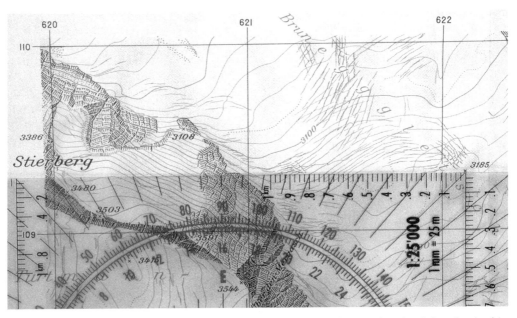

Figure 9. *Measuring the coordinates of spot height 3185 on a Swiss map (on the right edge in this photo). The coordinates are 622120 / 109300. We chose the scale on the map ruler—1:25,000—to match that of the map. To find the coordinates, we position the ruler so that the two scales intersect on our desired waypoint, as shown in the photo. Using the ruler, we measure the distance (120) from the waypoint to the vertical grid mark to the left (622), to obtain our easting coordinate of 622120. We do the same measuring downward, to obtain the northing coordinate of 109300 (tick mark 109 is on the map's left margin).*

UTM coordinates are expressed as two numbers: the first number describes the east-west axis ("easting") and the second describes the north-south axis ("northing").

Write down the coordinates for each waypoint in your notebook, in the space you provided for it next to the waypoint name. Double-check your work; your life may depend on it.

Enter waypoints into the GPS. Follow the manufacturer's instructions for entering waypoints into your receiver. Be sure you correctly set the correct map datum and position format on your GPS.

Entering waypoints by hand is tedious work. A complicated route involving lots of waypoints can take an hour or more to enter. Give yourself enough time to do a good job and avoid mistakes. Once you have the waypoints entered, create a route by stringing them together. Even though you can navigate from one individual waypoint to the next without first creating a route, the route feature makes following your line easier.

When using a computer, you also need to be sure that map datum and position format are correctly set on both the software and the receiver. Connect the GPS to the computer with the appropriate cable and upload the waypoints. With a computer you can also create a route by stringing waypoints together, then upload both the route and the waypoints at the same time.

Use other waypoint sources. Besides locating, measuring, and obtaining waypoint coordinates directly from your map, there are two other common waypoint sources.

You can obtain waypoint coordinates from someone else—a friend, the Internet, or a published source. Though these may save you a good deal of work and give you a good idea of where a route might go, you must confirm that they indeed indicate the best route by plotting them on your map yourself. Do not skip this critical step.

Also, as noted in the beginning of this discussion, you can record waypoints as you travel for use on your return or on a future trip. This can work well, depending on the recording and backtracking capabilities of your particular GPS. Most can be set to record your track as you travel, then you can save that track into the GPS memory as a route. Remember, when you have visibility you will be much more comfortable getting close to hazards such as open crevasses or cliff edges than you will in a whiteout navigating with GPS. Go out of your way to keep your track away from hazards.

Following a GPS Route in the Field

When following a GPS route in the field, also keep your map handy with your route and waypoints marked and named on it, so that you can understand better where you are at any moment and also verify that you are indeed headed for the correct next point.

You can use your GPS receiver either in continuous navigation mode or spot-check mode. In continuous navigation mode, your receiver is left on as you travel. Its display uses arrows and lines to indicate your course and your deviation from it as you go. The unit also indicates your distance to the next waypoint, its direction (bearing), the amount of time it will take you to get there given your current rate of travel, and your heading (current direction of travel). This is a very easy way to move between waypoints, but it uses up batteries very quickly.

In spot-check mode, you travel most of the time with the unit turned off, following a compass bearing or other travel line, periodically turning on the unit to gauge progress and accuracy. This mode saves batteries, though it does slow you down, because the receiver takes a little while to relocate the satellite signals each time it is turned on.

Some GPS receivers have an integrated magnetic compass; others determine direction by tracking the unit's movement. In the latter case, you cannot use the compass to determine direction when you are standing still; you need to maintain some minimum speed. Whichever kind of unit you have, you should still carry an ordinary compass for taking bearings from your map and shooting them accurately in the field, or in case the batteries run out or the unit malfunctions.

At very slow rates of travel—for example, when post-holing in deep snow—it is much easier to follow a compass bearing than the GPS display. The display responds slowly to small movements at low speed, and this can be confusing. If your GPS has a magnetic compass, you can use it in continuous navigation mode even at slow speed; just ignore the display and follow the bearing. Otherwise, it is best to use a traditional compass bearing and the GPS in spot-check mode.

Remember to check your first "known location" waypoint to confirm at the start that the GPS is working correctly, that the coordinates that you have entered are correct, and that the datum and position format settings of your receiver are right.

In general, GPS receivers are fairly reliable. However, one time our GPS was unable to acquire the satellites it needed to locate itself even after many, many minutes of trying, despite the fact that we were high on a peak with much open sky. We don't know if the reason for this difficulty was due to the electrical activity in the sky that day or perhaps related to a war effort in some distant part of the world. Either way, we were reminded of the importance of being able to switch back to traditional navigation methods at any time.

The GPS provides a lot of fascinating information and a strong temptation to focus on the display, head down and oblivious to all else, when following a route. This is a dangerous tendency. Keep using your other tools: map, compass, and altimeter. Avoid trusting in a single source of information, and be sure that data from all sources agree. Above all, continue to look around, watch for hazards and errors, and be sure that your confidence in the GPS is not leading you into other problems.

CHAPTER 5

Climbing on the East Ridge of the Breithorn,
Switzerland

Alpine Rock

Alpine rock climbing is much more challenging and complex than rock climbing at the crag, for many reasons. The alpine environment includes a host of hazards not normally encountered on simpler rock climbs, many of which can best be managed only by moving quickly. Mountains present a great deal of distance to cover, often entailing snow, ice, and glaciers in addition to the rock climbing challenges. The remoteness of alpine rock routes requires commitment and self-sufficiency, as well as emergency preparedness.

But one of the greatest distinguishing factors between crag and alpine climbing is the fact that mountains entail a huge amount of easy and moderate terrain in addition to sections of more difficult climbing. The constantly varying difficulty requires a variety of movement and protection techniques to match, providing varying levels of security. The climber must make careful risk management decisions with practically every step, use the right technique for the right purpose in the right place, and move the team efficiently through variable terrain and conditions.

This chapter covers risk assessment and rope management techniques for efficient travel on easy and moderate terrain; anchoring and belaying considerations for the alpine environment, including use of terrain belays, running belays, and short pitch belayed climbing; a review of rock anchors and belaying methods geared to alpine priorities; and considerations and techniques specific to descent.

We assume the reader has quite a lot of preexisting knowledge and experience in rock climbing. The mountains are not the best place to learn and experiment with leading on rock, belaying, placing protection, and building anchors. It is better to master these skills in the controlled environments of gym and crag. Specifically, we assume the reader has experience leading on rock, placing traditional protection, building rock anchors, belaying both a leader and a second, switching leaders on multipitch rock, and rappelling. We also assume the reader has knowledge of the following common knots: figure eight followed through and on a bight, butterfly knot, girth hitch, clove hitch, double fishermans bend for joining ropes and cord, water knot for joining webbing, and prusik and autoblock hitches for ascending ropes or for other rescue applications. Although it is extremely important for alpine climbers to be self-sufficient and know how to rescue themselves, we cannot adequately cover self-rescue in this book. Resources for learning all of these assumed skills are listed in the bibliography.

MOVEMENT SKILLS AND PROTECTIVE SYSTEMS

Any alpine rock route involves a continuum of tactics—modes of travel and levels of security—ranging from unroped, simul-soloing at one extreme to 5th-class belayed

Mountains require a variety of techniques to match terrain, and the ability to transition easily between techniques. Here, climbers move together on the South Ridge of the Lagginhorn, Switzerland.

pitches and even direct aid climbing at the other. The alpine rock climber constantly shifts between these, matching the degree of security to the likelihood and consequences of a fall. Since a climber's assessment of these will change countless times during a typical alpine rock climb, so too must the climber be willing and able to change tactics countless times and to do so as efficiently as possible.

Here we ignore "objective" terms defining difficulty, such as 3rd, 4th, or 5th class, and focus instead on this continuum of tactics and on the "subjective" process of choosing between them. After all, your choice of tactic is determined by your evaluation of difficulty and therefore defines that difficulty better than any arbitrary measures of steepness, exposure, or technical challenge. The goal of this decision-making process is always to travel as efficiently as possible while still addressing the risk of a fall. Three key elements contribute to this goal: routefinding (see Chapter 4, Routefinding and Navigation), movement skills, and rope management. This chapter primarily addresses the latter.

Applying the right tactic for the terrain requires you to form an opinion about the likelihood and consequences of a fall. You must determine how hard the climbing in the section ahead will be for you and, based on that, what degree of protection you need. This, more than anything else, will determine your protective strategy. Other factors influencing your decisions include your partner's ability, time constraints, rockfall hazard, weather, and

any other risks you have to manage simultaneously. Finally, you must look further ahead to plan for any transitions that you think may soon be necessary.

Throughout the following discussion, we progress from the fastest, simplest, and least secure tactics to slowest, most complex, and most protective.

CLIMBING UNROPED

Experienced, careful, and confident climbers can be sufficiently safe without a rope on terrain they consider easy, even if it is very exposed and consequences of a fall would be disastrous. Instead of the rope, they rely on their climbing ability and on good routefinding to protect them against a fall. There are many advantages to climbing unroped, chiefly the added speed and efficiency, which can actually increase safety in many ways. But beyond this, soloing can enhance the feeling of freedom and engagement that is at the heart of alpine climbing.

However, the psychological impact of exposure can have a huge effect on both the perceived and real risks of falling. The prospect of serious consequences usually affects our perception of this risk, even more than the difficulty of the climbing does. Our perception affects our emotions (fear!), which in turn very much affect how well we climb.

When less-experienced climbers choose to forego the rope, it is usually not a function of their confidence. Rather, it is because they don't know how to use the rope in a way that won't interfere or slow them down. The better you are at managing the rope while moving together (see below), the less it will encumber you. You will not need to resort to soloing in order to move quickly. You will have more options.

MOVING TOGETHER ON A SHORTENED ROPE

Belaying full pitches on easy broken terrain can actually increase risk rather than reduce it; the rope catches on things, it sweeps loose rocks from slabs and ledges, it creates rope drag for the leader, it complicates rope handling. There are many gradations of security between unroped soloing and full-pitch, belayed climbing. The first step toward greater security is to shorten the rope, and move together as much as you can, allowing you to belay only where it is truly necessary. Having the rope short simplifies rope management and allows you to move quickly and efficiently between belayed sections.

If your assessment of the terrain ahead leads you to believe or even just suspect that you might want the rope soon, strategize about the best place and time to put on harnesses. It may be more efficient to get harnesses and rope ready in advance of actual need if the terrain gets tricky above or if you want to take a break anyway.

Shortening the Rope

You and your partner both tie in as normal for belayed climbing, each at an end of the rope. You then take in over-the-shoulder coils and tie them off securely, as illustrated in Figure 10, to reduce the

length of rope connecting you and your partner. You may choose to divide the rope between climbers, or one climber may carry all the coils.

Practice coiling a rope so that you can coil an entire 50-meter rope and tie it off, as described above, in less than a minute. When dropping coils to lengthen the available rope, always peel the coils off one at a time, either directly off your shoulder or by first unloading all the coils into your hand. Dropping an entire pile of round coils onto the ground will result in a tangled, snarly mess! You have to try this only once (do it at home!) and you'll get the picture.

PRACTICE: SHORTENING THE ROPE

Practice taking in and dropping coils a few at a time to fine-tune the length of rope you have available. Tie in to an end of the rope, coil up about half it, and tie it off as described above. Now undo your tie-off, drop three or four coils, and tie off again. Repeat, taking in three or four coils, to end up where you were. It should take you no more than about 30 seconds to undo your tie-off, drop or take in four coils, and tie off again.

Moving Together

Once you and your partner are tied in and the rope has been shortened, one or both of you carry small coils in your hands as you go along (see Figure 11). Strive to move together smoothly and continuously. Watch your partner and anticipate changing

Figure 10a. *Coil around your neck using your left hand to control the coil size, with your elbow slightly bent. The rope is first pulled vertically, taut against the tie-in knot, before beginning the coiling.*

Figure 10b. *Stop coiling when you have the desired amount of rope left between you and your partner. Insert your right arm through the coils. The coils must be long enough not to impede your movement, but not so long that they fall off your shoulder or catch on obstacles and gear. It takes a bit of practice to get this length right. Push a bight of the available rope through your belay loop or tie-in knot.*

Figure 10c. *Pull plenty of slack through from the rope going to your partner. A 60-cm (2-foot) loop should do. Pull it back through the coils as shown, catching all strands.*

Figure 10d. *Tie off with an overhand around the strand going to your partner. Both it and the tied-off bight loop point away from you as they come out of the overhand knot.*

Figure 10e. *Finish by clipping the bight into your locking carabiner.*

needs, feeding slack out of your hand or taking it in to accommodate the changing distance between you.

Important: Simply by virtue of roping up in this way, you have not necessarily provided more security for either climber; in fact, you have increased the danger that if one of you falls, the other will likely be pulled off the mountain as well. What this tactic does is allow you to have the rope ready for use in more protective ways as soon as that is called for, yet in the meantime the rope interferes with your movement as little as possible. This tactic is useful if running belays and terrain belays are available (see the next section) or if you know or suspect you will want to belay occasional sections ahead—both of these are almost always the case in "easy" alpine rock terrain.

ADDING SECURITY

Security can be increased using a range of belay methods and options, which you must choose according to needs you assess moment by moment as you climb. Following are some ways to provide varying levels of security.

Figure 11. *Threading the rope among horns as a running belay. Arête du Table, Aiguille du Tour, France.*

Running and Terrain Belays

The rope can occasionally be placed across a ridge crest or over solid rock horns or other features as you and your partner climb simultaneously. Such running belays take almost no time to employ and effectively keep a party attached to the mountain in case of a fall. Look for them and take advantage of them as much as possible.

Figure 12. *Using the rock horns on ridge crests. The leader moves along the ridge, placing the rope over horns as they are encountered; the second unhooks them as they are passed. Dri Horlini, Switzerland.*

For example, when traveling together along a more or less horizontal ridge crest, stay on the crest as much as possible. Thread the rope between towers and horns as you go (see Figure 12). If you fall, the rope will snag around an obstacle or your partner can step or drop down on the opposite side of the ridge and serve as a counterweight to keep you from going very far. This tactic does not prevent falls, and even short falls by either climber can still result in severe injury. Easier climbing usually means more broken ground with ledges, horns, and other hard obstacles to hit. Your real protection on this kind of terrain comes from constant and careful assessment of difficulty and of your own climbing abilities and comfort level, more than the running belays you manage to get.

Short Pitch Belayed Climbing

As the climbing gets more difficult or more exposed, you may occasionally want to belay a move or short section on which a fall seems more possible and the consequences dire but the move or section is not long or difficult enough to warrant placing leader protection. This scenario differs from the one described above, where use of terrain belays allow you to continue moving together. Now your assessment of risk has changed; perhaps available features are too few and far between for your comfort, or the climbing is hard enough for either of you that you don't want both climbers moving through the tricky bits at the same time.

Short pitch belayed climbing, as

described here, in places where running belays are not available or are deemed inadequate, keeps the rope team on the mountain if either climber should fall. It helps to maintain momentum by keeping rope management as simple as possible and avoiding the many serious problems brought on by belayed climbing with long pitches and leader protection. It allows a quick and seamless transition to more sustained belayed climbing as difficulty increases (see Belayed Climbing with Protection for the Leader, below).

This tactic does have some important limitations, however. For example, injury may still be likely and even severe in case of a leader fall! In this scenario the old motto "The leader must not fall" is as true today as ever. However, because this tactic can provide good protection for the second, it is particularly helpful if one of your rope team is a stronger climber than the other (this, by the way, is why guides use this tactic so extensively).

The kind of "easy" terrain where this tactic is appropriate makes up the greater part of many alpine rock climbs and is the hardest kind to manage well. Climbers who know how to move together roped and to belay short sections as needed seem to fly up this stuff, while others can waste hours belaying long pitches on easy ground or take unnecessary risks climbing unroped or unbelayed.

This terrain is by definition reasonably low angle with plenty of features; the difficult sections are scattered and short. Take advantage of this, as follows:

- Blocky terrain offers many options for quick belays over horns or strong stances behind ridge crests and boulders. Use the fastest belay method appropriate to the angle and difficulty (see **Short pitch belay anchors and methods,** below).
- Look for frequent stance possibilities to keep belayed pitches as short as possible. Shorter pitches reduce the danger of dislodged rocks, rope drag, and snags.
- Go back to moving together whenever you can comfortably do so.

How much rope should you have available? The length of rope you keep available (that is, carried in your hand coils, not tied off over your shoulder) should be the minimum necessary to accommodate the difficult sections between stances. Having less rope out means fewer coils to carry as you move together, helping you climb better and more efficiently. It also simplifies rope management both by eliminating the need to reel in and organize rope you are not actually using and by minimizing the number of times you must undo coils and tie them up again as you transition between belaying and moving along together.

To determine the minimum rope necessary to have available, take a careful look at the terrain. How far apart are the features—rock towers, horns, flakes, both sides of the ridge, etc.—that you can use as anchors and belays? On highly featured and solid rock such as spiny granite ridges, belay possibilities are frequent, so you can get away with a shorter length of rope. On smooth faces or on poor rock there may be fewer options, so you will need more rope to reach a good stance. In most cases 6 meters (20 feet) will be about right. Consider 15 meters (50 feet) a maximum for the purposes of moving together with short belays, as opposed to sustained belayed climbing (see Belayed Climbing with Protection for the Leader, below). If your rope is too short, drop a few coils; if it's too long, take some in.

Short pitch belay anchors and methods. In this context, your belays should be as easy and fast to implement as possible, while still being adequate for the job. The challenge is to form an opinion not only about the likelihood of a fall, but also about the maximum potential force the fall would generate and the direction of that force. Here, as always, the benefit of speed and simplicity entails costs; the quickest belays tend to have less holding power than more-elaborate anchored belays, and they require more skill to control. The importance of time saved must be balanced against these potential drawbacks.

Another important consideration is that some belay methods allow rope to move through the system much more quickly than others. A belayer unable to keep up with a second will generate too much slack, making a fall more serious. A leader moving quickly will be needlessly halted and perhaps pulled off balance by a too-slow belayer. Climbers can move very fast on easy ground. When belaying, you must

Horns can provide astonishing holding power, but their use for a quick belay requires skill and judgment, as well as solid rock features! Breithorn, Switzerland.

not become the factor that limits your partner's speed!

Rock horns. Passing the rope over or around rock horns is often the fastest and simplest possible belay option and can provide very effective belays, especially when belaying a second (see Figure 13). Inspect the horn carefully to be sure it is part of the bedrock or solidly attached to it, not merely sitting on a ledge or wedged into a crack—this may sound obvious, but loose horns can often look deceptively strong, especially when they are very large. Thump it with your hand, pull out on it, kick it, etc. Be picky. Just because someone else left a sling on it doesn't mean it's good. Pass your rope around the horn, analyzing the direction of the potential fall force to be sure it will not cause the rope to pop off. Also take care that your hand will not be pinched against the rock and make you lose control of the belay. Obviously, the horn must protrude enough to hold the rope predictably and not be so sharp that it will cut the rope.

This extremely quick belay can provide a surprising amount of friction, depending on the type and texture of the rock, and it often requires little strength to hold. We use this method often while guiding and find that it provides adequate security not only for our partners, but also for ourselves, keeping us attached to the mountain even though typically, when using this technique on a secure stance or large

Figure 13. *A simple belay using a rock horn. Point Lachenal, France.*

ledge, we do not anchor ourselves to anything.

This method is much trickier to use for belaying a leader, though it can be done. Fall forces are much greater in the case of a leader fall, and the position and movement of the rope can be harder to predict and control. If the rope snags on any other features as the leader falls, the result is an upward pull that pops the rope off the horn and leaves you with no anchor. If the rope subsequently comes loose from its snag, the force of your partner's fall may well pull you off too.

Sitting belays. These can be quite effective—fast to set up, take down, and move rope through. Sitting belays—in which the fall force is absorbed by the stance of the belayer—very often are more than adequate for the potential fall forces on low-angle and relatively easy ground (see Figure 14). Variations include hip belays, in which the rope is passed around the belayer's body to obtain friction, or belays using a friction device on the belayer's harness. In either case, the belayer's strong braced position itself constitutes the anchor of a sitting belay, although he or she may choose to clip in to a separate anchor as a backup if the stance alone is not adequate.

In choosing between sitting belays with or without a device, anchored or unanchored, be sure that your choice offers an adequate margin of safety, keeps up with the climber, and transitions well into whatever is likely to follow. Below is a description of the four different sitting

PRACTICE: BELAYING AROUND HORNS

Find a boulder field and wander through it with a rope and a partner, finding horns and blocks to practice belaying with. Loop the rope over edges and around horns and hold your partner's weight using only your hand on the rope. Try different configurations of rope and rocks to get a feel for the friction you can generate and to learn its limits. Practice both taking in rope and letting it out while belaying over horns, to judge the relative ease or difficulty of controlling rope position and limiting slack.

You should quickly become adept at identifying solid horns and blocks and at seeing the best way to place the rope around it to hold securely, given a particular direction of force. With practice, it should take you only a few seconds to spot a usable terrain feature, visualize how the belay will work, and judge how it will react under load.

Warning: Large boulders are often unstable. Look for a boulder field that has had several centuries to settle down. A good sign of stability is the presence of lichen, which takes a very long time to grow. Avoid boulders resting on a glacier. As the glacier melts, the overlying rocks continually move and settle into new positions. The next time you find yourself on a rock-covered glacier, notice how unstable the areas of deep rubble are.

eases above, it is easy to transition from this belay into moving together. However, if the next pitch is steep and requires a belay for the leader, you will need to switch to another belay method. An unanchored sitting hip belay is not a good option for belaying a leader on steep ground because it is easy to lose control of the belay or to drop your partner through inattention. It is very dynamic; that is, the rope tends to slide through quite a bit in the case of large fall forces. This carries a real risk that the belayer's hands or

Figure 14. *Many climbers like to clip the "hot" end of the rope, that going to the climber, through a carabiner on the harness to help keep control of the belay during a fall. Our view is that this is unnecessary—if fall forces are high enough to make this a concern, then the hip belay is a poor choice, with or without the carabiner.*

belays and the slightly different applications appropriate to each:

- **Unanchored, braced sitting hip belay:** This option has the least amount of holding power but it is the quickest to set up and take down, and it allows you to take in rope very fast, making it ideal for bringing up a second on easy ground. If the difficulty

Figure 15. *A braced sitting belay with a belay device. Be sure the pull is low and that the feet are well braced. Dri Horlini, Switzerland.*

body could be injured by rope burn. Whenever you anticipate a large fall force (which is the norm in leader falls), you should choose a more powerful method such as the plate device or Münter hitch (described next).

■ **Unanchored sitting belay with a plate device or Münter hitch:** This is a good alternative to a hip belay when a large pack or cramped stance makes it difficult to quickly establish a hip belay or if you need a bit more holding power than the hip belay can provide (see Figure 15). You will not be able to take in rope quite as quickly, so it may be a bit awkward if your second moves toward you in a big hurry. Being unanchored, this belay is also not the first choice for belaying a leader unless you are really well braced.

■ **Anchored hip belay:** This is rarely used in rock climbing these days. The same factors that call for an anchor—potential for high loads or poor stance—also suggest the need for a belay method more powerful than the hip belay. However, since the hip belay does offer the advantage of allowing the belayer to move rope very quickly to keep up with a fast climber, it's possible to imagine circumstances in which this could be a good choice. If you have a marginal stance but also only moderate potential loads and a quickly moving climber—common in steep snow climbing but rare on rock—then the

anchored body belay might be a reasonable option.

■ **Anchored sitting belay with a belay device or Münter hitch:** This last variation of the sitting belay is useful for belaying a leader. The high friction of the belay device or Münter hitch combined with the security of an anchored stance makes for a strong belay. The downside for easier climbing is that this belay is the most complicated to build and therefore the most time- and equipment-intensive. Reserve it for when you anticipate higher fall forces and a simpler solution is not possible.

Trees. A runner or cordelette tied around a tree can be a very quick and solid anchor (see Figure 16). You can girth-hitch the runner or, if you have

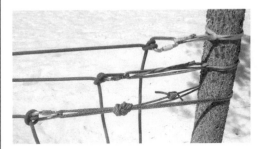

Figure 16. *Three ways to use a tree as an anchor. The top sling is simply girth-hitched around the tree, simple and effective. The middle uses a double sling wrapped around the tree then tied in an overhand with both ends into the anchor carabiner. The bottom method is the strongest but also the slowest to tie and untie. It uses a cordelette.*

enough material, tie a knot in it. Avoid triaxial loading—pulling in three directions on the carabiner used to clip in, as illustrated in Figure 17. In this unstable situation, the direction of pull will shift the carabiner and cause the load to pull straight out on the gate. The gate is the weakest part of the carabiner and fails at a much lower load than when the pull is along the axis of the carabiner.

With your anchor built, you can either belay direct (see **Direct belaying a second,** below) or use the anchor as a backup to a sitting or harness belay.

Slings around rock horns. As with a sling on a tree, you have your choice of either using a direct belay off the sling on the horn or using the horn as a backup to a stance.

Figure 17. *Two BAD ways to use a tree. The upper example pulls in three directions on the carabiner (triaxial loading), never a good idea. In the lower example, the gate of the carabiner against the tree could be pushed open, severely weakening it.*

When slinging a rock horn, inspect it for sharp edges or crystals. Webbing and cord under tension cut very easily. If you find reason for concern, use two independent strands of material (see Figure 18). We have in rare cases gone so far as to dull sharp edges by pounding them with another rock.

A sling that is too tight for the horn or block may end up multiplying the forces if the angle at the master point is too wide. Multiplying forces in this case increases the danger that sharp crystals and edges can cut the sling. Multiplication of forces is a concept you learned from building complex anchors at the crag, but it can easily be forgotten in the context of single-point anchors such as slung rock horns. As with multipiece anchors, keep this angle under 90 degrees if possible, and remember that the forces on the sling at 120 degrees are doubled.

Application: the judgment call. When using any belay anchors or methods, carefully determine the minimum level of security you need to provide an unquestionably strong belay, and choose your anchor and method accordingly. The need for speed does *not* justify settling for a doubtful or inadequate anchor or method. Provide adequate security, first and foremost, and increase speed in other ways or on other parts of the climb.

Once you have decided you would like a belay, your next steps are to carefully assess the greatest potential fall force, then to choose an anchor and/or a belay method that provides at least the minimum level of

Figure 18. *A single-point anchor using two slings around a rock horn.*

security needed to make you absolutely confident that you can hold that potential force.

BELAYED CLIMBING WITH PROTECTION FOR THE LEADER

As the climbing grows steeper, more exposed, more sustained, and more difficult—5th-class rock—the leader begins to place intermediate protection. Sometimes this tactic is needed only briefly; other times, it is used for pitch after pitch of steep, hard climbing.

If a leader fall is considered a real possibility, the objective of this tactic is no longer simply to keep the team on the mountain, but to protect both the leader and the second from injury in case of falls, particularly on the leader's part. Once the leader starts placing protection, the belayer should be anchored and/or braced.

In the following section our goal is to identify and discuss rock-climbing considerations that are especially important in the alpine environment and to describe any variations of technique that are particularly useful in this environment. We also selectively review some elements that may already be familiar to readers. We do this for instances in which we feel the issues are important enough to be especially emphasized or, more particularly, in the case of techniques we believe may not be as widely known or practiced as they deserve to be.

How Long to Pitch It Out?

The decision to begin belaying pitches does not necessarily mean that it is best to run them out as far as the rope will allow. For example, if 5th-class climbing alternates with easier climbing and the difficult sections are short, belayed pitches will also be short. While this example is obvious, determining the ideal length of a pitch in general is a lot more complex. In some situations, shorter pitches are more efficient; in others, longer pitches are more efficient. When sorting this all out, consider the following points:

■ If communication with your partner is particularly important, shorter pitches are preferable. For example, you may want to stop above a difficult or dangerous crux in order to provide support to your second, be it the simple reassurance of being able to see and hear you or the more material support of a tight rope or coaching.

■ If rope drag or snagging is a concern— for example, on very broken terrain or a wandering line—shorter pitches are preferable.

■ Where potential belay stances are plentiful and anchors are easy to find, build, and dismantle, you can get away with shorter pitches.

■ Where sheer terrain or rock type makes anchors complex and time consuming to build, more advantage is gained by longer pitches, because they maximize forward progress relative to time spent on anchors. This is particularly true on long snow or ice faces, for example, where you may even prefer to use extra-long ropes.

■ Considerations of the terrain may dictate the length of your pitch. For example, you may need to stop short in order to take advantage of a good belay

Climbing on the Breithorn Traverse, Switzerland

stance or anchor opportunity, given harder climbing or lack of belay options above. Conversely, you may be forced to run out a pitch to the bitter end through lack of stance opportunities.

Leading with Tied-off Coils

It is not uncommon for the leader to take a belay and place intermediate protection while still climbing on a shortened rope—that is, with tied-off coils (see Figure 19). For example, this may be appropriate if the 5th-class climbing alternates with easier climbing and the difficult sections are short or on a short but difficult step where the leader wants a high degree of security but knows the climbing will soon ease again. In these situations, it is best to drop only enough coils (plus a little extra just in case) to get through the hard sections. This tactic minimizes the need to handle rope that is not actually being used and also speeds the

Figure 19. *Traditional 5th-class climbing on a shortened rope. Be sure the coils are securely tied off and the tied-off loop is clipped in to your locking carabiner as well. Aiguille du Peigne, Chamonix.*

transition back to the faster tactic of moving together. The choice between climbing with tied-off coils versus having the entire rope readily available hinges on two main factors:

- Whether there are reasons to prefer short pitches in general (such as the need for communication, snag potential, or rope drag danger)
- Whether short pitches are feasible (lots of stance and anchor opportunities)

In any case, if you do decide to lead with tied-off coils, be sure to have enough rope out. Adjusting rope length in the middle of a lead is difficult and possibly dangerous; err on the conservative side. If you discover you need more rope, it is best if the belayer is the one to drop coils. This requires good communication between you, so you must be able to both see and hear each other.

Leading with the Entire Rope Available

The following are some specific factors that would lead you to drop coils and have the entire rope available:

- The hard climbing appears to go on for several hundred feet or more.
- Anchors or stances are hard to find and build.
- There is uncertainty about the availability of belay stances in the terrain ahead. You don't want to climb into positions where you are out of rope and cannot find a belay stance. Having more rope out means more options.

In the end, when deciding whether to drop or carry coils, strive always to use the technique best suited to the terrain but also to minimize changes in strategy; dropping a large number of coils off your shoulder takes time, as does taking them up again.

Belaying Options and Alpine Considerations

In this section, we depart somewhat from common cragging practices in order to emphasize variations that could save time in the mountains. Here we specifically assume the reader has familiarity with and competence in belaying both a leader and a second, using a plate device on the harness.

Alternating leads versus a single leader. Crag climbers often alternate leads, exchanging and rearranging the rack at each belay stance. This gives each climber an equal chance at both the challenge of leading and the ease of following. This is a common practice in the alpine as well; however, it may be more efficient in some cases to have one climber lead all of the climb or for blocks of several pitches. If time is of the essence, have the stronger climber lead most or all of the pitches. Even with climbers of equal ability, leading in blocks of several pitches yields fewer time-consuming and momentarily vulnerable exchanges of the rack. This strategy also gives each climber a rest between pitches and is particularly helpful on long ice faces where the climber's legs need a rest after a full rope length of front pointing.

Belaying a leader off the harness. This is the traditional method of belaying, using a plate or tube type device on the harness. This method is as useful in the mountains as it is at the crag. Remember that you should be comfortable, braced, and tied in snugly in line with the anchor and the expected direction of pull.

Direct belaying a second. Our preferred option for bringing in a second is to belay directly off the anchor (see Figure 20). A direct belay frees your position, since you no longer need to be braced, snug, or in line with the anchor. Freedom to move about allows you better visual or verbal contact with your partner. Holding a fall is easy, with no stress on your body. You can take in rope much faster, using your whole body and big arm movements to move lots of rope with each pull. Escaping the belay in a rescue scenario is vastly simplified, because the load need not be transferred from your harness to the anchor; it is already there.

With any direct belay, the anchor must be unquestionably strong. If you lack sufficient confidence in your anchor, you can either work to improve it, or you can belay off your harness with a braced stance that protects the anchor from load. In difficult climbing, however, we almost always build anchors fully capable of supporting a direct belay, and most of the time, this is the preferred method for belaying a second.

When you are direct belaying a second, the master point of the anchor should be at about the height of your head or shoulders. The belay device needs to be high in order to allow you freedom of movement and the ability to take in large amounts of rope quickly.

Figure 20. *Belaying a second directly off the anchor using a Münter hitch as the friction device. The direct belay allows freedom of position, fast rope movement, and easy escape in case of problems. If space is limited in the master point of the anchor, the belayer can clip in to the "shelf" (the strands above the knot in the cordelette or sling), as shown here.*

Direct belaying with a friction device. When belaying directly off the anchor, you have two main choices of device: a Münter hitch or an autoblocking plate device such as the Petzl Reverso or Reversino. A traditional plate or tube type device should not be used for a direct belay.

Münter hitch. Also called the "Italian

hitch," the Münter hitch uses the rope and a belay carabiner to create great friction when the rope is weighted—enough friction to arrest even severe falls. When the rope is not weighted, it runs freely with low friction.

With the Münter hitch, the brake position is the same as the operating position—the brake strand is parallel to the rope going to the climber—so the belayer need not move his or her hand in order to arrest the fall. You can operate the Münter from several feet away if needed. You can also use a Münter hitch to belay a leader, by building it on the locking carabiner on your harness. It requires no equipment other than a suitably shaped locking carabiner—a so-called pear-shaped or Münter carabiner (see Figure 21).

The Münter hitch can twist the rope badly, especially when the rope is loaded for a significant distance, such as when lowering. You can overcome this tendency by deliberately fighting the twists (forcing them through the hitch), but this requires effort and attention. Do not use the Münter for rappelling unless you truly have no other option! The twisting is too hard to counteract when you are rappelling.

Autoblocking belay device. An autoblocking belay device works as a ratchet, allowing you to take in rope as your partner comes up but locking automatically under the load of a fall. Like the Münter hitch, it can be operated from a few feet away, allowing you freedom of movement. It offers a couple of advantages over the Münter hitch. It is a hands-free

device, so you can let go of the rope completely and not lose control of the belay. This generally contributes to a safer belay—assuming, of course, that you don't go off and eat a sandwich while your second moves up and generates slack. It runs more freely when not loaded, so you may be able to stand farther from the anchor if desired. It does not twist the rope. An autoblocking belay device has two slots to accommodate two separate strands of rope, which makes it a better choice when climbing on double or twin ropes, or when belaying two climbers simultaneously on separate ropes (an application appropriate mainly to guides). Most autoblocking belay devices can also be used as a tube or plate-type belay device for belaying off the harness and for rappelling.

One disadvantage of the autoblocking belay device is that it is difficult to pay out slack once the rope is weighted, so if your partner falls he or she will have to unweight the rope somehow before you can provide slack. Also, some older models are unsuitable for belaying a leader off your harness. When buying an autoblocking belay device, be sure to select a model that is equally good for both direct and off-the-harness belay methods (see Chapter 3, Preparation and Equipment).

To use the autoblocking belay device for belaying a second in direct belay mode, clip it to the anchor master point with a locking carabiner and place the rope in the device with the load strand coming out of the top of the device, as shown in Figure 22. Use a

Figure 21a. *Learn to build the Münter hitch on the belay carabiner. Place the rope through the carabiner and grasp the "cold" strand (the side not going to the climber). Hold the rope as shown in preparation for the "twist."*

Figure 21b. *Turn your hand to make the twist.*

Figure 21c. *Fold the twist over and into the carabiner.*

Figure 21d. *Lock the carabiner to finish.*

locking carabiner to secure the loop. Take in rope by lifting up on the rope coming into the device at the top and simultaneously pulling down on the rope coming out the bottom. Thinner single ropes, such as 10-mm or narrower, pull more easily through an autoblocking belay device than thicker or fuzzy single ropes.

Direct belaying a leader. It is possible to belay a leader directly off the anchor, using a Münter hitch or belay plate. Though not commonly used in North America, the technique offers the advantage of isolating the belayer from the forces of a leader fall. This reduces the odds of losing control of the belay and also of belayer injury. However, there are some disadvantages as well.

■ Your anchor must be multidirectional—that is, able to withstand a strong upward force. Although this is frequently the case in cragging contexts

Figure 22a. *Belaying a second with an autoblocking belay device off a two-piece self-equalizing anchor. The belayer is clipped in with a clove hitch. The belay device, a Trango B-52, is hung off the belayer's tie-in carabiner.*

Figure 22b. *Belaying a second with an autoblocking belay device directly off a single-bolt anchor. This anchor, on a ridge crest on the Aiguille d'Entrèves, on the France-Italy border, was placed by local guides and positioned to belay a second, not for holding leader falls.*

159

with many bolt anchors, in the mountains the simplest anchors are more often unidirectional, such as slings around horns. Anchors constructed with gear such as nuts, cams, etc. are much more complex and difficult to build when you must protect against a strong upward pull (see **Protection from an upward pull,** below).

■ The easiest device to use for direct belaying a leader is the Münter hitch. Be aware that with the Münter hitch, it may be difficult to manage the twists and pay rope out quickly enough to keep up with your leader. On alpine terrain, a leader is often able and eager to cover easy ground quickly, and if you cannot keep pace with his or her movement, you will waste valuable time or, worse yet, pull the leader off balance.

■ The normally high position of a direct belay anchor makes it harder to pay out rope quickly than with a harness belay.

Tying in. A belayer's tie-in to the anchor may be snug or loose, depending on whether the belayer is to belay a leader or a second, whether the belayer chooses a direct belay or a harness belay, and whether the belayer is on a small and tenuous stance or a large and comfortable ledge:

■ When employing a direct belay of a second, consider tying in long if your stance and situation allow it. Tying in long gives you more freedom, increases comfort, and often allows you to place yourself where you can see your partner.

■ Still another option when belaying a second directly off the anchor is not to tie in to the anchor at all. This sounds radical, but imagine you are on a large ledge and about to transition to easier

---

TIPS: EFFICIENT LEADER CHANGE-OVER WITH AN AUTOBLOCKING BELAY DEVICE

If you are swinging leads up 5th-class rock or ice and belaying the second directly off the anchor, you will need to transfer the belay from the anchor to the belayer's harness as he or she climbs by. With a bit of coordination, this is quick and easy.

■ Both climbers should have an autoblocking device.

■ Once the second has reached the stance and transferred the rack in preparation for becoming the new leader, the belayer "steals" the leader's device and uses it to establish the new belay on his or her harness.

■ When ready to leave, the new leader then "steals" the device from the anchor and begins to climb.

By trading devices this way, you don't need to tie the climber in as you make the transfer. You need only one device per climber, as long as it can work both off the harness and off the anchor.

climbing above, where you will not belay a leader but will shorten the rope and move together. As you belay your partner, you stand away from the edge and your hands on the rope give you stability. Not tying yourself in eliminates several maneuvers and saves you time. Be aware of other risks, of course, such as obstacles to trip over or even simple distractions that could be dangerous if you are not anchored.

■ When belaying a leader or a second off your harness, tie in short to avoid being pulled off your stance and shock loading the anchor or losing control of the belay. Adopt a position or braced stance so you won't be jerked around in the event of a fall.

Although almost any "hard" knot will do for tying in to a belay anchor (figure eight or overhand on a bight are traditional favorites), a clove hitch tie-in is more versatile; it allows you to quickly and easily adjust length until you are perfectly comfortable. Avoid using a specially designed daisy chain. They are not as adjustable as a clove hitch, they lack the rope's dynamic, shock-absorbing qualities, and they are extra weight.

Protecting from an upward pull.
When a leader falls after placing intermediate protection on a pitch, the rope is pulled upward, toward the protection that held the fall. The belayer's body weight and bracing usually prevent this upward pull from affecting the anchor. But if the force of the fall is enough to lift the belayer off the stance, he or she can be injured or lose control of the belay by hitting an obstacle on the way up.

This is actually more of a concern in the cragging environment, where climbers often push their limits and severe leader falls are not unusual. In the mountains, leaders are less tolerant of the possibility of severe falls, hence such falls tend to be rare. In those situations where this is a real risk, you can manage it in several ways. Most often, bracing and a very solid stance are sufficient to keep the belayer on the ground or ledge. Consider this tactic first.

If you need more protection from an upward pull, you can either build an upward component into the anchor—many anchors are inherently multidirectional to some extent anyway—or you can anchor the belayer down. Which you choose should depend on comfort and convenience for the belayer and on simplicity and efficiency. Keep in mind that much of the fall force will be absorbed before it ever reaches the belayer tie-down or the upward-pull component of the anchor. Rope stretch, friction at the top protection piece, any slippage through the belay device, and the inertia of the belayer's body being pulled from the ground all contribute to diminishing the upward force on the anchor; a simple wrap of the rope around a large boulder can often be enough.

Constructing Belay Anchors
Situations in which the belayed climbing is difficult and sustained tend to have steeper and less-featured rock. Natural terrain

belays such as horns, trees, or good places to brace are few. Belay anchors must be stronger, more reliable, more stable, and easier to use. The decision-making process for building belay anchors includes the following questions:

- Where should I build it?
- What belay method will I use?
- How should it be constructed and evaluated?

These questions are interrelated. For example, the decision to belay directly off the anchor versus off your harness may influence how and where you construct your anchor. Conversely, the location of your anchor may limit your choice between direct or harness belay.

Choosing where to build the belay. Many considerations play a role in deciding where to stop and build a belay anchor. Two of them—desired pitch length and terrain constraints—are discussed in the preceding section. Beyond these, consider the following factors:

Comfort. Everything else being equal, it is preferable to pause on a ledge rather than hang your butt over the void! Cramped or awkward stances slow the changeovers between leaders and increase the likelihood of serious mistakes such as dropping things. Wherever possible, try not to force yourself or your partner to deal with an uncomfortable position or location.

Visibility and communication. Whenever possible, place your belay so that you will be in sight and/or hearing of your partner. Poor communication can be unnerving, and it often results in wasted time.

Efficiency of anchor building. Be an opportunist—watch for places where you can build an anchor quickly and easily. If you find a good horn or a big tree, consider stopping your pitch short, especially if you are not sure the possibilities above will be as good.

Convenience for where the route goes next. If you can identify the line of the route ahead, place your belay where it is convenient for the next pitch; for example, where you will get good visibility, minimal rope drag, and protection from any possible leader-generated rockfall.

Safety. Clearly, this overrides all other considerations. Locate your anchor where the belayer will be reasonably safe from objective hazards.

Choosing the belay method. At the same time that you are answering the questions of where and how to construct your anchor, you need to decide how you will belay. The choice is essentially between a direct belay off the anchor and one off the harness or body. We discuss the pros and cons of various belay methods in Belaying Options and Alpine Considerations, above, but we mention them again here to emphasize the point that your choice of belay method both influences and is influenced by factors of where and how you construct the anchor. Also, consider what happens on the route above you and how your chosen method will transition efficiently to the upcoming climbing.

Constructing and evaluating belay anchors. In this section, we assume the reader has knowledge of how to place and evaluate individual pieces of protection and how to build secure rock belay anchors. Here we concentrate on those aspects that maximize speed and efficiency and are, therefore, most applicable in alpine climbing.

An alpine belay anchor can take many forms, varying in response to the specific needs of the situation. In the mountains, these are more complex than at the crag, and the alpine climber must think a bit more creatively. Because of the underlying importance of speed and efficiency in mountaineering, alpinists must take advantage of time-saving options when available.

Many climbers are taught an acronym to help them construct and evaluate anchors. There are many variations, but most use similar terms. Below we list the common interpretation of one such acronym, ERNEST, adding a uniquely alpine twist or two.

Equalized

Crag interpretation: Anchor components should be equalized.

Alpine interpretation: In a multipiece anchor, this is usually a good idea, but the reason has more to do with the desirability of creating a single anchor master point (for clarity) than it does with the need to evenly distribute the load among anchor components. On a single-piece anchor, such as a rock horn or ice bollard, there is, of course, no equalization.

Redundant

Crag interpretation: If any one piece or component of an anchor should fail, there are others backing it up.

Alpine interpretation: In the mountains, single-piece anchors are common: a rock horn, tree, ice bollard, single bolt, single picket, ice screw, or simply a braced belay stance each may be adequate. The alpinist needs to be comfortable making this judgment.

No Extension

Crag interpretation: The failure of one component piece should not create a shock load on the others.

Alpine interpretation: This is true only if there is some doubt about the strength of the individual pieces. If all pieces are unquestionably good, then there is little chance that one will fail, hence speed considerations may trump concerns about extension.

Strong and Stable

Crag interpretation: All pieces should be strong and stable.

Alpine interpretation: The question, How strong is strong enough? becomes important. Overbuilding anchors (while better than underbuilding them, obviously) is a more serious error in the alpine environment than at the crag. Potential fall forces vary with terrain type and steepness. To maximize efficiency, alpinists should assess such forces when they position and build anchors.

Timely

Crag interpretation: This is vague. Some climbers define timely anchors as correctly located, others as quick to build and take apart.

Alpine interpretation: Here the alpinist's concerns are the same as those of the crag climber. Both correct belay location and time efficiency are critical in the mountains.

We like to add an A for "Applicable" into the mix (EARNEST). The alpinist has a bigger box of tricks than the crag climber, from wrapping the rope around a horn to all the complexity of a multipiece anchor. With more options, climbers must be sure

Figure 23. *A two-piece, pre-equalized anchor using one cam and a sling over a horn. Simple and effective, this anchor meets all the requirements of EARNEST.*

their choice applies well to the particular needs of the situation. Look at each belay individually, analyze its particular purpose, and remember that your choices must be in keeping with overall concerns about momentum as well as other hazards and considerations.

Single-point anchors. Many perfectly adequate anchors consist of only one component. In the mountains, these are almost always a rock horn or a tree (see Short Pitch Belayed Climbing, above) and occasionally a bolt. If there is any doubt about the strength of the single piece, do not use a direct belay. Instead, belay off your body from a braced stance, backed up by the piece.

Multiple-piece anchors. When you are building multipiece anchors in the mountains, speed and simplicity are of greater concern than at the crag. Although the following discussion deals with complex anchors, use simpler solutions wherever possible.

How many pieces should be in a belay anchor? When constructing belay anchors using traditional rock gear, most climbers are taught to use at least three different pieces, placed among at least two different cracks or other features. In many cragging areas, this is the norm. However, such hard-and-fast rules simply do not apply in the alpine environment, which should be evident by our discussions up until now. Rather than thinking about numbers, learn to match the potential load with your evaluation of the strength of the individual pieces, the distribution of forces throughout the anchor, and your level of confidence that the gear will hold under expected loads applied in expected directions of pull.

What about equalizing the anchor and creating a master point? The various parts of a multiple-piece anchor are usually tied together to distribute the force among them and to create a master point—a single clip-in point—for the belayer. Two simple and common methods for doing this are pre-equalization (also known as static equalization) and self-equalization (sometimes call X-equalization or the "Magic X").

- **Pre-equalization.** This (see Figure 24) is a good choice if the climber can correctly identify the direction of fall force beforehand and equalize the runner or cordelette in that direction and if this direction will not change substantially. It creates redundancy, but perhaps more importantly, the knot creates a clear master point, easy to see and clip in to without much potential for error. This is especially important in anchors with three or more components.

  Use either a long runner or a cordelette to tie the anchor together. A figure eight or overhand knot is fine for building the master point. In fact, if our cordelette is too long, resulting in a master point being lower than we want it, we often use a figure nine or 10 or 11 or more—that is, we will add twists to the knot to take up cordelette material until the master point is exactly where we want it.

Figure 24. *A three-piece pre-equalized anchor with two cams and a horn, tied together with a cordelette. Carefully analyze the direction of expected load, and pull the strands between the pieces in that direction before tying the knot.*

- **Self-equalization.** The component pieces are connected with a sling pulled down in a V shape with a twist in one strand, as shown in Figure 25a (Figure 25b shows self-equalization of three pieces).

  The main advantage of a self-equalized anchor is that it is faster and simpler to build and break down. Another advantage is that the sling can adjust to changes in the direction of

Figure 25a. *Self-equalization of two pieces. There is no redundancy in the sling, but this anchor has the advantage of using minimal gear and is quick to build and take down.*

Figure 25b. *Self-equalizing with three pieces. To check that you have the Xs properly in place, look at the strands of webbing coming out one side of the master carabiner. Each of the three strands should go to a separate piece, as shown here.*

the load, keeping the tension on each piece roughly equal. This allows it to be used where the direction of pull may change or be hard to predict. However, this advantage all but disappears when more than two components are involved.

The main disadvantage is that the master point is harder to see and clip in to quickly and infallibly, especially with

anchors of more than two components. Another disadvantage is that this method does not prevent extension if one piece fails, so do not use it if there is any doubt about any of the component pieces.

■ **Self-equalization with limiting knot.** To reduce the extension problem of a self-equalizing anchor, you can tie a limiting knot on one side of the sling, as shown in Figure 26. Usually this knot is tied in the longer arm or on the side nearest the more suspect piece.

- **Hybrid.** A combination of self- and pre-equalization within the same anchor can help solve a number of problems (see Figure 27). For example, it allows you to isolate weaker pieces while retaining some degree of self-equalization or simply to tie together multipiece anchors where the gear is spread out and a single sling or cordelette is not long enough.
- **Choosing your method.** In two-component anchors whose individual component pieces are unquestionably

Figure 27. *In this hybrid anchor, the two upper pieces are self-equalized. These are then pre-equalized with the lower piece. The advantage here is simply that we can distribute the force throughout the anchor using only two single slings.*

bombproof, self-equalization is often preferable for its speed and simplicity. With its very low likelihood of failure, the question of extension and shock loading becomes unimportant.

When the component pieces are more numerous or distant from each other, or when you have less confidence in any of them, then pre-equalization is usually best (see Figure 28).

Figure 26. *A limiting knot in a self-equalized anchor.*

Figure 28. *Here the belayer is tied in with a clove hitch and is belaying with a plate device. She has run the climbing rope through a carabiner on the master point to serve as a first piece of protection and to reduce potential fall forces. A cordelette was used to pre-equalize the anchor components. Mount Whitney, East Buttress, California.*

Fixed anchors. Fixed anchors placed by previous climbers are common on alpine routes where a rappel descent follows the route of ascent. They also are found in areas where the rock doesn't lend itself to placing wedges or cams, making bolt or piton anchors necessary.

Fixed anchors can be great time-savers.

They can help with routefinding, if only to confirm that you are indeed on route, as you suspected. However, they can be deceptive, so beware. Sometimes a rappel anchor will make good sense on descent but is not in the best location for the way up, being slightly off your best climbing route, in an inconvenient or uncomfortable stance, or not necessary at all. Keep your brain turned on, even when the presence of fixed anchors seems to make things easier.

To ease traffic or to facilitate passing on a crowded climb, you may be better off not using an available fixed anchor. If you can build your own anchor off to the side, continue on above, or stop short below the fixed anchor, you may save time by not getting involved in the chaos of a mobbed fixed anchor (see Passing Other Parties in Chapter 2, The Alpine Environment).

Just because anchors are fixed and established does not necessarily make them good. We have discovered many wobbly anchors on very popular routes over the years. A horn may be loose even if it has a lot of webbing wrapped around it. Pitons loosen or corrode with time. Trees die. Fixed anchors in the mountains are usually the product of "committee work"—a self-appointed committee composed of members who never see or talk to each other or even know who else is on the committee. Everybody changes, adds elements to, and subtracts elements from an anchor as they see fit. Tangles of webbing, mystery knots, hidden gear, and inadequate equalization of the various components of the anchor are the norm.

Many fixed anchors are made up of multiple components taking a variety of forms, from bolts to trees to knots in cord or webbing, slung chockstones, wooden wedges—you name it. It is quite possible for an anchor to be adequate even if none of its components taken individually is

very inspiring. Look at the integrity of each piece and the manner by which the pieces are connected to each other, in order to develop an opinion about their collective strength (see Figure 29). Do not hesitate to change some components or their connection, if doing so will improve the anchor.

While the best thought-out fixed anchors are connected with chain, steel cable, or other semipermanent material, in the mountains most are built on the fly

Figure 29. *A good two-bolt anchor. The leader has used the top bolt to serve as the first piece of protection, to reduce the potential fall factor.*

and tied together with webbing and cord. These materials have a limited life span, and climbers continually make improvements and adjustments, most commonly adding more sling material. While generally a good thing, this eventually creates a rat's nest of tangled nylon.

Do both yourself and other climbers a favor by cleaning up existing anchors. Usually this means improving or replacing the webbing that brings the parts of the anchor to a common master point, but it may involve more (see Figure 30). When you are evaluating and improving fixed anchors:

- Check that the various components are sound—horns, pitons, nuts, threads, etc.
- Carefully inspect how the anchor is tied together. Understand how each piece of cord or webbing contributes. If some of the material is hidden around the back side of a block or thread, rotate it to examine all of it.
- Remove damaged, frayed, burned, excessively aged, or superfluous sling material. Keep a knife handy for this.
- If necessary, retie the webbing to simplify the anchor or master point, to equalize the load among its components, or to create redundancy among multiple pieces of webbing.

Once, while we were rappelling off the Aiguille Blanche de Peuterey on Mont Blanc, two pitons constituting a fixed anchor both looked good but could be pulled out by hand. We whacked them back in and that was enough adjustment to give us confidence to use them.

Figure 30. *The original anchor consisted of the two fixed pitons up and left and all the old sling material. Not wanting to trust only the two pins, we added a cam in the crack on the right and pre-equalized it all together with a double runner.*

Using Single, Half, or Twin Ropes

Ropes fall into three broad categories: single, half, and twin. Each type is used in a different way.

Single-rope technique. This is by far

the most common method of protecting 5th-class rock climbing and is useful in all types of alpine mountaineering. Compared to half or twin ropes, single ropes are thicker, stronger, and heavier. Their greater strength is necessary mostly to provide adequate resistance to cutting over sharp rock edges. The greatest advantages of this method are less rope to carry and easier rope management when belaying, stacking, coiling, etc. The greatest disadvantages are that you can only rappel half a rope length, and if the strand is cut by falling rock or over an edge, there is no backup.

Double-rope technique. This is used when climbing with half ropes. Half ropes are narrower in diameter than single ropes and are used together, the leader climbing on both strands. Even though double-rope technique involves twice as much rope as the single-rope method—and entails more rope management problems—it has several advantages. Each half rope is designed to be strong enough to hold a leader fall on its own (backed up by the other rope), so the leader can alternately clip one strand or the other to each piece of protection. This reduces rope drag in situations where the climbing route traverses or wanders. Two strands are less likely to be cut over sharp edges than a single strand. In the event of a leader fall, double-rope technique reduces the maximum force transmitted to protection and to the falling climber, because a smaller, more elastic strand of rope absorbs the initial force. This also means the climber falls farther, however. With a double rope, you can rappel twice the

distance that is possible with a single rope.

Twin-rope technique. Twin ropes are essentially two thinner strands doing the same job as a single rope. In contrast to half ropes, neither strand of a twin rope is designed to hold a leader fall on its own, so both must be clipped in to each piece of protection (see Figure 31). Therefore, twin ropes are not as useful as half ropes for reducing rope drag or fall forces. However, they do allow longer rappels, similarly to half ropes.

Figure 31. *Mike Powers using twin ropes on the Blaitière's Red Pillar, France. With twin ropes, the leader clips both strands in to all protection points.*

Choosing your rope technique. The main difference between alpine rock climbing and rock climbing at the crag is the greater need for speed. Of all the considerations mentioned above, rope management has the greatest impact on speed. Because rope management is so much easier with a single rope than with either double- or twin-rope techniques, a single rope is usually the first choice unless there is a strong reason to prefer half or twin ropes. If your descent will involve rappels that are unavoidably longer than half a rope length, your second choice would be twin ropes or a single rope and rappel line (see Descent, below). If you need to make long rappels, if protection is complex and difficult to arrange, and if the climbing is hard enough to require lots of protection, then you may want to bring half ropes.

The need for long rappels is relatively

Figure 32. *The belayer is tied in to this two-bolt anchor with one strand of the double rope to one bolt and the other strand to the other bolt. This is a fast and simple tie-in method on a two-piece anchor when swinging leads on double ropes.*

rare. Many climbs utilize easier routes for the descent, and the broken terrain means rappels tend to be shorter. Most good guidebook descriptions indicate whether a route has a rappel descent or not and also the length of the rappels. There is always the possibility that you might have to back off a route partway up, requiring long rappels. Assess your abilities, the weather forecast, and any other factors that could force an unplanned rappel descent.

Tying in to the anchor with half or twin ropes. With half or twin ropes, you have more options for tying in. You can tie each strand separately to one anchor component and use your body position to equalize between them (see Figure 32), or you can create a master point to which both ropes are tied, just as in single-rope technique. The best choice is a function of several factors:

- Are you swinging leads, or is one climber leading all the pitches? If you swing leads, it may be quicker to tie the climbing ropes directly in to the anchor components, at least if there are no more than two components. This avoids the added step and gear needed to create a master point. Because there is no master point, you must belay the second off your harness.

  On the other hand, if one climber leads all the pitches, then the second needs to tie in to the anchor upon arriving at the belay. Creating a master point at the time the belay is built makes this much quicker and simpler.

- Will you want to belay your second off your harness or directly off the anchor? If you want to bring up the second using a direct belay off the anchor, then you must create a master point for this task in any case. You might as well use it to tie in to as well. This is the situation in Figure 33.

- How many component pieces does the anchor have? When your anchor consists of more than three component

Figure 33. *Tying in to an anchor with a master point. Double up the strands using a clove hitch. Leader's-eye view, looking down on the belayer—the leader has clipped a quickdraw in to the top nut as a first piece, to reduce potential fall factor.*

173

pieces, it is usually much simpler to create a master point using a cordelette. In this case, both rope strands are tied together into the master point.

Managing the Rope

Good rope management is essential to good time management. The less time you spend coiling, moving, restacking, and untangling rope, the more time you have for other important tasks, such as outrunning the coming thunderstorm or avoiding afternoon rockfall.

Rope management also entails a safety issue: the rope must run smoothly when you are belaying. The leader needs to have freedom of movement and not be jerked or brought up short by twists, knots, or other results of poor rope handling. The rope must be conveniently placed and correctly stacked.

Stacking. If you are on a ledge where you can stack the rope and it will stay put, stack it near the belayer, so that he or she can reach the rope and deal with any problems should it become tangled around rocks or roots, etc. The leader's end must come off the top of the pile. When swinging leads, this is straightforward. Pile the rope neatly as you belay in your second. When he or she begins leading the next pitch, the lead strand is already coming off the top of the stack. If, however, one of you leads all the pitches, you may have to restack the rope at the beginning of each new pitch, with the leader's end always on top. You can make this easier by keeping the rope in a neat and compact pile as you bring in the second.

Before beginning the next lead, "pancake flip" the pile upside down so that the lead strand comes cleanly off the top again.

If there is no place to stack the rope on a ledge, lap-coil it across your tie-in strand as you bring in your second. Try to keep all the loops about the same length—ideally, about down to your knee. When belaying the leader out, stay ahead of the game and drop a coil at a time before you actually need it. If one person is leading all the pitches, then flip the whole stack of lap coils over and onto the second's tie-in so that the leader's strand again feeds cleanly from the top.

Managing double ropes. This can be tricky. At the start of belayed climbing, stack each rope separately, with the leader's ends coming out the tops of both stacks. Once climbing is underway, however, it becomes complicated and time consuming to continue stacking each rope separately. You are better off treating the two strands as one and stacking them together. If twists occur, they will accumulate near the bottom of the stack. This should not be a great concern except on very long pitches.

On lead, if you clip each rope in to alternating protection, keep the strands clear of each other and untwisted in order to reduce rope drag. If you clip both ropes together to each piece, as in a twin-rope system, then treat them as a single strand and essentially ignore the twists unless they start to hinder the belay. When belaying, keep your little finger between the strands in order to keep the strands untwisted as they go into the belay device. The ropes will behave very much better if they are exactly the same length! Avoid using ropes whose length varies by more than a meter.

Racking Your Gear

Racking for alpine rock climbing differs somewhat from normal crag climbing. If you will be shortening the rope and climbing with tied-off coils, rack your gear and slings on your harness gear loops (see Figure 34), not over your shoulder where it

Figure 34. *Racking gear on your harness keeps it from interfering with your rope coils. Twisting, knotting, and carefully stowing slings and cordelettes prevents them from dangling too low, where they could snarl on rocks, shrubs, or your crampons.*

will inhibit changing the rope length.

However, this does slow down the transfer of the gear to a new leader, so if you swing leads on sustained 5th-class rock, it might make more sense to have at least half the rack on a shoulder sling to make this transition easier. If one person does most or all of the leading, having all or most of the gear on the harness is best. Your locking carabiners, autoblocking belay device, and cordelette can be racked farther back on your harness and out of the way. You will need them only occasionally and only at belay stances. On easy ground, put unnecessary gear away in your pack.

DESCENT

Popular myth states that most climbing accidents happen on descent. Actually only about a third do. Nevertheless, many dangers are particular to descending: fatigue, a hurry to get down, mentally relaxing one's guard, bad snow conditions or coming bad weather, lack of familiarity with the descent route. The descent requires as much consideration and planning as the route up.

PLAN YOUR DESCENT

On the way up, you have the option of retreat if things don't go well. By contrast, there's no turning back once you start down. If you fail to plan this portion of the climb, things can get serious pretty quickly.

Routefinding

Descent routes are often different from the route of ascent and may even be on a side of the mountain you were unable to see on the approach. Gather all the information you need to find your way down. Anticipate the possibility of cloudy weather. On some large glaciated peaks, especially those with rounded, windswept summits, finding the start of the descent in poor visibility can be the hardest part. Be sure your whiteout plan addresses this common problem.

Equipment

Know what gear you will need for the descent. Normally, what you used on the way up is more than adequate for the way down. However, this may not be the case in the following two common scenarios.

The first is on a multiple-rappel descent. You may need to replace anchors left behind by other parties if the anchors are poorly located or untrustworthy due to age, wear, or damage. Normally all you need for this is plenty of sling material or a cordelette or two, which you will already have with you on most climbs. But if your route has a long multiple-rappel descent, you may want to plan ahead and bring a little extra backoff cord or webbing. You can also scarf material from existing off-route anchors or use webbing gleaned from your cleanup efforts on overbuilt anchors—assuming the material is still in decent shape, of course.

For example, as they descended the Aiguille Verte in France, Mark and his partner Chris once found half a stuck rope that had been cut off and abandoned by a previous party. Chopped-up bits of this rope made great rappel anchors for the rest of their descent. Of course, before you trust your life to such scavenged material, inspect it carefully. In an emergency, you can even start chopping off bits of your own climbing rope after you run out of everything else.

The second common situation in which you may need to plan your gear specifically for the descent is when the ascent route is on rock but the descent is on snow or glacier. Different footwear, perhaps an ice ax, crampons, or other equipment may be needed.

"PLANNING" AS A LEARNING EXPERIENCE

Once while descending from a memorable climb of the Sunribbon Arete on Temple Crag in the Sierra Nevada, we met with an unexpected concrete-hard frozen snow slope. We had planned poorly, assuming any snow would be soft. In our desire to go light, we had brought only sneakers and our rock shoes and no snow or ice gear. Although the slope was not steep—only 20 degrees—we had to rappel, using frozen-in rocks for anchors. With a light ice ax, we could have created bollard rappel anchors or even chopped steps. We were lucky there were rocks frozen in the snow!

DOWNCLIMBING VERSUS RAPPELLING

On moderate terrain, downclimbing is generally faster than rappelling. While the act of rappelling itself can be quite quick, the transitions between rappels are time consuming and the anchors can be complex to evaluate and to build.

Downclimbing on exposed, easy terrain is a crucial alpine skill whose importance is typically underestimated, and which requires practice. This takes time but yields huge results in increased reliability, speed, and confidence.

Facing In or Out?

When you are downclimbing, the angle and difficulty of the terrain will dictate whether you face in or out. Facing out is much faster and allows better visibility; strive to do this as much as possible. Place your feet deliberately and precisely. Use hands, arms, legs, or buttocks where needed for friction and stability. On long steps, your back foot can unexpectedly hang up, pitching you forward, so small steps are preferable, even if this means using smaller footholds. Be careful, since falls while facing out are particularly difficult to stop.

Facing in feels more secure but is slow. With your eyes close to the rock, footholds below are harder to see and evaluate, and it is harder to pick out a route. The terrain below looks harder and steeper than it truly is. This is especially the case in shallow gullies or low-angle chimneys. When you do resort to facing in, keep gear, loose clothes, long hair, and other impediments to visibility out of the way, and turn around frequently to gauge whether you can turn and face out once more.

Belayed Downclimbing

If the going gets harder, you may eventually reach a point where unbelayed downclimbing of any kind does not feel secure. If the difficulties are short and not too hard, and if one of you is a more confident climber than the other, it might be faster at this point to downclimb using the rope to belay rather than to rappel.

If you have been moving together on a shortened rope up to this point, the transition into belayed downclimbing is very quick and natural. If you are the stronger climber, belay your partner down the difficult section using the quickest belay method that will provide adequate security—often a braced body belay or a quick wrap of the rope around a horn. Watch your partner downclimb, and gauge how difficult you think it will be for you. Your partner can coach you through the crux or help you locate your next foothold, place protection for you as he or she descends key spots, or at the very least give you a quick belay around a handy block to keep you both on the mountain should you fall.

Lowering the first person can be much faster than having him or her downclimb. If you plan to lower, use a direct method, such as a Münter hitch on the anchor. With the Münter hitch, you'll need to counter the tendency for the rope to twist. Stack the rope so that it feeds cleanly into your hands, stand in a location where you can see the person you are lowering the entire time, and lower slowly at a constant speed.

RAPPELLING

Although downclimbing is generally preferable to rappelling, often we have little choice in the matter. Try to rappel only when it is clearly the fastest, safest, or only option.

Rappel Anchors

Earlier in this chapter we discuss evaluating and improving fixed anchors and using natural features such as rock horns, trees, etc. Rappel anchors also have their own specific issues in addition to those mentioned earlier.

Retrieving the rope. When inspecting rappel anchors, evaluate how hard it will be to retrieve the rope. An anchor's location, position, or configuration can make it difficult to retrieve the rope because of friction. Burned or excessively worn webbing at the spot where the rope threads through the anchor is evidence of difficulty in retrieval. Adjust the anchor as needed so that this rope-threading point will allow an easier pull. There are several ways to do this.

Extend the pull-through point. If the anchor is set back too far from an edge, extend the point at which the rope connects to it (see Figure 35).

Use rappel rings or carabiners. On long rappels, the weight of the ropes and friction of rope on rock can complicate retrieval. To solve this problem, climbers

Figure 35. *Extending the anchor to make the pull easier. Notice the knots creating redundancy in the sling. This is a good idea wherever there are sharp edges or the potential for abrasion.*

often incorporate rappel rings of various kinds into the anchor and thread the rope through these rather than through the webbing. Such rings take various forms: rolled aluminum or welded steel rings and "quick links" with a threaded sleeve closure are common types. You can carry these and add them yourself as needed to anchors that you find or create. You may prefer to leave a carabiner as a rappel ring, especially on preexisting anchors, because it is faster and easier to clip a carabiner in to webbing than to untie and retie the old webbing through a ring.

If the anchor already includes a rappel ring, inspect it inside and out for any cracks or for grooves worn by ropes pulling through. This is clearly a critical point: it is the only thing connecting the rope to the anchor. If you have any doubt about its trustworthiness, back it up with a carabiner or webbing loop as in Figure 36.

Figure 36. *Backing up a carabiner with a tied nylon loop. Here we want the carabiner to permit an easy pull and also the cord loop for extra security. Adding a separate loop can also back up any suspect connection point such as frayed webbing or a worn rappel ring.*

Leaving gear behind. Sometimes there is no anchor where you need one, or the anchor that exists doesn't inspire confidence. In either case you may need to leave behind some of your own rack. A disinclination to do this creates a psychological barrier against reinforcing a chancy anchor. Sacrificing gear is painful, we know—but don't be deterred! After all, how much is your life worth to you? If you find yourself raiding your rack for rappel anchors, chances are things are not going as you planned so you may have few options at that point, but there are a couple of ways you can economize your precious gear when improving existing anchors.

Existing anchors rarely need to be replaced entirely. Most often you need only to improve them. You can do this either by beefing them up or backing them up.

Beef up dicey anchors. This entails adding a new permanent element to the anchor. Ideally, equalize the new element with the old so that anchor components share the load. Use an equalization method that prevents shock loading should any element fail (see Figure 37).

Back up dicey anchors. By contrast, backing up a suspicious anchor allows you to safely test it under load. If it passes the test, you may decide to retrieve the backup and take it with you. Your backup must be connected to the anchor in such a way that it holds none of the test load, or you will not actually test the existing anchor's strength and, hence, defeat your purpose (see Figure 38). Fatal accidents have occurred when

Figure 37. *When you beef up an anchor, make sure you equalize your new element(s) with the whole. In this scenario, the cam on the right is to be left behind. This is expensive, but if you don't trust the anchor without it and can find no alternative, it's well worth it!*

backups held some of the load during the first person's rappel and the anchor later failed when the second removed the backup and then fully weighted the unreinforced and untested anchor for the first time.

Test the anchor by sending the heaviest person down first, while the backup is in place. Load this climber up with extra gear or the heavier pack. The second climber

should carefully watch the anchor for any movement or problems and then decide whether to leave the backup in place or remove it and trust the original anchor alone. Compare the two anchors in Figure 39. Seeing the anchor hold the heavier climber may give reason for more confidence. If you both weigh roughly the same or if you still don't trust the anchor, you

Figure 38. *When you back up an anchor, make sure that the connection of backup to rope is completely independent of the anchor being tested, that your backup is capable of holding all the load in case the anchor being tested should fail, that it is positioned appropriately for the direction of potential load, and that it is slack, holding none of the load during the test!*

Figure 39a. *A good rappel anchor on the Aiguille du Peigne. The rock "neck" is quite solid.*

might not ever feel confident enough to remove a backup, in which case leave it in place and rappel with peace of mind. It's your call!

Backing up rappel devices. This is occasionally advisable, most often for two reasons: if you fear you might have trouble maintaining control of the rappel, or if you need to stop and perform some other task during the rappel. Set a backup on the rope *before* you start your rappel under the following conditions:

- You are likely to have to stop during

your descent to do some work such as untangling rope or searching for, improving upon, or building the next anchor in the absence of a ledge.
- There is real danger of rocks or other objects falling from above.
- Your attention and focus are not optimal because of some difficulty or stress: the need to rush, wind blowing the ropes aside, the route follows a radically

Figure 39b. *A frightening rappel "anchor" on the descent of Sabre, in the Southern Alps of New Zealand. This single rusty piton bashed into a dirty, grassy crack is an accident waiting to happen. Not finding another option for a better anchor here, we opted to simply downclimb.*

traversing line, poor weather, etc.
- The rappel is steep and long.
- You are carrying a heavy pack.
- Your ability to grip is compromised because the rope is narrow in diameter, brand new, single strand, wet, or icy.
- You just feel like having a backup!

The above list suggests that backing up a rappel is the rule, not the exception. This is not strictly true. Many rappels are short and straightforward, with the ropes running clean and visible to the ground or ledge. Very often you are relaxed, attentive, and not too rushed and there is no real hazard of falling objects. In these conditions, you may well choose to dispense with the backup.

Backing up the rappel using a prusik loop. The method we describe here both backs up your rappel and prepares an easy way to get your hands free in mid-descent to deal with any snarls or problems. This method involves minimal fuss and interferes relatively little with your rappel. However, note that this method does *not* prevent you from accidentally rappelling off the ends of the rope.

Place a small prusik loop (see Figure 40) on the rope downhill from your belay device, and clip it to the leg loop on your harness with a locking carabiner. This functions as an extra "hand," to hold you in place even if you let go of the rope entirely. As you rappel, slide this prusik down the rope with your brake hand as you go. When you want to stop and free your hands, let go of the prusik and be sure it grabs before you let go of the brake strand of the rope.

Adjust the prusik loop to just the right length. If it's too short, you won't get enough wraps to hold. If it's too long, the prusik knot will bunch up against your rappel device and fail to grab. Experiment with the length of your prusik loop until you get it just right. Store your prusik loop girth-hitched around one of the gear loops on your harness so you always have it handy.

Extending the rappel device. If you have

Figure 40a. *The two-wrap prusik knot. If this doesn't hold, try three wraps. Neatness counts! Remember, when rappelling on two strands of rope, the knot must be built around BOTH strands.*

Figure 40b. *Build your prusik knot around both strands of the rope, as shown. Clip the prusik loop to the leg loop of your harness using a locking carabiner. Make sure the prusik knot cannot touch your rappel device, or it will bunch up against it and not grab. Hold the prusik knot loose to rappel; release it and let it tighten to stop.*

trouble getting the length of your backup cord right to prevent the prusik knot from bumping up against your rappel device, you can extend your device away from your harness by girth-hitching a sewn runner through your belay loop and placing your device on this, as shown in Figure 41.

The extra space created between your backup and your rappel device makes it

easier to operate your backup properly, makes it easier to keep both hands on the brake strands—helpful when dealing with twists—and can reduce the risk of clothing or hair being sucked up into your device. Use only sewn runners for your extension.

Using a "fireman's" belay. Once you arrive at the bottom of a rappel, you can back up your partner's device from below. Hold the ends of the rope and keep your

The autoblock is a good alternative to the prusik. It has less gripping power but is more releasable under load. It will extend a bit when loaded, so be sure you have enough distance between the knot and your rappel device. Again, build it around both strands of rope when rappelling.

Figure 41. *Extending your device with a girth-hitched runner makes it easier to manage the backup, allows you to brake with both hands, and facilitates the prerigged rappel (see Prerigging rappels, later in this chapter).*

eyes on your partner. If he or she loses control of the brake or wants free hands, pull down hard on both strands to brake.

Knotting ends. Climbers have died rappelling off the ends of the ropes. The only sure way to safeguard against this is to remain ever vigilant and attentive. You may choose to knot the ends of the rope, but doing so requires equal vigilance and also introduces other problems:

■ The knots may hang up on flakes, shrubs, horns, and other objects. This is especially true when the wind is blowing and the ropes extend out sideways along the cliff. In these conditions, if you wish to knot the ropes you should carry them down the cliff with you, rather than throwing them. See **Coiling for feeding on descent,** later in this chapter.

■ It's easy to forget the knot is there when you go to pull the rope through the anchor above. In this case you may be truly stuck. Knotting the ends is not a license to space out.

We normally knot the ends of the ropes only in situations where rappelling off the ends of the rope seems a real possibility. A good example is a long, steep rappel ending in the middle of a wall with no good ledge. Knotting ends is especially important in this case if other distracting or difficult conditions also exist. However, if you know the ropes will reach the ground or a big ledge, then knots are usually more a hindrance than a help.

Use one half of a double fishermans knot at the end of each strand. Knot each end individually, leaving each strand free to twist independently without twining around the other.

Joining Knots

When joining two ropes of roughly equal diameter for a two-rope rappel, use a flat overhand knot (see Figure 42). This knot is preferred because it "flips up" and presents a flat surface to the rock when it is pulled over obstacles, making it less likely to jam in cracks or catch on edges.

Snug the knot down carefully and thoroughly, pulling hard on all four strands individually. Rope tails should be 30 to 45 cm (12 to 18 inches) long, because the flat overhand has been known to invert and travel under very big loads. Do not tie backup knots in the tails; this defeats the purpose of snag-free sliding along the rock.

When joining ropes of significantly different diameter (more than 3-mm difference), use a double fishermans knot. Again, do not tie backup knots. The

Figure 42. *Rappelling on a 10.5-mm rope joined to an 8.2-mm rope with a flat overhand knot. The thicker rope is threaded through the descending rings.*

bulkier this knot is, the greater its tendency to jam and snag, and it is plenty strong enough as is.

When using ropes of unequal diameters, pass the thicker of the two through the descending ring or anchor point and arrange ropes so as to pull on the thinner one for retrieval, as in Figure 42. Because the thinner rope stretches more, the ropes will shift at the anchor as you rappel. As long as the larger-diameter rope is passed through the anchor, the joining knot will eventually jam, limiting the movement of the rope.

If your ropes are of equal diameter, it doesn't matter which side of the anchor the knot is on, but look carefully before you leave the stance, and remember which strand to pull!

Retrieval Lines

As discussed earlier in this chapter, using a single rope reduces weight but limits the distance you can rappel compared with half or twin ropes. Use of a retrieval line can extend this potential rappel distance without adding the full weight of a second rope. A retrieval line can be a lightweight cord or even several joined lengths of cordelette or narrow-diameter rope. Any material strong enough to withstand the hard pull of retrieval without breaking will work.

Examine Figure 43. The climbing rope passes through the anchor and is joined to the retrieval line using any joining knot, a flat overhand in this case. Find the midpoint of your total combined rope, including the retrieval line, and situate this midpoint at the anchor. Tie a very small bight with a butterfly knot on the retrieval side of the anchor, and clip this back to the rope on the other (rappel) side with a locking carabiner. This fixes the climbing rope in place so that you can rappel on the single strand of the climbing rope on the rappel side. When you rappel, the butterfly knot jams at the anchor. When you pull on the retrieval line, the carabiner slides freely along the strand of the climbing rope. With this method, you can have as many knots or

Figure 43. *Rappelling on a single strand with a retrieval line. The climber's left hand holds the retrieval line.*

joins in the retrieval line as needed to get it to the required length.

Warning: Rappelling on a single strand makes sharp rock edges extra spooky. It is also slipperier than rappelling on two strands—use a high-friction rappel device and consider backing it up with a prusik loop as described above.

A note about the butterfly knot. In our own climbing, we use the butterfly knot in only two different situations: with the retrieval line method as described here, and in glacier travel to help a single climber arrest a crevasse fall. Even though this knot is seldom used, it is worth learning for these applications, where it truly is the best choice. In the rappel application, it is extraordinarily useful because it is far less prone to jamming in the rappel anchor than a figure eight, making for a much easier retrieval.

Rope Management During Rappel Descents

Much time can be lost because of poor rope handling in pulling and setting up rappels. In addition to the pointers below and in the following section on refining transitions, think about teamwork and having all climbers "at work." Anticipate what will happen and what jobs need to be done.

Clipping in. You must, of course, untie from the rope during rappels, so improvise a clip-in runner: girth-hitch a single runner to the belay loop on your harness, and clip in to the anchor using a locking carabiner. Clip in as soon as you get to the anchor.

Coiling and throwing. Round coils or

lap coils both work for gathering the rope in preparation to throw it down the cliff. In either case, your coils must be very small and the two strands should be coiled separately. For most rappels, a sequence like the following works best:

- Coil the upper (closest to the anchor) half of one of the strands of the rope. Throw this down the cliff, being sure to keep the lower end of the rope with you—gently step on it or have your partner hold onto it.
- If you want a knot in the end of the rope, tie it now, then coil up the remaining rope and throw it down the hill. If you use round coils, try to throw them with an uncoiling spin, so that they uncoil in the air (see Figure 44).
- The weight of the first strand as it falls may cause the ropes to slide through the anchor. Prevent this from happening by tying a knot and clipping it to the anchor, by having one of you hold the ropes, or by stepping on them gently.
- Repeat this procedure with the other strand.

Coiling for feeding on descent.
Throwing ropes on windy days can be an invitation to disaster, especially when the ends are knotted. An alternative is to carry the coils down with you in such a way that the rope feeds into your device from coils on your harness. This is also a good thing to do when rappelling down on top of another party, to reduce rockfall or to avoid throwing ropes down on them. This technique has great snafu potential, and close attention to detail is vital to make it

Figure 44. *This climber is throwing small round coils underhand, so that they open up and uncoil in the air. Note the stopper knot to keep from rappelling off the end. She has already thrown about half of this strand, which can be seen running down the slope below. The middle of the rope is threaded through the anchor and also clipped with a knot to a carabiner to keep it in place and prevent it from slithering down the hill under its own weight.*

work. It is best to practice it at the crag and work out solutions to potential problems. Here's how it works:

- Extend your device to help ropes feed cleanly into the device.

- Place a prusik loop backup on the ropes downhill from your device, as described above. You need your hands free to deal with tangles.
- Using lap coils (never round coils), coil one of the two rappel strands. Start with larger coils—about half a meter (2 feet) to a side—and make them progressively smaller.
- Clip a shoulder runner to a gear loop on your harness, cradle the coiled rope in the runner, and clip the other end of the runner with another carabiner also to your gear loop. The strand to your rappel device must feed from the front of the coils.
- After coiling one side, coil the other in the same way. Put one strand of the rope on one side of your harness and the other on the other side, like saddlebags.

Efficient Transitions

Transitions between rappels can be made much more efficient if you think ahead, divide your labor, and work together as a team.

Getting off rappel quickly. Once you have clipped in to the anchor at the base of a rappel, don't wait to remove the rope from your device before yelling "Off rappel!" Instead, yard a bunch of slack through your device right away and call "Off rappel" once you've done this. Your partner will then have enough slack to begin his or her rappel while you free your device at your leisure.

Pulling and resetting joined ropes. If the preceding rappel was long and you are therefore near the end of the ropes, then one of you should find the end of the rope being pulled, feed it into the new anchor, and thread it through as the other pulls the rope down. If your previous rappel was relatively short, then it may be quicker to begin pulling without threading the end and untie and retie the rope-joining knot as soon as it arrives at your stance, to avoid having to thread a large amount of slack through the new anchor. Begin pulling down on the appropriate strand and when the rope-joining knot

Figure 45. *Carrying the ropes with you as you rappel. Extending the device makes this much easier. Neatness counts!*

comes within reach, quickly tie a temporary overhand knot and clip it in to secure the ropes while retying the knot. One climber reties the rope-joining knot while the other continues pulling.

Prerigging rappels. One way to spend less time on transitions is to prerig your rappels: both you and your partner place your rappel device on the rope at the same moment, at the top of the rappel (see Figure 46). This cuts in half the time needed to rig, since two people working simultaneously take no more time than one.

1. Extend the device away from your harness (see Extending the Rappel Device, above). Otherwise, as the first rappeller weights the rope on the descent, the climber left at the top will be pulled into the cliff or the ground—very uncomfortable. Never use a figure eight device or Münter hitch with an extension: the twisting effect will wind the rope and the extension around each other.
2. Once both climbers are rigged, the first one descends. Upon hearing "Off rappel," the second simply double-checks the rig and begins descending after unclipping the clip-in runner.

Stuck Ropes

Despite the best efforts, ropes do occasionally stick on retrieval from a rappel anchor, which can be a huge time drain as well as quite dangerous. Foresight and prevention are obviously vital. Situations with high rope-snag potential are often foreseeable, particularly in high winds or

Figure 46. *Prerigging the second person to rappel. The climber on the left has her device set up with an extension. Because the stance is small, she also remains clipped in to the anchor with her daisy. As soon as the person on the right gets to the next stance and unweights the rope, the second can start down. The climber on the right does not need an extension.*

on low-angle terrain with lots of cracks, horns, blocks, or shrubs just waiting to eat your rope. A shorter rappel, where possible (using one rope instead of two, for instance), can help forestall the worst snags. Here are a few other tips to avoid problems as you go:

1. If the rappel anchor ring or webbing

is situated so that your rope is against the rock where it passes through the ring, set up your ropes so the strand you pull down is against the rock. This helps to avoid the problem of the rope being pulled pinching the other strand, sticking it.

2. As you leave the stance, make sure that the strands coming from the anchor run clean and straight into your device, with no twists. As long as you use a plate, autoblocking belay device, or carabiner brake, the ropes won't become twisted as you descend unless you spin in the air.

3. As you begin your rappel, carefully position the ropes so they run untwisted over any edges, and avoid cracks or notches where the joining knot may jam.

4. While rappelling, look for and avoid rope-eating features. Likely suspects are inside corners with cracks just larger than the rope's diameter, as well as horns, flakes, trees, and shrubs.

5. At the bottom of the rappel, carefully keep the strands straight as you remove the rope from your rappel device. Separate them and see them run cleanly all the way to the anchor if it's visible, to be sure the strands are not twisted as you pull.

6. If you can safely move around, seek a good position to pull from, where the ropes will fall away from trees, horns, loose blocks, and other potential problems. If possible, get a bit away from the cliff to where you can see the anchor above.

7. Pull the ropes as carefully and gently as you can, watching for any signs of misbehavior. If the rope runs near something on which you think it will snag, change your position and angle of pull if possible.

RAPPELLING AS ENDURANCE SPORT

On our second rappel off the summit of Patagonia's Cerro Torre, one of our ropes blew off to the side as we pulled it down, wrapping neatly around a sharp flake. We had been climbing nonstop for the previous two days, with only a couple hours of chilled half-sleep, and were in no mood to reclimb anything. In the declining light of the setting sun, we were able to free the stuck rope with only a modicum of fiddling. We rappelled through the night, nodding off at stances, trying with limited success to stay alert. Some 30 rappels later, at about 7:00 the next morning, on the very last rappel above the warmth and security of our bivouac, the ropes stuck again. Up again, reclimb another pitch—brains so fuzzy we now can't recall the reason for the problem. We do recall, however, the relief of being off the climb, staggering down through the boulders on the lower glacier, thanking the powers that be that during the nearly 35 rappels necessary to reach terra firma, only twice did the ropes misbehave.

If despite your best efforts the rope does jam, here are a few tricks to help you coax it down:

- First of all, make sure you are pulling on the correct strand and not just trying to force the joining knot through a rappel ring or webbing at the anchor.
- Change your position and angle of pull to get farther from the cliff if possible.
- If you know or suspect that the rope is stuck in a crack, try pulling on the other strand if you still have access to it; sometimes that can unjam the caught strand.
- If you can see that the rope is caught on a horn, flake, or tree, jerk the slack vigorously upward and to the side to try to flip it off the obstacle. Use a lot of slack and large, vigorous motions to create a large open loop at the obstacle. Be careful not to pull rope-ensnared loose blocks down on yourself!

In the rare case that none of these strategies works, you will have to climb the pitch to free the rope yourself, unless there is some good Samaritan above you who can come to the rescue. The following are three possible stuck-rope scenarios, each suggesting a different response.

Stuck rope example 1. In the first scenario, you have access to both strands, but the ropes won't budge no matter how hard you pull on either strand. Place a prusik knot on both strands and either ascend the ropes to the anchor using a prusik system (see Chapter 7, Glaciers) or free-climb the pitch, moving the prusik up with you as a self-belay.

Stuck rope example 2. In the second scenario, you have pulled most of the rope down before it gets stuck, or it gets stuck while it is falling, so you have only one strand available to you. The terrain is reasonable to climb. Tie in to the end you have available and lead up the pitch, taking a belay and placing protection as needed. Once you free the rope, either downclimb or find/build a new rappel anchor.

Stuck rope example 3. In the third scenario, as in the previous one, you have pulled most of the rope down before it jams, so you have only one strand available to you. However, this time the terrain you rappelled is too difficult to free-climb. Your only option is to ascend the stuck rope itself using a prusik system. This is a horrifying prospect, since whatever the rope is stuck to is your only anchor, at least in the beginning. If you do not absolutely need all of the rope to get down safely, seriously consider chopping the rope and descending with whatever you have left.

If you absolutely do need the rope to continue, and no other climbers are above who can bail you out, then your next step is to make sure you have done everything possible to free it—you and your partner together pull as hard as you can, get your combined body weight on the rope, bounce and heave aggressively, pull from varying angles. If it still will not budge, at least you have tested it somewhat.

Next, decide whether you have enough of the rope down to allow you to lead on the available end while ascending the stuck strand using a prusik system. If you do, build a solid anchor for your belayer (if you don't already have one), tie in to the available end of the rope, and take a belay from below as you prusik up the stuck strand. Place gear and clip your lead strand in to it as frequently as possible. That way a leader fall is the worst that will happen if the snag suddenly comes loose.

If you do not have enough rope to reach the snag or suspect you might not, still place gear for protection as you prusik the rope. In this case, do not tie in to the available end. Your partner puts the rope through his or her device and holds it as if braking a fall, and you simply begin prusiking the stuck strand. Place gear and clip the rope in to it behind you as you go. Once you have placed a piece or two, pull up some slack in the rope behind you (your partner feeds it through his or her belay device), tie a figure eight on a bight, and clip in using two carabiners on your harness, reversed, opposed, and preferably locking. As you continue to ascend the stuck strand, this rope will begin to move through the gear and your partner will begin to pay it out through the belay device.

A loop will begin to form between your prusik knots and your tie-in knot. This loop could itself snag as it trails behind you, so keep an eye on it. Periodically stop and clip in to a new figure eight knot, then untie the old one and drop the resulting slack back down the cliff. Your partner must quickly pull the slack down through his or her belay device and recommence belaying as you continue up. Renewing your tie-in knot this way

ensures you do not run out of rope on the ground and limits the size of the loop formed as you climb.

DEBRIEF

Alpine rock climbing is often much harder than its grade indicates, for many reasons: pack weight, complex routefinding, length, weather, etc. As you apply the tools and techniques of rock climbing in this more challenging environment, your mountain sense and judgment constantly come into play, making the experience even more rewarding.

Keep a logbook of your climbs. Make corrections to your guidebooks, improve drawings and topos, create more accurate gear lists. Such practices train your memory and make learning easier. One day you may repeat the climb and find your previous notes invaluable, or someone else may benefit from the information. Always debrief your ascent:

- Did you use the best technique to suite the terrain, conditions, and other changing factors? Did you find yourself belaying in sections where you could have safely moved together? Conversely, did you move together when either you or your partner would have felt more comfortable with a belay?
- Was there any gear you needed but didn't have? Did you carry anything that you never used? Was your rope the right length for the route?
- Identify the important objective

hazards. Did you manage them adequately? Would you manage them differently next time?

- How was your routefinding? If not perfect—and it seldom is—replay your moves to determine where you went astray.

- Was the difficulty of the climb what you expected? Think of the entire climb, both the easy and the harder sections, the ascent and the descent.

- Did you keep to your time estimates or to guidebook time? If not, why not? If you did, congratulations are in order!

CHAPTER 6

Climbing on the Arête de Peuterey, Mont
Blanc, France

Snow and Ice

A glance at the photo above brings home the difference between alpine climbing and cragging! The alpine environment typically features snow and ice in all of its beautiful and various forms, which largely determine the flavor of any climb; cramponing on firm snow is a completely different experience from wallowing in bottomless powder or scratching on gray water ice. Alpine climbers must adapt to this variable medium and apply different climbing techniques and protective systems to meet a wide range of conditions.

This chapter focuses on understanding the nature of snow and ice and the daily, seasonal, and longer-term changes it undergoes; route selection and planning based on the different climbing conditions that result; strategies for climbing in different conditions; and movement skills and protective systems on snow and ice.

UNDERSTANDING SNOW AND ICE

Falling snow crystals, light and soft, gradually transform on the ground under the influence of wind, warmth, and time. The pressure of more overlying snow and daily cycles of melting and refreezing compact and eventually metamorphose snow into ice. On a given alpine climb, the climber may encounter many of these varied forms of frozen water.

Understanding these changes and the factors governing them helps you to predict the conditions you will likely encounter, choose routes in good condition, and climb them in good time and style.

SEASONAL CHANGES IN MIDLATITUDES

Most midlatitude mountain ranges (from about 25° north or south of the equator to near 60°) share a typical seasonal cycle of cold, relatively wet winters, with dryer and warmer summers. The major exception to this is the Himalaya, where weather cycles are uniquely governed by the summer monsoon. The rest of the world's midlatitude mountains receive most of their precipitation in winter and lose much of their snowpack in summer, resulting in a distinct, fairly predictable seasonal progression of changing snow conditions.

Winter

As winter approaches, temperatures drop, days shorten, and snow begins to fall in the mountains. In winter's cold weather, snow does not adhere well on slopes steeper than 45 degrees. Instead, frequent, normally small spindrift avalanches continually slide off steep slopes as the snow falls. Relatively warm, wet climates such as those in the Cascade Range and New Zealand's Southern Alps result in "stickier" snow that deposits more readily on steep ground.

Winter is perhaps the most difficult season for alpine climbing. Days are short. New snow makes travel difficult, sometimes impossible without skis or snowshoes. Even a small amount of new snow over talus or other rough, rocky ground can make the going slippery and treacherous, hiding holes and bad footing but being too soft to support body weight. Higher-angle rock is very hard to climb, with hand- and footholds hidden and every surface cold and slick. Steep ice slopes are hard and bare where cold new snow cannot adhere. In the dead of winter, big alpine ice faces can turn into sheets of bullet-hard, dark gray ice—extremely difficult to climb.

Winter does offer some advantages, however. Cold temperatures keep rockfall in check, and daytime warming is usually too little to dramatically change snow conditions as the day progresses, so climbing well into the afternoon is a more reasonable option in winter than in the summer. Solitude, the reward for a willingness to face harsh conditions, is far easier to find.

Spring and Early Summer

The arrival of spring brings important changes; the first and most significant is in temperature. Warmer storms bring moist snow that can stick to steeper faces. The dark, forbidding alpine ice sheets of winter turn white, and tracks appear on many of the great ice faces of the Alps as the climbing conditions improve.

Springtime in the midlatitudes also brings a daily melt-freeze cycle—a regular and sustained fluctuation of warm, sunny days and cold, clear nights. This pattern creates a surface crust that gradually grows thick and hard enough to support body weight while frozen. Once this happens, travel is fast and easy in the early morning but bogs down as the day warms.

Afternoon brings soft, wet, unstable conditions. The mountains seem almost to come alive in the warmth of the day; rocks held in place only by the support of frozen snow and ice lose their grip and tumble down. Wet snow avalanches cut fan-shaped swaths down faces. Snow evaporates on south-facing rock routes like steam on a mirror, leaving them dry and inviting—rock in direct sunlight can become surprisingly warm, even when air temperatures remain below freezing.

Midsummer

Relatively mild temperatures and drier weather make summer the most popular time to be in the mountains. Stable weather conditions and melt-freeze cycles continue to firm and consolidate the snow—a process that continues into fall, ending only with the first snowfall of winter.

A frozen, dense summer snowpack is a mountaineer's blessing. The traditional predawn alpine start allows a climber to take maximum advantage of these good climbing conditions. As the day warms, so does the snow—and a climber's feet sink deeper with each step, crampons don't bite as effectively, and rockfall hazard increases.

As the summer advances, the sticky spring and early summer snow begins to melt off the big alpine ice faces, and the gray underlying ice shows through once more. Climbing on these routes becomes both more difficult and more serious as progressive melting exposes and loosens more rock. In the warmest weeks of the summer, rockfall can be a serious problem.

Fall

With the arrival of autumn, long weeks of summer melt-freeze metamorphosis leave the snow at its firmest. As average temperatures drop, the snow freezes more quickly in the shade and stays frozen longer into the day. The mountains quiet down once again as short, crisp days decrease rockfall. The big ice faces look formidable in their dark, black-ice conditions, stripped of their cover of snow. Glacier travel can be a great pleasure. Although crevasses are open to their maximum extent, walking is easy on consistently firm snow. In crowded ranges, the tourists thin out. While the good weather lasts, autumn climbing can be a wonderful, tranquil experience.

Everything changes abruptly with the coming of the first snows, which not only hamper climbing, but also hide crevasses under thin and weak bridges. Even a light snowfall can signal the end of the season—a good objective on Friday can become utterly unreasonable by Saturday morning. Take this into consideration in your climbing plans, and know that this changing season requires flexibility of options.

SEASONAL CHANGES OUTSIDE THE MIDLATITUDES

The seasonal patterns may be very different in equatorial or arctic mountain ranges. In Peru and Bolivia, for example, the wild snow sculptures that make these peaks so photogenic—mushrooms, cornices, and fluted ridges—result from the fact that most of the Andean snowpack falls in the warm wet season from November to March, when new snow sticks to even the steepest surfaces. This is also a characteristic of Himalayan peaks due to the summer monsoon precipitation and dry, cold winters.

Though temperature and precipitation

patterns may vary radically from one range to another, the same principles of snow and ice metamorphosis apply. If you know which seasons are warm or cold, what time of year most of the precipitation falls, and typical daily temperature fluctuations, you can usually make a good general prediction about snow and ice conditions in any season for any range. (Note that predicting avalanche hazard and snow stability is much more complex, particularly in winter, for which much more detailed, time- and place-specific information is needed).

DAILY CHANGES

Diurnal patterns—sun and shade, day and night—greatly influence a climber's experience. Temperature fluctuations that rise well above freezing during the day and drop much below freezing at night stabilize the snow by gradually increasing snow density and grain size. These factors, along with the depth of nighttime freezing, determine how strong the frozen surface will be in the early morning and how long the good walking conditions will last. Here are a few general principles about how daily patterns influence snow conditions:

- A clear night usually brings a strong freeze, from the surface down. On clear nights, snow surface temperatures can be a good 10°C colder than the actual air temperature. A good hard freeze in dense snow forms a crust several inches deep, allowing good cramponing relatively late into the day, while a light, shallow freeze provides only a thin crust that is quickly broken down by the day's heat.
- Nighttime cloud cover means shallow freezing or none at all. Snow must be exposed to a clear sky to maximize radiative cooling. The greater the exposure, the more intense and deep the freezing will be.
- Enclosing walls of gullies also block exposure to the sky and will hold and reradiate the day's warmth back onto the snow well into the night. Snow often freezes less quickly and less deeply in gullies than on wide-open slopes.
- Snow in the shade continues radiating heat to a clear sky even after sunrise and tends to stay cold and firm until the sun hits it.
- The thin, clear atmosphere of higher altitudes intensifies nighttime freezing—there are fewer atmospheric impurities to reflect heat back to earth than at lower elevations.
- Wind can interfere with nighttime radiative freezing. In calm weather, radiative heat loss from the snow surface cools the thin layer of air just above the snow surface, and this contributes to freezing. Wind disturbs the process by carrying this cool layer away from the surface and circulating in warmer air.
- Wind during the day has the opposite result. It cools the surface by evaporation and at the same time carries away sun-warmed air near the surface and mixes it with cooler air. These effects together inhibit the sun's warming

influence, keeping the snow firmer for much longer, even in direct sunlight.

ROUTE-PLANNING CONSIDERATIONS

Various geographical features—glaciers, steep snow and ice faces, couloirs, etc.— are influenced differently by seasonal and daily snow cycles and current weather conditions. In planning a snow and ice ascent, consider the following:

- Learn the current condition of your proposed climb, either visually or by talking to local climbers and guides. Climbing a route in poor conditions may make it far more dangerous and difficult. If necessary, wait for your climb to come back into shape—often this does not take long, especially in summer. In any case, the climb will always be there another year.
- Select your equipment based on your knowledge of current conditions. Know what you can expect now, and avoid the trap of preconceived assumptions about the climb.
- Look to the weather forecast, especially to projected nighttime freezing elevations and daily maximum temperatures, to identify problems or hazards that can be expected to change over the course of the day.
- Consider where you want to be when temperatures rise above freezing, and plan your day accordingly (see Chapter 3, Preparation and Equipment). Estimate how quickly you will be able to travel through different sections of your route. You may need a contingency plan in case you are unable to keep to schedule. Determine how hard or dangerous retreat would be.
- A previous up track, especially in soft snow, can greatly ease and speed your travel. If you suspect your route will have a track already broken in, you may be able to adjust your time estimates accordingly. But in new snow, remember that even a moderate breeze can quickly fill in previous tracks.

Couloirs

Couloirs present attractive lines of ascent, allowing climbers to move quickly on terrain that is consistent and typically easier than the rock walls to either side. These rock walls can present opportunities for protection and belay anchors, however, which can often be quicker to place and more secure than snow and ice protection. Rock spikes frozen into ice can also offer strong and speedy protection or belays. Tap them with your hammer or ax to get a sense of their solidity by sound and feel.

Couloirs also present their own hazards, since every falling object funnels down them and can ricochet unpredictably. Below are a few considerations for climbing safely in couloirs.

Belay positioning. When leading, try not to knock ice and snow off onto your belayer or others below. As you look for a belay stance at the end of a pitch, anticipate where the next lead will go and consider the trajectory of falling objects. Place the belay anchor well off to the side or, better still, under an overhang or in some protected position.

Other climbers. Another party above you in a couloir can present a serious hazard. In soft snow, falling objects may soon come to rest and therefore be a lesser problem, but ice climbing is a different story. The solution is to plan your start time early enough to be the first party in the couloir. At the same time, try to avoid the sense of being in a race with another party. Not only does this spoil the enjoyment of the climb, but it also may cause both parties to climb carelessly, increasing icefall and the odds of making a mistake. If the couloir is wide enough, and if both parties agree, you may be able to climb side by side so that neither leader climbs above the other. All else failing, be prepared to abandon the climb and choose an alternative route if you can't manage to be first or can't find ways to protect yourself from the hazard of a party above.

Ridge Crests

Many classic snow and ice routes follow fantastic, sinuous, and narrow ridge crests. On such features, the climbing can be both technically easy and outrageously exposed—mountaineering at its finest!

Most ridges have a well-defined windward side, which almost always offers easier and safer climbing on firmer snow, avoiding any cornices overhanging the leeward side. Any previous tracks can make the climbing still easier and more secure. However, if a track softens up during the day, steps may become unpre-dictable and falls more likely. Again, timing is everything.

Sometimes the route follows the center of the crest. In this case, the ice ax is useless as a balance aid. Learn to walk comfortably without it. A common beginner's mistake is to seek support from an ax placed in the weak "Swiss cheese" of a sharp ridge crest. Leaning any weight on an ax in unpredictable snow brings unpredict-able losses of balance. Stand tall, relax, and rely on your balance. Move your feet slowly and place them deliberately, just as you do on boulders. Enjoy the open views!

Passing other climbers on an exposed ridge can be delicate. Where a well-defined track exists, usually one party will stop to let the other go by. The party that stops should get above or below the track. In the complex and usually unspoken rules of climbing etiquette, it is considered rude to stop in midtrail and force another party off the track to get around you. There is no rule about who yields, but generally the less-sure climbers are inclined to step aside.

For specific roped protective strategies for ridge crests, see Protective Systems on Snow later in this chapter.

Open Faces and Slopes

Climbing on open snow and ice slopes offers a vast range of route finding choices; you can wander almost anywhere. Even so, the line you choose to follow influences your exposure to hazards such as ice- or rockfall and avalanche, as well as the quality of the snow you encounter.

Large alpine ice faces tend to be fairly

consistent and sustained in steepness, typically between 45 and 60 degrees, and provide few obvious opportunities to rest. The most variable aspect of these routes is the surface texture—specifically, the amount and consistency of any snow or soft ice covering the harder stuff underneath. Your best choice of route is one that permits you to climb on soft ice or snow but also to place belay anchors in hard ice or rock.

Glacier Ice

Glacier ice is most commonly encountered low on a glacier, below the firn line. Usually the terrain is low angle, and the team is able to move fairly quickly through it. Because glacier ice is the result of gradual compression of névé, its density can vary tremendously, from little more than hard snow to transparent, bullet-proof water ice. Its surface texture varies greatly with weather and temperature. Hot days create a Styrofoam-like granular surface, while cold rains can erode this down to a glassy hardness.

Steep climbing on this type of ice is rare, usually occurring during practice sessions on broken areas of the lower glacier or when crossing a bergschrund. Higher on the peak, the route may entail difficult glacier ice at a serac barrier or a messy broken zone. If your route cannot avoid such passages, be prepared for difficult climbing and be sure you're capable of moving through it as quickly as possible.

For more information about travel and risk management on glaciers, as well as crevasse rescue, see Chapter 7, Glaciers.

MOVEMENT SKILLS ON SNOW

This section focuses primarily on firm, melt-freeze metamorphosed, nonwinter snow conditions. However, even in the period from spring to fall, there can be great variety in the types of snow a climber encounters, and we try to address that variety here.

In the preceding chapters, we repeatedly stress the fact that on most alpine routes, much of the day is spent on relatively easy ground. The same is true on snow; most of an alpine climber's time is spent on moderate-angle slopes. Even though such "easy" slopes can be plenty steep enough to fall from, and the consequences as dire as on more difficult ground, belays are rare—the moderate difficulty and the distance to be covered make them impractical. Under these circumstances, the consequences of sloppy technique can be disastrous. Unroped or unbelayed slips on snow are second only to those on rock as the most frequent causes of mountaineering accidents.

This fact makes it clear why snow climbing requires a rock-solid foundation of footwork ranging from easy walking to steep step-kicking on snow. Our discussion of movement skills begins with low-angle footwork, moving to techniques for steeper angles and harder textures, and finally to a range of supporting ice-ax techniques that vary according to the angle of the slope and consistency of the snow. Our starting point may look deceptively simple, but the movements involved are critical to security on steeper snow; in fact, steep snow

Climbing on the Minarets, New Zealand

climbing is a common Achilles' heel among even relatively experienced alpinists with otherwise good technical skills. Close attention to the basic details of step kicking and efforts to improve in this area will yield quick results.

CLIMBING FIRM SNOW

Dense summer snow, slightly softened by the warmth of midday to a foot penetration of about 1- to 5-cm (about ½- to 2- inches), is ideal for climbing. Often called névé,

this kind of snow is common in spring and summer in midlatitude mountain ranges. While careful step kicking is necessary on all but the gentlest slopes, crampons are typically not needed on snow this soft until the angle reaches 35 degrees or more.

Walking Pied en Canard

When traveling straight uphill on low-angle slopes, adopt a duck-footed position, also known as *pied en canard* (see Figure 47). **Note:** Because the French were among the first to describe snow- and ice-climbing progressions in a systematic way, their terms for these techniques are commonly known and used around the world; hence, we use them in this book.) Pied en canard improves your grip by keeping more weight on your heels and the inside edge of your boot. Here are a few tips when kicking steps in pied en canard position:

- Kick and slice your inside edges into the snow (see **Kicking steps in a diagonal line,** below).
- Use the small, shallow ridges that often run straight up and down the fall line in summer snow to your advantage by slicing your steps along either side of the crest—this reduces the effort needed to keep your steps level and your weight on your heel.
- Use trekking poles to help propel you forward and maintain your balance, allowing you to travel significantly faster and expend less effort. Keep poles short, with your hands at about waist height. Ice axes are generally too short to be much help on low-angle snow.

Choosing Straight Up or a Diagonal Line

As the slope gets steeper, pied en canard begins to feel uncomfortable, with your feet too splayed. You will be more comfortable either kicking steps aggressively straight up the hill or taking a zigzagging diagonal line up the slope. Your choice between these depends largely on snow firmness and to some extent on steepness.

A general principle of snow climbing is that the more you can spread your body weight along the length of your entire foot, the more stable and relaxed you will feel, helping you to climb more efficiently and safely. For example, imagine kicking your toes into a hard, frozen surface, compared to softer snow in which you can sink half your boot. In firm snow, it is more advantageous to take a diagonal path rather than going straight up the slope. This is because in very firm snow, kicking straight in forces you onto your toes and stresses your calves, whereas a diagonal path, with a sideways body position and a slicing kick across the slope, allows a distribution of

Figure 47. *Pied en canard on a low-angle slope*

204

body weight over your entire foot with your heel carrying its fair share.

In general, if the snow is soft enough for a boot to go about a third of the way in with one kick, a straight-up path is probably most efficient. In snow firmer than this, a diagonal path is usually best. Exceptions might be where constrained terrain such as a tight gully forces a direct line or where a steep step is very short and you can sprint without wearing out your calves.

Kicking steps in a diagonal line. Slice your foot into the snow to create each step, using precise and aggressive movements. The pressure of your boot hitting the snow should be directed both forward and inward, slicing into and removing the soft surface snow. The boot should seem almost to lock in place with a definite *kerchunk* as the lugs bite into the firmer snow beneath the soft surface. Snow shooting out from the front of your boot as you kick is evidence that you're doing it right.

Use the weight of your boot and leg to drive the slicing kick. In most summer snow, little effort should be necessary— you will soon be able to gauge the amount of forward slice and downward pressure needed to create a step that will not move or collapse as you weight it. Conserve energy by making as few kicks as possible to achieve adequate steps. Very firm snow may require as many as three or four swipes, softer snow only one.

The platform of your step should be more or less level. If your heel is too much downhill, you will tend to slide backward.

With each step, be sure that your weight remains spread across the entire foot, not concentrated on the toe.

When zigzagging a diagonal line up a slope, there is always an uphill leg and hand and a downhill leg and hand. Moving the uphill leg forward is an in-balance step into the in-balance position (see Figure 48a), whereas moving the downhill leg forward is an out-of-balance step into an out-of-balance position (see Figure 48b). Your out-of-balance step should be small— your forward foot placed just above and

Figure 48a. *Taking an in-balance step: a comfortable stance, with legs open to the slope and the uphill leg above and ahead of the downhill leg.*

Figure 48b. *Taking an out-of-balance step: the downhill leg steps forward.*

ahead of your other foot. Gain slightly more elevation with your in-balance step.

Kicking steps without crampons requires precision and confidence, both of which increase quickly with practice. Seek opportunities to play around on slopes with safe runouts, and strive to become ever more comfortable on steeper and firmer snow.

Choosing an angle of attack. The best angle of attack—the ratio of movement across the slope to movement up the slope—depends on the steepness and firmness of the snow, as well as on slope configuration. At too steep an angle, the

climbing becomes awkward and balance precarious. At too shallow an angle, time is wasted traveling across the slope instead of up. The goal is to ascend a snow slope securely and efficiently. Adjust your angle of attack to be as steep as is comfortable without compromising your balance.

TIPS: STEP-KICKING IN FIRM SNOW

If you find that you often slip while kicking diagonal steps, the problem is most likely one of the following:

- Your weight is too much on your toes.
- Your steps are not level (often related to the previous problem).
- You are stomping down on the sloppy surface snow rather than slicing it away.
- The snow is just too firm for the technique, and it's time to put on crampons.

Using the ice ax. On easy snow slopes, trekking poles may be preferable to an ice ax. They are a better aid to balance and save energy. As difficulty increases, eventually you will want your ax. When to break out the ice ax depends on such things as climbing skill, snow firmness, the consequences of a slip and hazards in the runout zone or on a crevassed glacier.

Once you have decided to use the ice ax, hold it in your uphill hand like a cane, with your hand over the top of the head. If you have used trekking poles up to this point, you might wish to keep one in your downhill hand while using the ice ax in your uphill hand. This can increase balance and security if the slope is not too steep or icy.

The ax can now serve as a balance point, as a partial anchor placed by either plunging the shaft into the snow or into old ice-ax holes, or as a self-arrest tool in the case of a fall.

Choosing piolet canne or self-arrest grip. The topic of self-arrest (see Ice Ax Self-arrest later in this chapter) gives rise to a controversy of sorts. Climbers love a debate, and the question of which way to point the pick—forward or backward—is one such long-running argument. The pick-forward position, with the palm over the adze, is known as *piolet canne*—French for "ice ax cane" (see Figure 49a); the pick-backward position is often referred to as the self-arrest grip (see Figure 49b).

The self-arrest grip is preferred in situations where self-arrest is a realistic risk-management strategy; for example, on heavily crevassed glaciers where it prepares roped climbers to arrest a crevasse fall as quickly as possible. The controversy arises when the self-arrest grip is used as a way to feel more secure on steep slopes. The problem is that most of the time, self-arrest is not a realistic risk-management strategy for steep snow. While inexperienced climbers might fall on slopes gentle enough that this technique may actually work, skilled climbers are unlikely to fall until the slope is so steep that self-arrest probably will not save them. Piolet canne, being more comfort-able on the hand than the self-arrest grip, makes for more aggressive and secure placements in firm snow and therefore provides better support and security on steep slopes. This preventive benefit arguably outweighs the questionable effectiveness of being more ready to self-arrest. Personally, we normally carry our ax in the piolet canne position unless we

Figure 49a. *The pick-forward piolet canne position is used most of the time and is integral to a number of useful ice-ax positions.*

Figure 49b. *The self-arrest grip maximizes readiness to catch a fall.*

feel there is both a real potential for the need to self-arrest and a chance that it might actually work.

Using the ice ax on moderate terrain. On moderately steep slopes, the ice ax is essentially used as a balance point like a walking stick. Carry the ice ax in your uphill hand. Establish a simple, regular, one-two walking tempo, moving the ice ax between counts (every two steps). On easy ground, move the ice ax while in the out-of-balance position. This conforms to your normal and natural walking sequence with arms and legs moving forward on opposite sides.

As the slope steepens, the ice ax becomes more important for additional security. Plunge the shaft deeper into the snow, using any existing old shaft holes. With the ax shaft deep enough in the snow, a short slip might be arrested before it becomes a fall, but even if you do not slip, the greater penetration gives more support for tenuous balance. On steep terrain, move the ice ax only while standing in balance, with your uphill foot forward. This less-natural sequence nevertheless provides greater security. Strive still to maintain a one-two walking rhythm without breaking stride to move the ice ax.

Turning corners. Establish the outermost edge of the corner with an out-of-balance step, before you turn (see Figure 50a). Your next foot placement will be oriented back in the opposite direction. At this point, you face into the hill for a moment with your feet in the duck-foot (pied en canard) position, as shown in Figure 50b.

Switch hands on the ice ax before stepping through into an in-balance position facing in the new direction (see Figure 50c).

Stowing ice-ax wrist loops and leashes. A wrist loop is sometimes useful on vertical ice, where it can support your grip while you hang on an extended arm with your tool placed over your head (see Movement Skills on Ice later in this chapter). It is also helpful to prevent you from losing the ax when chopping steps.

But a wrist loop is an unnecessary nuisance when you are zigzagging up moderate-angle snow slopes, especially when roped. When you turn a corner, the ax must be switched to the new uphill hand. Using a wrist loop means spending more time in a vulnerable and unstable face-to-the-hill position while removing the loop from one hand and putting it on the other. During this operation, a fall is more likely than at any other time. Gloves make this even more clumsy and slow. When climbers are roped together, everyone must stop to wait for each person to switch hands at the corner, consuming still more time.

A leash system connecting the ice ax to the harness is an alternative to wrist loops that solves this problem, but only at the cost of creating even more problems; it has no useful function in normal alpine climbing. It will quickly become an annoying distraction, especially if you ever want to remove your harness, wear a jacket over your harness, or quickly stow or holster your ice ax.

Therefore, on moderate to steep snow slopes, especially when zigzagging,

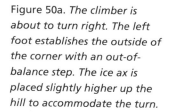

Figure 50a. *The climber is about to turn right. The left foot establishes the outside of the corner with an out-of-balance step. The ice ax is placed slightly higher up the hill to accommodate the turn.*

Figure 50b. *The climber turns the right foot into the new direction. Leaving the ice ax in place, the climber switches hands. The pick is then rotated away from the climber to point in the new direction.*

Figure 50c. *Without moving the ax, the climber steps the left foot through into the new direction. The climber again stands in balance, then moves the ice ax in preparation for the next step.*

remove the wrist loop from your ice ax and stow it in your pack. You can always get it out and reattach it when you encounter a section of prolonged step-chopping or very steep climbing. Instead of using a wrist loop, learn to keep a good firm grip on your ax. It's not that hard, especially since your instinct will naturally lead you to grip harder in exactly those circumstances where you most need the security the ax provides.

Kicking steps straight up. When kicking steps straight up the hill, the distance you take between steps is a compromise between comfort and energy expenditure—too close together makes too far apart makes stepping up strenuous and awkward. Experiment to find the step riser height that is most comfortable for you. If shorter climbers are following you and you care to make them happier, shorten your steps.

Kick your foot deeply into the snow to get the weight as far back on the sole of your boot as possible and to minimize strain on the calves. Two or more quick kicks may be necessary in firm snow. If you don't get about a third of your boot penetration with two to three kicks, it may be time for a diagonal line or for crampons if the slope is steep enough, the difficult section long enough, or the consequences of the runout nasty enough.

Using the ice ax in firm snow. On steeper ground, different ice-ax positions and techniques provide more support and security for harder climbing. *Piolet appui* refers to three simple ice-ax positions suitable when the snow gets a bit harder. These ice-ax techniques can be used with or without crampons. *Appui* means "support" in French, and this is a good way to characterize these quick and efficient uses of the ax. Individually, they are known as *piolet manche, piolet panne,* and *piolet poignard.* These positions all involve placing the hand on or near the head of the ax, with the pick in the snow. They all offer excellent support and balance. They apply on moderately steep slopes for the simple reason that on shallow slopes, they force you to bend over. Piolet canne would be a better choice for lower-angle slopes.

All three piolet appui ice-ax techniques are particularly well suited to firm névé, where pick penetration is at least a couple of centimeters (an inch or so). In hard ice, the pick can't penetrate and the tool wobbles uselessly, while in very soft snow it simply slices through and offers little support.

Piolet manche. Meaning "ice ax shaft," piolet manche is most often used when you are facing into the slope. The ice-ax shaft is held in your hand just under the head. The pick is pushed into the snow, as shown in Figure 51.

Piolet panne. Meaning "ice ax adze," this entails holding the head of the ax with your palm over the adze and the pick forward,

held between your thumb and forefinger. Keep the tool placement low for comfort. Drive the pick into the snow with a firm downward and inward motion (see Figure 52). Piolet panne is particularly efficient and supportive on descent, since you can reach very low, lean down on the adze with a great feeling of security, and climb down below the ax before making the next placement.

Piolet poignard. Meaning "ice ax dagger" in French, piolet poignard is also known as the high dagger position; it allows you to get the ax in high and is comfortable to place when you are facing sideways to the

Figure 51. *Using the ax in piolet manche position while climbing across the slope. Torres-Tasman Traverse, New Zealand.*

Figure 52. *Moving quickly with piolet panne on the Grand Traverse of Mount Cook in the Southern Alps of New Zealand.*

Figure 53. *Drive the whole shaft in soft snow if you can.*

slope as well as straight in. Hold the head of the ice ax with your fingers over the top and thumb under the adze, then stab the pick into the snow at or above head level. It is particularly useful on traverses where the slope above is too steep for other ice-ax positions.

Using the ice ax in soft snow. In softer steep snow, use the ice-ax shaft in the stake position: drive in the shaft of the ax, holding your hands over the head. Use both hands if necessary to get a sufficient depth of placement (see Figure 53).

Using Terrain Features

When putting in a track on snow, plan your route ahead as you go and identify a preferred line based on what you see some distance—usually at least 15 meters (50 feet)—ahead. Several factors determine the best line:

■ Take advantage of the best snow consistency for easy and secure step kicking. Plan your line based on how sun and shadow alter snow firmness.

■ Minimize time spent on steeper terrain. For example, when gaining a rising snow crest, such as a snow-covered moraine, climb to the crest on a line perpendicular to the crest, not parallel. When deciding where to turn a corner on a diagonal tack, look for minor features (tree wells, melt-out around boulders, wind scoops, etc.) that reduce slope angle or offer an island of security.

■ Maintain a critical and independent mind when following an existing track; consider whether altering it would better serve your party as a whole.

Cutting Steps

Typically, if you cut steps, you do so to handle very short sections of hard snow or ice where a bit of chopping would take less time than putting on and taking off crampons. It is also helpful when climbing with someone less experienced than yourself; a few steps chopped or enhanced here and there—even if you are already wearing crampons—can greatly increase that person's security and comfort at little cost to you.

A fall is generally not stoppable using ice ax self-arrest on the hard snow or ice where climbers normally choose to cut steps, so the steps must be big and secure, especially if crampons are not being worn. Consider cutting handholds also.

In firm snow, use the adze to slice each step into the snow, swinging the ax in a vertical plane. In ice, use the adze (or the pick, if the ice is too hard or brittle for the adze) to chop away hunks of ice with downward blows. Start at the end of the step nearest you, and work away from your body.

Use sideways blows to define the angle of the bottom of the step, and finish with downward blows to remove most of the ice.

CLIMBING IN SOFT SNOW

Climbing in deep, soft snow is very strenuous. This is one of the cases where a few secret tricks actually can help a great deal.

Putting in Your Own Track

When you are putting in your own track, try to walk in a straight line. Sight ahead to plan the location of turns. Check your trail behind you to gauge how well you maintain a consistent direction of travel. Use trekking poles for balance. Adjust the poles short, keeping your hands close to waist level. If a number of climbers are doing the same route and are breaking a difficult trail in new or soft snow, take your turn up front. Normally the fastest trail-breaker will gravitate toward the front of the line, but all climbers should at least offer to share in the work.

Use the weight and inertia of your boot, foot, and leg to compress the step into the snow. Avoid excessive stomping; instead, add just enough push at the end of your step to compress the snow to the exact point where it will support your weight without moving farther under your foot as you weight it (this takes a bit of testing and practice to determine). After you punch your step, pause for just a heartbeat to give the compressed snow underfoot a chance to set before you weight it. Weighting the step in the same movement with which you created it makes your foot sink deeper than necessary because snow moving underfoot has little resistance to further compression. Once the pressure is released, even just for an instant, the snow offers more resistance—often enough to allow you to stand on it without further collapse.

Following an Existing Track

When you are following a posthole or deep track, let your boot scrape a bit of snow off the side of the hole and into it with each step. This fills it in slightly, pads and spreads out the stress on the step, and reduces the chance that it will collapse as you shift your weight.

When traversing a steep slope in a deep track, initiate your step slightly to the uphill side of each hole, again scraping off just a bit of snow to fill it in a little.

Old tracks are especially helpful in breakable crust. If the steps do not support your weight, try stepping on the convex bumps and little ridges to one side or the other of the old track (convexities freeze more solidly at night than concavities because of their greater exposure to the night sky, so they sometimes support weight slightly better than the steps themselves).

Moving in Steep, Soft Snow

When deep snow gets steep, the going can be strenuous indeed. When it comes to moving quickly in these conditions, efficient technique is more important than fitness, though the latter is most definitely crucial. Keep your fastest leader or leaders out in front, relieving them as they slow down.

If the snow is too steep and deep for you to get your foot as high as you want, use your knee to create a depression in the snow into which you can then place your foot. Distribute your weight on your hands as well as your feet. Plunge the shafts of your ice tools into the snow above, weight them, and pull yourself up onto the higher step. Trekking poles held horizontally with both hands across the slope can also help.

Pacing

Climbing on soft snow is all leg and lung work. Establish a regular pace for your steps and for the number of breaths per step—both will vary depending on your speed and energy output. The tempo of breaths per step changes as slope angle changes, in order to maintain a fairly constant level of exertion. Regularity and consistency help you climb efficiently.

DESCENDING SNOW

Many climbers who are reasonably quick going uphill on snow waste much time and energy in descent. This is yet another learned skill that greatly increases safety and that looks deceptively simple when competently done. The good news is that with practice, improvement comes quickly and easily. On snow, as on rock, the more comfortable you can be facing out, the more quickly and efficiently you will move.

Descending a gentle snow slope truly is just walking and needn't take much thought. Trekking poles can be a big help, especially when the wind is strong, the snow is variable, or you are tired or carrying a heavy pack.

Plunge Stepping

As snow slopes approach 30 degrees or steeper, the plunge step is the technique of choice for descending. Mastering this technique allows you to descend more quickly and securely than you might have imagined possible, even on fairly steep and firm slopes.

1. Drop your weight straight down into the snow using the edge of your boot heel to bite in with each step. Do not stomp or kick your foot backward. Keep your foot level, or even point your toes slightly up, as you plunge your heel into the snow—this gets your heel to really bite (see Figure 54). Be aggressive, and come down hard on your heel. The more *oomph* you put into it, the deeper your heel plunges into the snow. This doesn't mean you must actively stomp—just commit the weight of your whole body downward onto your heel.

2. As you drop your weight into the snow, bend your leg slightly to avoid hyperextending your knee or excessive jarring.

3. Hold your ice ax in piolet canne off to the side; it is too short to easily reach the snow when you are going straight down the fall line. Point the pick forward, away from you. Do not hold it across your chest with both hands, in preparation for self-arrest. This impedes balance and makes slips and injuries more likely.

Plunge stepping is easier straight down

Figure 54. *The plunge step*

the fall line than on a diagonal and it is easier in undisturbed snow than in tracks. New boots with sharp sole edges grip better than dull or rounded boots.

Diagonal Plunge Stepping

In very firm snow, increase your sense of security by turning sideways and descending on a diagonal, plunging the shaft of the ice ax into the snow with every other step. The ax helps stabilize you and, with enough penetration, might help stop a slip.

Keep your ax in the uphill hand. While

standing in balance, reach down and sink the shaft deep into the snow (see Figure 55), using previous placement holes if the snow is firm and strong. With the pick backward in the self-arrest grip, you will feel more ready for a slip. However, the more preventive, pick-forward piolet canne position still allows a deeper and more secure placement, so it is worth practicing to become more comfortable with it.

Diagonal plunge stepping forces a hunched-over posture that interferes with the commitment of body weight to drive

Figure 55. *The diagonal plunge step, the ice ax in piolet canne position and plunged into the snow to the side*

boot placement. To compensate, use a bit more energy and stomp your heel down a bit harder than usual, using the boot edge as well as the heel to create your step.

As always, greater security comes at the cost of a slower, more energy-consumptive progression. Delay resorting to this method by continually striving to increase your skill at the faster, straight-down plunge step technique, practicing on steep slopes with safe runouts.

Facing In

On snow so steep or so firm that you can no longer comfortably face out, turn and face into the slope. Just as on rock, this much slower tactic inhibits visibility, routefinding, hazard awareness, and the sense of what is going on around you—hence, the importance of striving for skill and confidence facing out. Still, facing in is more secure, and all of its disadvantages are obviously far preferable than taking a bad fall! Your own skill and confidence level are the deciding factors when choosing to face out or in. When you do face in:

1. Remove equipment hanging in front of you that may obstruct your visibility.
2. Kick hard, using old steps if available. If there are no old steps, make your steps long to lose as much elevation as you can with each step. Small steps mean more work and a slower pace. Crampons add grip and security on firm snow (see Movement Skills on Ice later in this chapter).

3. Look over your shoulder frequently to see where you are going. Turn and face outward again as soon as the angle or snow conditions allow.

4. In soft snow, plunge the ice ax shaft into the snow, using either one or two hands. In firmer snow, use the ax in the piolet manche (see Figure 56) or piolet panne position. In piolet panne ("ice ax adze"), place the palm of your hand over the adze of the ax and push the pick into the snow with a downward and inward motion.

Figure 56. *Hugh Barnard using piolet manche while descending steep frozen snow on the Minarets, New Zealand*

Glissading

Glissading is in the finest mountaineering tradition. It's quick, and it's fun. But sliding down a snow slope also carries risks. Many disasters have resulted from glissading in the wrong place, at the wrong time, in the wrong way, or out of control. Follow these extremely important safety tips:

■ Know your route, especially your runout, including everything that you could encounter below—rocks, trees, crevasses, cliffs, or snowmelt streams beneath the snow.

■ Maintain good visibility ahead.

■ Avoid glissading on glaciers where the possibility of a crevasse fall exists.

■ Avoid glissading in crampons. They tend to catch and can easily break a leg or sprain an ankle.

■ Watch out for changing snow conditions or variations in the snow surface.

■ Stay in control!

The standing glissade, the sitting glissade, and the crouching or "three-point" glissade are the main glissade techniques. Here we discuss the standing and sitting glissades only, since, in our view, the "three-point" glissade, using an ice ax as a third point of balance, is less useful. Most slopes where it is employed can be handled as well or better with a standing glissade.

Standing glissade. The standing glissade is the most fun and is usually safer than a sitting position due to better visibility, more maneuverability and control, and fewer soft body parts on the snow. It definitely looks the coolest! Use your heels and the sides of your boots for

TIPS: SNOW-CLIMBING PRACTICE SESSIONS

Practice, practice, practice is the key to snow climbing. Unfortunately, not all of us are blessed with nearby steep snow slopes—we need to travel a bit to reach good practice terrain. Sometimes it seems the biggest challenge is simply to convince ourselves that an outing dedicated solely to perfecting snow climbing skills is worthwhile. It is. Here are a few pointers on how to direct your practice sessions:

- Wear boots, ice ax, helmet, and gloves. For a top-rope session, add a rope, harnesses, belay device, a few carabiners (for belaying as well as for the anchor), and a snow anchor.
- Find a safe practice area. Examine your runout zone thoroughly. Watch for rocks or other obstacles in the snow. Be sure not to jeopardize other folks in the area.
- Look for slopes with a variety of angles so you can practice a variety of techniques, and look for very firm snow that just allows a reasonable-size step to be kicked with one or two kicks. For the greatest skills development, you may need to time your practice session to match the daily warming and softening of the snow surface. Ski hills can be a great place to practice after the resort has closed for the spring. They won't appreciate you kicking a line of holes up their nicely groomed piste during the ski season!
- Push your limits, both in ascent and in descent. Setting up a top rope helps you to do this, as does finding steep rolls on a short slope with a safe runout. The hardest step-kicking task is putting in a good line of steps diagonally uphill—securely, fluidly, and efficiently. Spend extra time on this. Most climbers need to work harder on downhill technique than on uphill skills. Focus on descending, especially facing out on steep slopes. Work for speed and efficiency in your practice sessions. The importance of these skills is not apparent in short "snow school" sessions, but they loom large on an actual climb.
- Become ambidextrous with your ice ax by spending more time practicing on your "off" side than on your "strong" side. When walking on level slopes or using pied en canard straight up a gentle slope, carry your ax in your "off" hand.

steering and to help you maintain a reasonable speed. Snow consistency makes all the difference; in perfect summer firn, with just a shallow layer of soft snow on the surface and a firm base beneath, you can link turns like a slalom ski racer.

Bend your knees. To accelerate, rock slightly forward and flatten your foot on the snow. To slow down or to steer, rock back onto your heel and boot edges. The most effective way to stop is the "hockey stop," an abrupt sideways weighting of the boot edges.

Hold the ice ax in one hand, off to the side in piolet canne position. Point the pick away from your body. Your arms and hands should be held out wide, free to flail about as needed to maintain balance. If the slope angle is not quite steep enough, you can sometimes skate.

Sitting glissade. When snow is too soft or the slope not steep enough for a standing glissade, the sitting glissade is a fun alternative, providing the runout is visible, clean, and safe. Being down in the snow with limited visibility and using a sharp ice ax to control speed mean that accidents are common, so be careful. Particularly risky are snow-filled gullies. Though they offer nice avenues of travel, streams usually run underneath and the depth and strength of the overlying snow is impossible to determine. Watch out for rocks, which can rip your clothing, break your tailbone, or do other nasty things, and never wear crampons on a sitting glissade!

Sit in the snow and hold the ice ax in the *piolet ramasse* position (see Using an Ice Ax on Steep Snow and Ice later in this chapter). Place the spike in the snow near your hip and brake by pushing it down into the snow with one hand and dragging it behind you. The other hand holds the ax head steady; that arm should cross your body so that the entire ax remains on the "brake" side. Be sure to hold the ice ax head so that the pick points out to the brake side and away from your digestive organs!

To slow down, press the spike of the ax hard into the snow, right next to your hip. To some extent you can use the ax like a rudder, altering your direction perhaps as much as 10 to 15 degrees. Experiment with steering by varying the angle of the ax in

A CAUTIONARY TALE: GLISSADING

Early one summer season, SP Parker, Joe Demarsh, and I were just wrapping up a session of guides training on Mount Baker in Washington's North Cascades when we witnessed an unroped member of another party glissade straight into a wide-open crevasse in the Coleman Glacier. He dropped 12 meters (about 40 feet) down to where the ice walls slowly came together. He was "corked," squeezed between the constricting walls. His face was pressed against one wall and his frame pack, shoved high up on his back, was lodged against the other. As fate would have it, he wore no harness—and the rope was coiled and carefully stowed in his partner's pack.

I was lowered into the crevasse and immediately thought I was probably going to watch him die. The very tight crevasse, his lack of a climbing harness, and his already hypothermic state all spelled another unfortunate statistic. Eventually, however, after much effort, we were able to extract him. Following a bit of warming, he was able to walk down the rest of the descent.

He was lucky. To this day, I don't know whether he lost control of the glissade or was simply unaware of the hazards of his chosen route. Because he had climbed up this section of the glacier the day before, either explanation seems inadequate.

—Mark Houston

the snow or by digging in first on one side of your body, then on the other. Heels in the snow also help slow you down but spray up much snow in your face, making it tough to see where you are going.

Increase speed by straightening your legs and lifting your heels off the snow. Remove your harness or unbuckle your leg loops for still more speed. Use troughs made by previous glissaders for more speed and a slightly smoother ride.

In spring or soft snow conditions, a cushion of sliding snow can accumulate between your legs and underneath you as you glissade. These mini-avalanches are fun to ride and can smooth out an otherwise bumpy ride. Like all avalanches, however, they have a mind of their own and may not want to stop when you do. Wet snow has tremendous mass and will carry you with it if you become slightly submerged. Roll out of it off to the side occasionally, especially if it gets too big or fast.

PROTECTIVE SYSTEMS ON SNOW

There are several protective systems for climbing on snow. As always, the first and best consists of developing your climbing ability, knowing your limits, and not falling. This is particularly true on snow since it is impractical to belay everywhere that a fall would have serious consequences. The other strategies covered in this section include moving together roped but unbelayed; using belays, both anchored and unanchored; and using ice ax self-arrest.

MOVING TOGETHER ROPED BUT UNBELAYED

Climbers might choose to travel roped together but unbelayed on snow slopes for a number of reasons. These include:

- preparing in advance for transitions in technique
- short-roping, in which a more-skilled member of the party can help protect those less skilled, even while walking together
- glacier travel and crevasse rescue (see Chapter 7, Glaciers)

Preparing for More Difficult Climbing

Rope up early to be ready to belay as the slope steepens, a rock section is encountered, or some other difficulty calls for belayed climbing. Climbing together roped can save precious time that would be wasted putting the rope on and taking it off again every time you change strategy. If you believe there is a good chance you will want to belay sections ahead, don't wait until you find yourself teetering on a steep slope. Instead, rope up when it is easy to do so, before the going gets tough, using the method for shortening the rope described in Chapter 5, Alpine Rock, with one or both climbers carrying coils over a shoulder and tied off at the harness.

One or both climbers should carry two to three coils in hand, and the party should remain close together, 1.5 to 2 meters (5 or 6 feet). The less rope is out between climbers when a slip occurs, the less momentum and force are generated and the easier it is to arrest a fall. More rope means more rope stretch and some inevitable slack, both of which make for longer and harder falls. Moving close together also allows your party to present a small target in case other climbers fall above you. You are less likely to be "flossed" off the mountain if you are close together than if your rope is stretched out across the slope. Staying close together also helps your party move quickly, perhaps quickly enough to pass other roped parties you may mistrust.

Whereas on rock there are typically many opportunities for quick running and terrain belays, on snow such opportunities are rare and belays require more time-consuming anchor building (see Snow Anchors, below). Moving roped but unbelayed on snow therefore requires much more careful assessment of conditions and climbing ability than the same tactic on rock.

Short-roping

Yet another occasion to rope up and move together is when one member of a rope team can stop the fall of the other, either by simply pulling tight on a shortened rope while taking a braced stance or by self-arrest if necessary. Guides use this technique frequently. Short-roping works best when it is the lower climber who slips—it may not work at all if the upper climber falls, because of the momentum and speed generated before the lower climber can do anything.

Short-roping as a protective strategy

Short-roping can provide moving protection for the lower climber. Minarets, New Zealand.

entails more than merely traveling together and is very difficult to do effectively, especially on snow. Guides, who use this strategy extensively, must spend countless hours practicing. Without such practice, it is all too easy to actually increase your party's risk without even realizing it. Nevertheless, it has a place in recreational climbing in some situations if the uphill climber is more experienced or has better footing.

Short-roping is not an alternative to fixed belays when they are needed but, rather, an alternative to traveling unroped or with no other protective strategy. Consider carefully whether going unroped might actually be safer in your situation—for example, on snow so steep that the upper climber has little chance of arresting the slip of the lower climber. Also consider carefully whether a belay is justified despite the time it takes to set up. On steep and firm slopes, if the risk of falling seems significant and the consequences dire, belaying may be the only real option. If you do decide to short-rope, keep the following in mind:

- The most skilled climber should be uphill, in both ascent and descent. The upper climber (if paying very close attention) can often pull the lower climber back into balance before the slip becomes a fall, but if the upper climber falls, most likely both will take off.

- The team should move at the same pace, step for step, to keep the distance between climbers constant and rope management easy. The distance between climbers should be as little as possible without interfering with each other's movement—about 1.5 to 2 meters (5 to 6 feet) maximum.

- The upper climber should tie a small loop in the rope as a handle for the downhill hand, instead of carrying coils (as in rock). This allows an easier and quicker arrest of a stumble or slip, with no chance for momentum to build up. The downhill hand holds the loop while the uphill hand holds the ice ax.

- The upper climber should keep light tension on the rope to feel the lower climber's movements through the rope. If a slip occurs, he or she can sense it

and react immediately, before momentum builds up.

- Practice holding falls on steep terrain (safe runout, crampons off!) to learn the limits of this technique. This is part of a mountain guide's training—recreational climbers wishing to use this technique must do the same.

Moving on Ridge Crests

Ridge crests present excellent terrain belay opportunities on snow, as on rock. If a climber falls off one side, the other can stop the fall by stepping or jumping the other way. The rope is less likely to be damaged on snow in this scenario than it would be on rock, but the arresting climber has to get down onto the side opposite the falling climber, quickly, in order to stop the fall. This technique is also worthwhile to practice in a safe place, both to build confidence in its effectiveness and to train yourself to be decisive and quick in response to falls.

Lengthen the rope between climbers to 5 to 6 meters (15 to 20 feet), and have each climber carry a few coils in hand to provide some time to react to the other's fall (see Figure 57). Keep in mind that the climber in the lead cannot see the other's fall and therefore is at a disadvantage. If one climber is stronger than the other, he or she should go second.

When encountering sharp ridge crests too narrow to walk on or when climbing in gusty winds, consider traversing sideways along the ridge with a climber on either side. Shorten the rope between climbers to

Figure 57. *Snowy ridge crests provide a potential terrain belay. Each climber carries a few small coils of rope.*

about 2 to 3 meters (6 to 9 feet), and flip the rope along the crest as you traverse. Very steep slopes can be traversed this way, knowing that your belay is bomb-proof. Obviously, this will not work where cornices force one or both climbers to climb too far below the crest.

USING UNANCHORED BELAYS

When you decide that the only realistic risk management strategy is to belay, there are many possible options for anchors and methods, from using terrain features and/or body positioning to constructing a snow anchor. Just as on rock, the best belay on snow is the one that results when you do the following:

■ Realistically assess the degree of security required.
■ Seek the simplest and fastest anchor that will provide this degree of security.

Because snow anchors can be arduous to build, we start with quicker, unanchored belays.

Terrain Belays

Positioning the belayer's body behind terrain features can provide tremendous security on snow, just as on rock, with almost no expenditure of time or use of equipment. Moats or ridge crests are particularly useful for this. The belayer must be low enough behind the edge or into the moat so that he or she cannot be pulled from the stance (see Figure 58). The falling climber's weight will cut the rope into the lip, and the belayer will be pulled up and into the slot but is unlikely to lose control.

Unanchored Sitting Belays in Soft Snow

Sitting belays in deep, soft snow can be quite secure, even unanchored; in fact, these may be the most secure anchors available in very soft conditions (in firm snow, other options are usually better).

When establishing your sitting belay stance, dig a nice deep horseshoe-shaped trough in the snow. A saddle of minimally disturbed snow between your legs (see Figure 59) provides the resistance that constitutes the strength of this anchor. The softer the snow, the deeper your trough

Figure 58. *A braced belay in a small moat*

Figure 59. *An unanchored sitting belay in soft snow, with a Münter hitch on the harness*

should be. Once in position, dig in your boot heels and brace against the expected direction of pull.

The Standing Ax Belay

Of all the various boot-ax belay methods, the standing ax belay is the strongest and easiest to use. We include it here under Using Unanchored Belays because we can scarcely call an ax shaft plunged into the snow much of an anchor on its own; the belayer's body is an essential component of this "anchor's" strength.

This technique is most useful when you are standing on top of a steep bulge of snow, belaying someone below you. This method gives you a good view down the hill (see Figure 60), so you can watch your partner carefully, and allows you to take in rope quickly.

1. On the less steep snow at the top of the bulge, kick out a platform large enough for your two feet.
2. Place the ax in the back of the platform, vertically if you are on a slope or slightly tilted back if you are on level ground. Stomp it down to the head. If it goes in with anything less than about six well-aimed stomps, the snow is probably too soft for this belay method and you should use a different one.
3. Clip a locking carabiner to the hole in the ax head. If the carabiner won't fit, put it around the shaft before you stomp in the ax. Clip the rope through the carabiner.
4. Stand with both feet on top of the ax.

Figure 60. *Standing ax belay. Both feet are on the ax, though this is difficult to see in this photo. Alternatively, the belayer could move back, away from the steep slope, and belay simply off the harness, unanchored. Using the ridge crest in this way would provide a strong belay, but does not offer visibility of the climber below.*

Be sure the rope runs freely through the carabiner.

5. Use a shoulder belay as shown in the photo below: run the rope up under your arm, up your back, over the opposite shoulder to the front of your body, and hold it in front, with the brake-hand thumb upward. Alterna-

tively, you can use a hip belay, clipping the hot end through a carabiner on your belay loop to keep the rope on your hip. Do not use a higher-friction belay device such as a Münter hitch or plate. These lock up too easily and are more likely to cause the belay to fail.

Although we consider this to be the most useful version of boot-ax belay, it does share the same serious limitations with other versions:

- The strength of the anchor may be difficult to gauge. No boot-ax belay is very strong.
- Boot-ax belays are not useful for belaying a leader; severe fall forces would likely overwhelm this relatively weak anchor.
- These belays are not appropriate for belaying crevasse crossings, because once a fall is caught and the anchor is loaded, it is extremely difficult to escape the belay, since the belayer's body position is a component of the anchor.

USING ANCHORED BELAYS ON SNOW

One thing common to all the anchors described in this section is that the direction of pull in the event of a fall must be as nearly parallel to the snow surface as possible—no snow anchor will withstand a strong outward pull. Keep the pull low by building your anchors well uphill from your stance or belay device.

Direct versus Harness Belay on Snow

For belaying a leader on snow, a harness belay (as opposed to a direct belay) is obligatory since snow anchors are almost never multidirectional. For belaying a second, a direct belay is still desirable with any anchor strong enough to withstand whatever forces might be applied to it (in fact, belaying off the harness in snow means the comfort factor is of greater importance than on rock, because the belayer must sit in cold or wet snow). However, by the nature of the medium, snow anchors can be weak or hard to assess and predict. Making them unquestionably strong enough for a direct belay tends to be more time consuming and arduous than on rock, therefore the harness belay is more frequently advantageous in this medium.

In a harness belay, the stance itself is the belayer's first line of defense, reducing the load the anchor must hold. The anchor in this case serves as little more than a backup (albeit a critical one) to the stance. The belayer should tie in tight with no slack between him or her and the anchor; establish a solid, braced stance; and belay the climber using a friction device on the harness.

Snow Anchors

There are several ways to build a solid snow anchor; the choice usually depends on the consistency of the snow.

T-trench (aka "deadman"). T-trenching means burying a strong, linear object such as a picket or ice ax deep in the snow. A sling attached to the center of the object is a clip-in point. Such anchors can be extremely strong and relatively quick to build. Larger items such as skis or packs can be even more solid but take longer to bury.

To create a T-trench, use your ice ax adze to dig a trench perpendicular to the anticipated direction of force—this is the top cross-bar of the T. First score a line through the snow with your pick, defining the front face of your trench. The desired depth depends on the consistency of the snow. In very firm, metamorphosed snow a trench 20 to 25 cm (8 to 10 inches) deep may be enough, while in softer snow you might need to dig 60 cm (2 feet) or more. Make the trench a bit longer than the object to be buried. The snow in front of your T-trenched object constitutes the strength of this anchor; avoid disturbing this snow as you build and use your anchor.

Dig a slot perpendicular to your trench, running in the direction of anticipated force—this is the stem of the "T" (see Figure 61). It must be no shallower than the first trench, or a pull on the rope will jerk the buried object upward.

Attach a sling to the object to be buried. In the case of an ice ax, girth-hitch a long sling around the shaft. The pull point should be slightly nearer the head of the ax rather than at midpoint, because the head will provide more resistance to shearing through the snow than will the spike. When burying a picket, clip a locking carabiner in to the center hole. If your picket has no holes, girth-hitch the middle of the picket.

Figure 61. *Building a T-trench anchor with a picket. After checking that positioning is correct, pack snow in on top of the picket.*

Place the object horizontally in the cross-bar top of the T and bury well, packing snow into both the trench and the slot, then pull hard on the sling to see how your anchor reacts to loading.

If you wish to reinforce your anchor, place two pickets or ice tools vertically into the snow in front of the T-trenched object.

Snow pickets (aka snow stakes). Pickets are designed to be driven into hard snow, in addition to T-trenched. When hammered in, their strength depends on the snow's consistency. A single picket can be strong enough to haul a car from when the picket is pounded into thoroughly metamorphosed and frozen summer or autumn snow. But in sloppy, slushy snow; new snow; powder snow; or light snow containing layers of ice, driven pickets can pull out under less than body-weight force.

The same strong snow that provides

Belaying a leader off the harness tied into a T-trenched ice ax.

extremely strong picket placements also makes for strenuous work pounding them in and pulling them out. When driving pickets into the snow, keep in mind the following:

■ Pickets should be driven in to at least two-thirds their length. If you can't get this depth, or if it takes more than about 20 hammer strokes to do so, then it might be appropriate to find another type of anchor such as ice screws, bollards, or a rock anchor if possible.

■ Hammer the picket in at an angle of about 10–15 degrees away from the direction of pull, using strong, full-arm swings.

■ As you hammer, notice the resistance, especially any changes in resistance. If the picket goes in easily and quickly (less than about 10 good hard swings), or if it suddenly goes in much more easily than before, your placement is weak. A second picket equalized with the first may solve the problem, but in

227

very bad snow, using a T-trench or another type of anchor is a better choice.

■ If you are unable to get the picket in all the way, tie it off using a carabiner in the clip-in hole nearest the snow surface. Lacking holes, girth-hitch a runner near the surface.

■ For belays, place the picket at least 1.5 to 2 meters (5 to 6 feet) uphill of your stance to keep the pull low and close to the surface of the snow (see Figure 62).

■ To remove a picket, assume a braced and well-balanced stance above the picket and pull straight upward. If it does not come out easily, tap lightly straight down on the end of the picket with your hammer or ice ax adze, while pulling upward on the picket at the same time. If that doesn't work, pound and pull harder. Do not pound the picket sideways, which will dent and damage the edges and make it harder to place the next time.

Figure 62. *A direct belay from two pickets pre-equalized. The belayer stands well below the anchor to prevent any outward pull on the pickets.*

Figure 63. *Two ways to carry pickets: the top one is stuffed horizontally between the pack and the climber's back (be sure to clip it in to something!); the lower one is clipped in the middle to a harness gear loop.*

Bollards. These are trenches dug around plugs of snow or ice into which a sling can be placed or the rope slotted (see Figure 64). Bollards are particularly useful for rappels, because no gear need be left behind. A bollard's strength is only as great as that of the snow it is made of; the softer the snow, the larger the bollard must be to ensure the rope will not cut through.

It is difficult to generalize about appropriate bollard diameter. In dense summer snow, a bollard will typically be about 1-plus meters (3 or 4 feet) in diameter; in softer snow, much larger. If dense summer snow is frozen in the early morning, as little as 50 cm (20 inches) could be adequate, while in powder snow a

Figure 64. *Rappelling off a snow bollard. Notice the rappeler's position, keeping the pull low on the bollard. This bollard is a little over a meter in diameter.*

bollard will not hold no matter how large you make it. The best thing is to play around with bollards in different types of snow, testing them fully to see how they behave. As a practical matter, there may be little point in making bollards any larger than about 2 meters (about 6 feet) in diameter—in snow this soft, a different anchor method such as a sitting hip belay or buried skis would be a better choice.

When creating and using a bollard in snow, make sure of the following:

- Use the adze of your ice ax to chop the groove, which must be deeply cut and "positive"—that is, you must be sure the rope will stay in it. The groove must be equally deep along its entire length. Any shallow places may pull the rope off the entire bollard.

- At the downhill end, your grooves will point to a theoretical meeting point below the bollard. Make sure this point is well down the hill, describing a long U or teardrop shape rather than a circular plug.

- In very firm snow, use existing terrain features whenever possible to reduce the amount of chopping needed. Ridge crests or edges of moats are particularly useful—often you can simply chop small notches for the rope to run through. If the back of the feature is not steep enough to keep the rope from sliding up and over the top, cut a deep groove across the back to hold the rope in place.

- When rappelling, position the rope carefully in the groove, and as you set up your device, take great pains to stay low and to keep both rope strands on the snow surface until you have descended a few feet, so that you don't inadvertently pull the rope up out of its seated position.

If you are uncertain about the quality of the anchor or the snow, you can reinforce a bollard as follows:

- Place padding material in the top groove to inhibit the rope's tendency to cut through soft snow. Almost any material will do: tree branches, rocks, sticks, clothing, etc. Make sure the rope will stay in the groove and not pop off the padding. If you are rappelling, this material must be left behind.

- Drive ice tools, pickets, etc. into the snow at the top shoulders of the plug, and place the rope above them, forming a triangle. This is a good way to reinforce a soft bollard for belaying or lowering purposes, but it is not so helpful for rappelling, since the last climber down will not be able to trust the anchor after removing the reinforcement, which you presumably will be loath to leave behind—pickets may be dispensable, but you will want to keep your ice tools with you!

Snow flukes. A snow fluke is a small aluminum plate that is buried in the snow, with an attached steel cable for clipping in. As snow anchors, flukes have severe limitations: they are difficult to place in frozen or very firm snow; loose, powdery, or slushy snow or ice layers within the snow can render them useless. The range of snow conditions where a fluke is useful is therefore quite limited, and where it can be used, a T-trenched object is stronger. We have essentially stopped carrying flukes on our own alpine climbs for this reason and do not recommend them as an essential part of a snow climbing rack.

> ### TIPS: DESCENDING ON A REINFORCED BOLLARD
>
> A reinforced bollard can still help a party descend quickly, even if the reinforcement will not be left in place.
> - Have your strongest climber descend last.
> - Others rappel or are lowered off the reinforced bollard.
> - They find or build a (hopefully) very strong anchor at the bottom of the pitch and belay the last climber from below.
>
> This is risky for the last person but still may be faster than everyone downclimbing with equal painstaking care.

USING ICE AX SELF-ARREST

There are many good sources for learning the procedure for self-arrest (see the bibliography). In keeping with our emphasis on more advanced skills, we refer readers unfamiliar with the technique to those sources and limit ourselves here to discussing the place that self-arrest occupies in the context of overall security on snow.

Any useful discussion of self-arrest as a component of protective systems on snow must start with a realistic look at its limitations. As we mention above, self-

arrest does not always work. A slip can easily occur on slopes too steep or too firm to arrest effectively. Or the distance available to arrest may be too short to successfully stop before hitting an object or sailing over an edge. This is not to say that you shouldn't bother to learn and to practice the technique, much less that you shouldn't fight as hard as you can to arrest a fall. On the contrary; quick reflexes combined with thorough practice and training in self-arrest could possibly save your life when all else has failed. But before you put all your eggs in the self-arrest basket, be sure there are no more reliable baskets at hand.

Self-arrest is a response to a mistake. Usually the mistake consists of a fall or slip on snow, but it could also be an out-of-control glissade or a crevasse fall. Look for ways to reduce the probability of these mistakes: improve your snow climbing technique; glissade only where you can be sure of a safe runout; learn to better identify, assess, and avoid crevasse hazard; stick to climbs within your party's ability; and be willing to turn back if the going proves harder than expected. Above all, choose a more protective strategy, such as belaying, anywhere the probability and consequences of a fall are enough to worry you and you consider self-arrest unlikely to succeed.

The critical factors determining success or failure of self-arrest are slope angle, firmness, and the amount of time the sliding climber has to execute the maneuver. On firm snow at angles greater than about 40 degrees, there is little chance of pulling off a good self-arrest, especially when wearing crampons. The technique is more useful when roped to a beginning climber who might fall on lower-angle slopes or in the case of a crevasse fall, where the team is typically on lower-angle terrain and may have the benefit of a moment's warning. However, steep slopes above crevasses merit belaying, because rope team arrest is unlikely to be effective.

If someone on your rope team does fall, don't wait for the pull. If you wait, it may be too late. Run or dive in the opposite direction before the rope tightens on you. The weight of your body moving away will absorb much of the fall's energy, greatly increasing the odds of a successful team arrest.

MOVEMENT SKILLS ON ICE

We first learned to climb alpine ice among the seracs of the Coleman Glacier on Mount Baker in the Cascade Range and later taught countless clinics for aspiring alpinists in this same wonderland of glacial ice. Through this experience, as well as through our adventures farther afield, we have come to believe that developing good footwork wearing crampons is among the most important skills for the alpinist and that endless repetitions of movements—up and down, back and forth—are the building blocks of good footwork.

This section focuses on movement skills for climbing in crampons, both on hard ice and on frozen snow. We also cover a

variety of ice ax positions appropriate to different angles and firmness of snow and ice slopes. This section ends with a few observations for dealing with soft snow while wearing crampons and for cutting steps on hard ice.

DECIDING WHEN TO USE CRAMPONS

Deciding when to put crampons on, when to take them off, and indeed whether to bring them along on an outing at all is not always obvious or easy. In making these decisions, you balance a number of variables:

- relative ease or difficulty of walking with or without crampons
- degree of security gained, or lost, from wearing crampons
- time it takes to put crampons on or take them off
- length and difficulty of the terrain for which you want crampons on (or off)
- weight of crampons

Below are a few pointers that may help you balance these factors and make a decision:

- Bring crampons on climbs where you think you may encounter firm frozen snow, steep slopes, or dangerous runouts. If such terrain is not technically difficult, consider bringing lightweight aluminum crampons. They will not stand up to prolonged use on mixed ground or water ice but are ideal for frozen névé or soft glacier ice.
- As you approach the part of the climb that calls for crampons, begin looking

for safe, convenient spots to put them on, even if this means doing so before you actually need them. Avoid climbing up into steep terrain, only to be forced to don your crampons in an awkward or tenuous place. We have seen even expert climbers drop crampons while making this transition in cramped stances—one of these was a famous French climber instructing on a guide's course!

■ As the day warms and the snow softens, take crampons off once you can feel secure without them. Your feet will feel lighter, and you will reduce the risk of snagging your clothes, a common problem in deep snow.

■ Sticky snow balling up in crampons is a serious hazard! Antibottes (anti-balling plates) are standard equipment for alpine climbing—use them (see Chapter 3, Preparation and Equipment). Take crampons off if they are balling up.

■ Climbing rock while wearing crampons is yet another extremely important climbing skill to develop (see Mixed Climbing later in this chapter). When crossing short sections of rock or even long sections of dirt, it can be much faster leaving crampons on than stopping to take them off, only to put them back on again a short distance later. Do not worry about dulling crampons by walking on rock or dirt. They are easy to sharpen—and you should keep them sharp! Besides, wearing out gear is part of alpinism. As a good friend of ours says whenever he accidentally skis over a rock: "They make new ones every day."

■ Practice putting crampons on and taking them off quickly. You should be able to take them out of their protective bag and get them on your feet, ready to go, in less than a minute.

■ Being on a glacier does not necessarily mean you must put on crampons. Base your decision on snow consistency, not on glaciation.

PUTTING CRAMPONS ON

In firm snow, you can put the crampon on the snow and step into it. In soft snow, put your crampons on with your foot raised up out of the snow. Practice both ways. Put your harness on before your crampons! Most crampons have a right and a left foot, defined by the shape of the crampon and/or the straps. The buckles always go on the outside of the foot, similarly to gaiters. This reduces the chance of snagging and tripping into a potentially nasty fall.

Place the toe of your boot in the crampon first, then the heel. If your crampons have a heel lever, snapping it in place usually helps to seat your boot into the back of the crampon. In fact, with some models of crampons, the heel of your boot will not fit into place properly until the lever is snapped shut. The heel lever should close with a definite *thump* and stay shut without the help of the strap. The strap should fasten around your ankle and serve as a backup, not the primary means of keeping the heel lever in place.

USING CRAMPONS ON EASY TO MODERATE TERRAIN

Crampons commonly have 10 points facing down and two front points facing forward. Techniques for walking and climbing with crampons range from simple walking to duck-footing to zigzagging back and forth across the slope using a "flat foot" technique to kicking straight in on the front points. The full range of these techniques is the focus of this section.

The choice of which technique to use at any given time depends on the skill and confidence level of the climber in relation to the steepness and firmness of the slope. For that reason, the discussion here is organized according to techniques used rather than slope angle or difficulty.

As we progress from quicker and simpler crampon techniques to more complex (those more suited to harder climbing), remember that as you become more skilled, you can safely use these faster, more efficient techniques on ever steeper terrain. Security comes from matching your abilities to the terrain and not just the technique to the terrain.

Walking

On low-angle slopes, walking in crampons requires no specific skills. Even a novice becomes a pro after 30 meters (100 feet) as the strangeness of the sensation disappears. Walking with a slightly wider stance helps to keep crampons from snagging on each other or on pants, legs, or gaiters.

Pieds à Plat

The earliest crampons had no front points. Climbers flexed their ankles to keep the boot soles parallel to the snow, maximizing penetration of all crampon points. The various foot positions used to achieve this are collectively called *pieds à plat,* or "flat foot" technique. With your feet flat on the surface, your weight is distributed across your entire foot, favoring a relaxed, energy-efficient stance. Modern crampons are now equipped with front points, but pieds à plat is still the technique of choice for the moderate-angled slopes that make up the vast majority of snow and ice terrain in the mountains.

Pied en Canard

On gentle slopes, adopt the "duck-foot" position, pied en canard. Splaying the feet slightly outward allows for a more balanced stance and more weight on the heels (see Figure 65).

Taking a Diagonal Line with Pieds à Plat

On steeper ice slopes, just as on snow, climbing directly uphill with pied en canard grows awkward, and it becomes more comfortable to turn sideways and ascend diagonally. The goal is to distribute weight across the foot, especially on the heels, and to preserve a natural, relaxed, and upright stance. However, while security on snow comes from aggressive slicing and digging with the boot edge, on ice it comes from the penetration of the crampon's down points,

Figure 65. *Walking in pied en canard.*

Figure 66. *Standing in balance with pieds à plat and piolet manche. Notice that the feet are pointing across the fall line, even though the direction of travel is diagonally uphill.*

so good footing requires a very different movement. When cramponing, let your ankles roll downhill, to bring your boot soles more or less parallel to the surface and to penetrate all crampon points equally (see Figure 66).

Ideally, your uphill foot should point more or less straight across the fall line, but changes in slope angle will force you to change your foot position in order to preserve both a natural upright stance and weight over the heels. On very low-angle slopes, the toe can point slightly uphill, while on very steep slopes it may need to point just a bit downhill. The downhill foot

(when standing in balance) often points slightly downhill.

- Gain most of your elevation with your in-balance step. The out-of-balance step should be kept relatively small, with the feet close together (see Figure 67). Otherwise, when it comes time to step up, the crampon points on your lower foot will tend to shear out of the snow before you have safely transferred your weight, sending you on a potentially long slide.

- Swing your boot and leg in an arc as you make your out-of-balance step, letting the weight of the swing drive your points into the ice. Getting adequate penetration in very hard ice may require more active stomping.
- As you weight your foot, let the ankle relax and roll downhill. The boot upper will press hard against your leg and ankle. Avoid the sensation of edging—in fact, actively strive *not* to edge.
- Use footholds and ledges when possible, and set a steady pace. Remember, you may have thousands of feet to go.

Figure 67. *Taking the cross-over, or out-of-balance, step. Feet are close together, the crossover foot pointing slightly downslope.*

Using an Ice Ax with Pieds à Plat

On moderate to steep snow and ice slopes, the ice ax is used in combination with pieds à plat in a number of different ways, all of which are primarily meant to help maintain balance. For the most part, these ice ax techniques are limited in their ability to stop a slip, but they do help you avoid the slip in the first place.

An ice ax long enough to reach the ground on flat terrain is too long and awkward to use on steeper ground, where it is really needed. A useful length for most alpine climbing is 60 cm, both short enough to be useful on somewhat technical ground and long enough to provide support on moderately steep slopes.

Piolet canne ("ice ax cane"). Piolet canne—the use of the ax as a cane—is the basic application in classic mountaineering and is the preferred ice ax technique for the vast majority of the time when pieds à plat cramponing is used. Piolet canne technique on ice is nearly identical to that in snow (see **Kicking steps straight up,** earlier in this chapter). The only difference is that on a very hard surface, a bit more vigor may be needed to set the ax; also be sure the spike of the ax doesn't slip unexpectedly.

Changing direction. On ice just as on snow, changing direction is often the most precarious moment in ascending a slope pieds à plat. Plan your movements carefully to maintain balance. The sequence is basically the same as that described for kicking steps in snow, with the minor difference that your outside corner step should be taken with the toes pointing slightly uphill to provide a more stable position facing into the hill.

CLIMBING ON STEEP TERRAIN

When the going gets truly steep, you will be forced to turn and face the slope, bringing the front points of your crampons into play in order to feel secure. The point at which this happens could vary anywhere from 20 to 50 degrees or so, depending mostly on surface firmness, which can range from bullet-proof black ice to perfect Styrofoam-like frozen névé. Your personal skill and experience level will be a major factor. A highly experienced alpinist may think nothing of using pieds à plat on a steep slope with a fatal runout, where a beginner would be wiser to face in.

Front Point Cramponing

When front pointing on ice, follow these tips:

- Kick your boot straight in, keeping your heels low to prevent up or down movement as you shift weight and to reduce calf muscle strain. Use shin muscles to actively point your toes upward as you kick with a bent leg.
- Once you have placed your foot, shift weight onto it quietly, without rocking your heel either up or down or from side to side. See if you can "step" up onto it without moving your foot at all.
- Kick your toes in perpendicular to the plane of the ice, striving for equal penetration of both front points. Adjust the angle of your kick as the plane of the ice changes. If the ice is concave, the toes of your feet must diverge in a

Figure 68. *Keep the feet level and bring the knees in close to the ice by bending at the ankles.*

Front-pointing with a relaxed stance—knees and hips in, shoulders out, heels low

duck-foot position. If it is convex, pigeon-toe in. In both cases, your point penetration is still equal and your toes remain perpendicular to the ice surface.

■ Keeping heels low, bring your knees in to touch the ice (see Figure 68), to reduce strain on your calf muscles and to stabilize your position.

■ Generally, small steps are better than large ones, because they make it easier to shift your weight onto the higher foot without unwanted movement of the lower foot.

Pieds Troisième

Pieds troisième (*troisième* is derived from a similar foot position in ballet) consists of front-pointing with one foot and flat-footing with the other (see Figure 69). This technique combines the opportunity for rest afforded by flat-footing, with the security of facing into the slope. Pieds troisième is the best technique for long, uniform, and fairly steep slopes of alpine ice or frozen snow, such as the classic north faces of the Alps in firm snow conditions. When using pieds troisième technique, observe the following:

■ Occasionally switch feet to avoid burning out the calf on your front-point side.

■ Rest with the weight on your flat foot, the front-pointing foot a little higher, the knee bent slightly. Take advantage of shelves, ledges, or lower-angle terrain to make this tiring technique easier.

Figure 69. *Mike Powers using pieds troisième. He moves his tools while his weight rests comfortably on his sideways (right) foot. Ice tools are in piolet manche.*

Using an Ice Ax on Steep Snow and Ice

In the snow climbing section above, we present the three ice ax techniques of piolet appui—piolet panne, piolet manche, and piolet poignard. These positions are equally useful when you are wearing crampons. In fact, they are perfectly suited to frozen firm snow and combined with pieds troisième they form an ideal way to climb many classic routes. In addition to these, several more ax positions are useful on steeper slopes.

Piolet ramasse. In French, *ramasser* means "to collect or gather"; the piolet ramasse technique entails pulling the ax in toward your body as you traverse. An elegant technique, originally developed to help push the limits of flat-foot cramponing on steep slopes before front points were introduced, it is used only occasionally these days—facing in has become more commonplace on this type of terrain. But piolet ramasse is still quite useful for traversing in places where the slope above steepens or a cramped situation makes the various appui techniques awkward.

Hold the ax comfortably with your downhill hand over the adze and your uphill hand around the shaft just above the spike. Point the pick horizontally forward, away from your body, holding it between your thumb and forefinger (see Figure 70). Do not use the self-arrest grip here, or you'll tear up your clothes (or worse!).

Standing in balance, bend forward slightly and place the spike into the snow about as far away as you can reach, with the ax head slightly higher than the spike and the shaft diagonally across your body at about chest height. Take two steps—out of balance, then back into balance—for each ice ax placement. Make your steps small to avoid running into the shaft; you will quickly get a sense of how far away you must place the ax.

Remember that the ax is only a balance point, and keep your weight centered on your feet. If you lean into the slope, your feet will tend to shear out.

Figure 70. *Piolet ramasse: the ax pick is point forward, across the slope.*

Piolet ancre ("ice ax anchor"). This entails swinging the ax like a hammer and driving the pick in strongly to create an anchor, hence the name. More than just a balance point, a well-placed tool in piolet ancre can actually hold a slip, assuming you have a good grip on the shaft. Piolet ancre is virtually the only technique that provides adequate security on ice steeper than about 50 degrees or on snow at more than about 60 degrees.

Because its application is on steep snow and ice, piolet ancre is almost always used in combination with front pointing or pieds

239

troisième. (In the good old days, climbers used piolet ancre in combination with pieds à plat in an elegant but twisted, over-the-shoulder tool swing. This difficult and strenuous technique is no longer seen much since the advent of front points, generally only in instructional courses to lend a bit of historical perspective and to give the instructor a nice opportunity to show off—we all need a creative outlet of some kind.) When climbing on front points or in pieds troisième on less-steep snow, using piolet ancre with one hand alone and some other, less-strenuous technique such as piolet manche or piolet panne in the other hand can provide great security as well as smooth, rapid progress.

Grasp the shaft firmly with your hand at the bottom, very near the spike. Avoid the temptation to choke up (grip too high) on the shaft, which will result in a weak swing and/or cause the spike to bounce the tool off the ice.

Practice your aim, striving for precision and efficiency. The better your aim, the fewer swings of the tool and the less brute force you will need to get a secure place-ment. You will quickly appreciate how strenuous removing a too-deeply driven pick can be, especially on steep ground. Look for depressions or old tool placement scars, and try to nail them with your pick on the first try. Take advantage of top-rope ice climbing sessions to learn to gauge the quality of your placements and make do with the minimum necessary penetration.

Piolet traction. This is used on very steep ice, typically at angles of 60 degrees or more, where pure front-point cramponing is the norm. It is basically the same ice ax placement technique as piolet ancre, but the steeper angle of the ice results in the tools taking some of the climber's body weight and providing the purchase necessary to move upward (see Figure 71). With piolet ancre, the climber's weight is still centered over the feet and the tools are placed "just in case."

Piolet traction is inherently strenuous, even for the most muscular athlete, and

Figure 71. *Mike Powers using piolet traction on the North Face Triangle of Mont Blanc du Tacul—left foot in pieds à plat to relieve strain on the calf muscle.*

technique is vitally important to conserve strength. As the angle of the ice approaches vertical, body position becomes increasingly important. The trick is to prepare for each new tool placement by getting the shoulders and head away from the ice while standing comfortably in balance. This body position allows better visibility, better balance, and a better swing for the next tool placement.

As you prepare to swing and place a tool, get centered under the other one—that is, your feet should be spread wide to either side beneath it. If your soon-to-be-the-only-weighted-tool is too far off to the side, you will "barn door" (swing out to the side) when you remove the other one. Keep your heels low, and bring your knees and hips in close to the ice. Arch your back to get your shoulders away from the ice. Swing your tool from this position. Once your pick is placed, pull down on it aggressively to test and set it. Avoid any rotating or pulling outward as you move up higher in preparation for another placement.

On ice this steep, wrist loops may be useful, largely because they reduce the effort needed to hold on (at least on traditional straight-shafted alpine axes). This said, modern axes with ergonomic shaft grip designs and gloves with nonslip palms reduce the need for wrist loops—more and more alpinists climb even very steep ice without them. "Leashless" climbing can be a great pleasure. It simplifies the task of placing and removing ice screws on steep ground, for example, where getting one hand free to work while hanging on with the other can be difficult! But be careful not to drop your tools, particularly at belays, where they should be holstered, clipped in to your anchor, or placed securely out of the way.

If you do use wrist loops, correct length is extremely important. The correct length enables you to hang off the wrist loop with a relatively relaxed hand. If the loop is too long, your hand slides down off the spike. If the loop is too short, you "choke up" and can't get a good swing. The loop should be taut around your wrist when your hand is grasping the very bottom of the shaft, with your little finger almost on the spike.

Ice tool movement patterns. On near vertical ice, there are two basic patterns for moving tools. Parallel tool progression keeps hands at about the same level whenever you move your feet. One tool is moved up, then the other to about the same height, and then both feet are moved. This pattern is psychologically reassuring but slow. Alternating tool progression is faster and more efficient but may feel a bit less secure. A single tool is placed above, the feet are moved up, the other tool is placed higher, the feet moved again, and so on. By moving the feet with each tool placement, you can climb higher on each tool and therefore use fewer total tool placements to cover a given distance.

Use alternating tool progression when following steep ice, both to move more quickly and to become comfortable with the technique. When leading, many ice climbers begin with parallel progression and gradually move to alternating progression as they develop skills.

DESCENDING ICE

On ice, as on snow and rock, becoming as comfortable and competent as possible with fast downclimbing techniques (facing out as much as possible) improves your efficiency and safety.

Descending with Pied en Canard

Pied en canard is the fastest technique for descending moderately steep ice slopes up to about 45 degrees. It provides good

Figure 72. *Descending with pied en canard. The ax is held off to the side in piolet canne position.*

visibility and a comfortable, centered stance. Turn your toes outward in a V and walk straight down the fall line, rolling ankles to the inside with every step (see Figure 72). The duck-footed position helps keep your feet flat, because ankles flex more easily from side to side than they do backward, especially in stiff boots.

As with the plunge step, hold the ice ax in piolet canne position off to the side. Beware when using it as a balance point on hard and smooth ice—if the spike slips, you may be thrown off balance, actually increasing the likelihood of a fall. Slips on even low-angle water ice can be very serious.

Turning Sideways

As the slope steepens, turning sideways to the hill allows you to get more support from the ice ax. The sideways position helps keep the downhill foot flat and is psychologically more comfortable. It is slower and requires more effort than facing straight downhill. Remember always to keep your weight centered over your feet, and avoid leaning on the ax.

Facing In

Descending facing in is common when the terrain steepens to more than about 45 degrees. On firm snow, front points will bite well and large, quick steps can be taken. With the ice ax, use piolet panne if you can get enough pick penetration to feel stable; otherwise, crouch and place the ax with piolet ancre as low as you effectively can, then front-point down until you must remove the ax and repeat.

When the ice is hard, downclimbing is more difficult. It can be hard to keep heels low when kicking in front points on descent, and there is a tendency to reach downward with the toes, bringing the heels up. Kick as low as you can on a fairly stiff, straight leg, tensing your quadriceps and shin muscles together to keep your toes pointing upward as much as possible.

Using Abalakov Rappel Anchors

The Abalakov anchor (named after its inventor, the Russian climber Vitali Abalakov) is often the preferred anchor for rappels on steep, smooth ice. Bollards can also be chopped in ice, but an Abalakov anchor is typically faster to build in very hard ice and is definitely easier to use. On a route where other climbers have left Abalakov anchors for their descent, you can often incorporate them into your own ice screw belay anchors to beef them up and/or to save time on the way up. A well-constructed Abalakov anchor in good ice can be amazingly strong.

An Abalakov anchor is made by drilling two holes that intersect in a V at the back, then threading webbing or cord through the holes and tying it in a loop. Place a long (22-cm) ice screw diagonally into the ice twice, to form an equilateral triangle as shown in Figure 73a.

In Figure 73a, the screw on the left is partially backed off but remains in the hole to help visually guide the second screw placement to the convergence point. If you have only one long screw, remove it and replace it with a shorter

Figure 73a. *Drilling the holes for an Abalakov anchor*

Figure 73b. *Using the hook to pull the cord through*

Figure 73c. *The finished Abalakov anchor*

screw inserted halfway in to serve as the visual reference, and reuse the long screw for your second hole.

Once the holes intersect, push one end of your cord or webbing into one hole until it reaches the back—you should be able to see it in the other hole. Insert a sharp hook (made of clothes hanger wire or commercially made) into the empty hole, and "fish" until you catch the cord or webbing (see Figure 73b).

Pull the cord through, tie your loop using a single or double fishermans knot in cord or a water knot in webbing, *et voilà!* You are ready to thread your rope through the loop as shown in Figure 73c and rappel.

Although the amount of ice comprising the anchor may look small, the Abalakov is a strong anchor when carefully placed in good ice. For additional security, this anchor can be backed up with a temporary ice screw or combined and equalized with a second Abalakov anchor.

PROTECTIVE SYSTEMS ON ICE

A fall on ice, even a short one, is usually very serious. Speed and momentum build up quickly. With ice tools in hand and crampons ready to catch on any little ledge, stabbing injuries, shoulder separations, and ankle sprains are common. While successfully self-arresting on steep snow is very difficult, it is virtually impossible on ice. Therefore the strategy of moving together on a shortened rope is much less helpful on ice than it is on rock

and snow, and the transition to belayed climbing comes earlier, on much lower-angle terrain. For this reason, our discussion of protective systems on ice dives right in with ice anchors for belaying.

ICE SCREWS

Ice screws are by far the most common anchoring tool used in this slippery medium. A well-positioned and properly placed ice screw is normally strong enough to withstand the high forces of a leader fall. However, a screw placed poorly or in weak ice can fail under modest forces.

Placing Ice Screws

Look for solid and consistent ice, free of cracks and air pockets. On an alpine face, good ice may be found under "Swiss cheese" ice full of air holes and pockets or a layer of snow. Chop down through any surface nastiness to find the ice that you want. Old glacier ice can be either quite good or complete junk; scrape away at the granular surface and look for dense, consistent, hard ice. Bulges and convexities tend to fracture and shatter more readily than concave areas, so place screws and construct anchors in flat ice or gentle concavities whenever possible.

Once you have found a good spot in solid ice, chop a small starter divot with the pick of your ice tool. When starting the screw, tilt it slightly toward the direction of the load. Tests indicate that in good ice, screw placements are strongest when tilted a few degrees toward the direction of pull. The opposite is true in ice exposed to warmth or sunshine, where screws will eventually melt out—here you should tilt the screw slightly away from the angle of pull (in bad ice the placement is suspect no matter which direction you point it!).

Place the teeth of the screw into your starter divot, and press on the end of the screw while rotating it in. Press as hard and as long as needed to get the threads to engage. Once you can remove your hand without dropping the screw, rotate it all the way in, using the handle, until the hanger is flush against the ice. Chop away any ice that inhibits the last few turns. If the ice fractures into loose "dinner plates" as you go, break these out so that the ice remaining is solid.

Feel for consistent resistance to rotation throughout the placement. Any change in resistance is usually a bad sign. If it suddenly becomes much easier to rotate, you have hit air, snow, or water—try again in a new spot. If the screw suddenly will not rotate in any more, you have probably hit rock. Trying to force it in farther will damage the teeth. Either back it out and try again in another area, place a shorter screw (if you have one) in the same hole, or, if you don't think you can do better in the ice nearby and the screw protrudes no more than an inch or so, simply clip it anyway, keeping in mind the placement's limitations.

Constructing Ice Screw Belay Anchors

One of the most important attributes of an ice screw belay anchor is the location of the stance. Because climbing on such a brittle medium often involves dislodging copious amounts of ice shards large and small, your belay stance must be in a safe and comfortable position, well off to the side of the plumb line of the next pitch, where material raining down will not hit the belayer.

A typical belay anchor consists of two good screws placed in solid and consistent ice. First, decide exactly where you will want to stand while belaying. This will determine how high you place your first belay screw—ideally about face height or slightly higher. If your stance lacks a natural ledge, chop a small platform where at least one foot can be placed sideways.

Next, place your first screw, clip a carabiner to it, and run the rope through the carabiner to have some protection while placing the second screw. The second screw should go in above the first, at a minimum distance of about 30 cm (12 inches), or farther away in brittle ice.

Connect the screws with a runner or cordelette using either self-equalization or pre-equalization, as described in Chapter 5, Alpine Rock. If both screws are good, self-equalization is generally best, because it is faster and consumes less gear (see Figure 74). If one of your screw placements is less than perfect, try another spot. If you simply cannot get the quality of screw placements you want, add more screws if possible until you are convinced that collectively the anchor is good. In this case, pre-equalize all pieces.

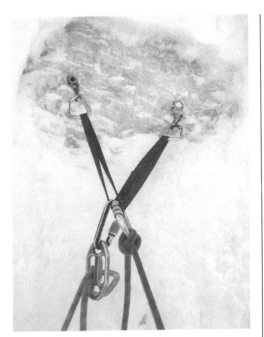

Figure 74. *Belaying a second off two screws self-equalized using a single runner. We had to chop through a few inches of snow to get to good ice underneath, typical of many north faces. The device used for this direct belay is an older-model plaquette called a GiGi. Athabasca North Face, Canadian Rockies.*

Before unclipping the rope that you ran through your first screw, pull up some slack and tie in to the master point of your anchor using a clove hitch in a locking carabiner.

Belay your partner directly off the anchor with an autoblocking device or, alternatively, redirect the rope through a carabiner or quickdraw on one of the screws and belay off your harness.

Before the leader leaves the stance to begin the next pitch, run the rope through a carabiner or quickdraw attached to the upper screw, to reduce the potential fall factor (see Figure 75).

Figure 75. *An ice screw belay anchor and stance. Here, a double sling was used to pre-equalize the two screws. The rope running through the quickdraw on the top ice screw reduces the fall factor on the anchor. It also directs the pull on the belayer's body upward into the anchor rather than down. The belayer leans on the anchor for a relaxed and stable stance.*

LEADING ON ICE

A leader on ice cannot afford to make mistakes: even a short fall can result in serious injury. Adding to the consequences of a fall is a leader's tendency to place less protection on ice than on rock, mostly because ice screws typically take more time and effort to place than rock protection.

When placing an ice screw, chop a small platform with your adze tool to enable you to get a foot sideways while you work; this is equally helpful to your partner, who can use your same step while removing the screw. If the ice is very hard or the climbing difficult, place an ice screw early on the pitch. Resist the temptation to place your screws high; a placement at about rib level allows much more efficient body mechanics as you push in to seat the screw. A long pitch of 55-degree smooth ice is harder than it looks. While no single move is difficult, the length, the lack of opportunities to rest, and the weight of the climbing rope all take their toll. Stay calm and in control. If you start to get nervous, stop and place a screw.

Climbers on alpine ice faces frequently run it out, using little or no intermediate protection. However, when assessing the need for protection, take into account your confidence, the quality of the belay anchor below, the consistency of the ice and its influence on both difficulty and the quality of your intermediate protection, the presence of climbers above you, your relative need for speed, and—last but not least—the psychological effect on your partner of seeing you climb with little or no protection!

TIPS: MOVING FAST ON ICE

- Use long ropes to reduce the number of pitches.
- The second might climb more quickly without tools or using minimal tool placements.
- Lead in blocks, rather than swinging leads.
- Run out your pitches to the very end of the rope until you have virtually no slack left. After placing the first of your two belay anchor screws, have your partner take you off belay as you continue to build your anchor. Because the leader has no more rope left, there is functionally no difference between being on belay and off at this point.
- After the leader places one of two belay screws, the second can remove one of his or her two screws, waiting for the "Belay on!" call to remove the second screw.

FOLLOWING AND CLEANING AN ICE PITCH

Following an ice pitch with a belay from above provides a safe opportunity to move fast, minimizing the depth and vigor of tool placements and conserving physical and emotional energy. Use piolet panne or piolet manche whenever possible. Look for old tool placements, and hook your picks in them rather than swinging and driving your tools.

Practice removing screws efficiently with one hand, to conserve time and arm

Changing over at the belay. Mike, on the left, has just followed the pitch below and is about to lead the next. While he takes gear from Kathy's harness, he remains temporarily anchored with the plaquette with which he was belayed. Meanwhile, Kathy is transferring the belay to a plate on her harness. The changeover will take less than a minute.

strength on steep ground and to reduce the chance of dropping something. Unclip and rack quickdraws before removing screws. Once you have removed the ice screw, clean old ice out of the core before you rack it; otherwise, the frozen plug may freeze into the screw as you continue climbing, making it very hard to place again when the time comes. Clear the screw by banging the head of the screw on your hammer or ax. Never tap the screw's teeth or threads, because nicks and dings make them harder to place. Alternatively, in temperatures above freezing you can place the screw's teeth end in your mouth and blow the plug out—but do not try this in subfreezing temperatures!

MIXED CLIMBING

Looking at the latest issue of *Horrendous Ascents,* one might get the impression that all mixed climbing involves radically overhanging limestone walls and hooking picks on desperate dime edges while clipping quickdraws into a line of bolts 1 meter (3 feet) apart. In the mountains, things are usually a bit different. For most mere mortals, alpine mixed climbing simply means climbing moderate rock while wearing crampons. This is often the most efficient way to deal with circumstances such as a short section or pitch of rock on an otherwise mostly snow or ice route, a ridgeline alternating between rock and hard snow, or a skiff of new snow or rime ice on 3rd- or 4th-class terrain. Such situations are routine in the big hills, and they usually involve easy climbing, often no more serious than exposed walking.

ROCK CLIMBING AND SCRAMBLING IN CRAMPONS

The importance of developing competence at easy rock climbing and scrambling in crampons is often overlooked. Watching a skilled climber do this is as inspiring as any other demonstration of a highly developed skill and helps to awaken an appreciation for this seemingly unglamorous component of expert alpine climbing. Start by practicing simple walking in crampons on relatively flat but rough, rocky ground. The trick is to find foot placements that do not rock side to side and that allow weight distribution across the length of the foot. Allow the ankles to roll slightly to whatever direction is required to keep the foot stable. Move the feet slowly and deliberately.

Cramponing on steeper rock requires precise footwork. Front points hold amazingly well on even the smallest of holds, but they must be placed carefully and not move as weight is transferred. Find places to practice more challenging moves in crampons. Look for practice sites with easy climbing in obscure, environmentally nonsensitive locations, unattractive to rock climbers. A good practice area can be level or slightly inclined, with rocks ranging from about 15 cm (6 inches) to 1.5 meters (5 feet) in diameter. Possible locales might include boulder fields, beaches, or dry creek beds; in an urban setting, look for areas where large rocks were used for some sort of landscaping—perhaps as part of an overpass or road cut—so long as they are stable and you can stay away from traffic.

Traverse back and forth, up and down, working to increase balance, speed, and comfort. As you gain confidence, introduce some variety: walk in slow motion, pause on one foot. Create a small circuit on which you can time yourself. Do not wear a pack; this only increases risk with no benefit. Your goal is to learn how the crampons react underfoot and to train your proprioceptors (local nerve centers in your ankles) to respond adroitly.

For practicing, use an old pair of crampons, one that you don't mind destroying, and set a goal of eventually destroying them completely! On soft rock, such as limestone, this may take some time; on granite, a few good sessions will show significant wear.

USING YOUR HANDS

Mixed climbing often involves the use of hands on cold snow- and ice-covered rock. Use the thinnest, tackiest gloves possible to provide good traction and feel for the rock. Test frozen-in handholds by a firm tap with the heel of your hand. On short passages of only a move or two, consider letting your ice tools hang from your wrist loops.

SHOULDERING THE AX

A quick way to stow your ax while keeping it readily available is to slot it behind your shoulders between your back and your pack, as shown in Figure 76. Hold the head of the ice ax with one hand in the self-arrest grip, and stuff the spike under your pack shoulder strap on the opposite side, so that it points away from your body (go in above the sternum strap if you have one). At about midshaft, push the shaft back behind your shoulder, while rotating the head of the ax over and behind your head and stuffing it down along your back and between it and the pack. The pick

Figure 76. *Climbing with ice ax shouldered*

should point down between your shoulder blades and the adze should stick out a bit over your shoulder. Drop or push the head down to rest as low as possible between the shoulder straps of your pack so that it doesn't interfere with your head movement as you look up.

Stowed this way, the ax can work its way up and out under certain circumstances, especially while you are downclimbing rock and facing out. Watch out for this; and, of course, remember your ax is back there when you take your pack off!

CHAPTER 7

Climbers on Palcaraju Oeste (Ranrapalca behind), Cordillera Blanca, Peru

Glaciers

A party of climbers setting foot on a glacier begins a complex task of routefinding while assessing the level of risk posed by hidden or hard-to-see hazards. A number of decisions must be made: where to go; how or even whether to rope up; how to manage the team's movement as they travel together; where to consider belaying. The climber in the lead must be able to identify and follow the best route, recognize signs of hidden crevasses, and decide how best to approach a visible or suspected crevasse. The rest of the team must know when the leader is approaching hazards, how to adjust rope tension and position in response, and what to do if someone does fall in.

These decisions and tasks collectively make up a strategy for glacier travel. The key elements of this strategy are:

- route selection and routefinding
- hazard assessment
- choice of protective strategies, based on degree and type of hazard
- efficient movement of the rope team
- emergency preparedness (crevasse rescue)

This chapter addresses each of these in turn but first looks at glacier structure and movement, because understanding these underlies all of the above elements.

FORMATION OF GLACIERS

Glacier travel is tricky because of the mazelike complexity of crevasse fields as well as the hazards presented by hidden or hard-to-identify crevasses. An understanding of glacier structure helps climbers to recognize and negotiate these problems and to find as direct and safe a line of travel as possible.

Glaciers form anyplace where winter

snowfall exceeds summer melting. Over time, as ever more weight is added from above, the snow compacts and eventually becomes ice. At some point, gravity starts the whole mass creeping downhill. The ice deforms as it is forced over uneven bedrock. It stretches and thins over steep slopes or bulges and piles up on level benches and concavities. Many glacier features and glacier hazards are the result of this deformation.

Glaciers are divided into an *accumulation zone,* the upper part of the glacier, where there is an annual net gain of snow, and an *ablation zone,* the lower part of the glacier, where the winter's snowfall completely melts each year; these two zones are separated by the *firn line.* The term *firn* denotes dense summer snow and also refers to the surface snow in the accumulation zone. In midlatitudes, the firn line is clearly visible in late summer—lighter snow above and old, bare ice below.

Crevasse Formation

Crevasse formation is perhaps the most important glacier phenomenon to climbers, because whether hidden or visible,

Low on the ablation zone of the Mer de Glace, Mont Blanc Massif, France. Crevasses such as these are a great place to practice skills and have a fun day exploring.

crevasses are the greatest obstacle to safe travel on glaciers.

Tensile stress. Crevasses are surface cracks formed in response to tensile (stretching) stresses within the glacier. Such stretching is usually caused by differing rates of movement of the ice as it flows downhill. Crevasses form perpendicular to the direction of the stretch. They then travel downhill along with the entire glacier mass, deforming further as they go. Where there are tensile stresses in a number of directions, such as when the ice flows over a rounded knob, intersecting crevasse lines form and may cause the ice walls to break into unstable towers called seracs.

Heavy winter snow partially fills and conceals open crevasses. Nevertheless, it is possible to predict the likely locations of hidden crevasses by understanding where tensile stress is likely to occur and recog-

The Glacier du Géant, France. Mont Blanc is behind on the right. The bergschrund is clearly visible under the North Face of the Tour Ronde on the left. Concave areas are generally crevasse-free compression zones. Learn to correlate the location and direction of crevasses with stresses in the ice caused by flow over varied bedrock.

nizing the signs of it. Crevasses form most readily where the terrain steepens, and such terrain is usually quite obvious both on the map and to the eye.

Particularly crevasse-prone is the top of a roll, where the slope begins to steepen and drop away below. Crevasses are also common where parts of a glacier are stretched due to differing flow rates. In a typical valley glacier, the ice flows fastest in the center, where it is thickest, and more slowly at the thin edges. As the ice in the glacier's center pulls away from the ice at the edge, tensile stress results. Marginal crevasses form at the glacier's edge in response to this stress. These usually point uphill toward the center of the glacier at a 45-degree angle—perpendicular to the direction of stress.

Compression. Where the underlying bedrock flattens out, glacier ice slows down or piles up, and crevasses narrow and disappear. Such areas are called compression zones. Ice also converges in troughs between ridges and bumps. Benches, bowls, gullies, and junctions where two glaciers meet all offer potential for compression and often crevasse-free travel. Discerning and linking together such zones is the key to finding relatively safe travel corridors.

ROUTEFINDING

Routefinding on glaciers, just as in other contexts, requires constant shifting between the big picture and the close-up perspective. Climbers must scrutinize subtle surface details for signs of hazard, correlate these signs with the overall structure of the glacier, and at the same time keep track of where they are, where they want to end up, and how they plan to get there.

On glaciers, the distant view is of the utmost importance because it shows the general layout of compression zones and crevassed areas. A maze is much easier to analyze when viewed from above than from within. Note and memorize major crevasse patterns as soon as a glacier comes into view. Also identify areas of potential serac hazard that may be hidden from view later on.

At the same time, begin to identify your proposed route. You will almost certainly modify it later, but try to form a provisional plan as early as you can. As your view changes, you will gain new information to help you improve your route. Link crevasse-free troughs with level compression zones to create the best line. Compression zones may be hidden over the tops of bumps, but changes in steepness can help you predict where areas of easier travel are likely. The low-angled ice just above an icefall or a steep broken area is often rife with deep, long crevasses, which become bigger and more problematic the closer they are to the drop. As you approach from below, these may not be visible, but you can assume their presence.

As always, memorize major terrain features and locate your proposed route and notable hazards relative to them. These landmarks will serve as valuable guides to keep you on track and away from the worst problems later on when everything becomes harder to see and recognize in the foreshortened, near view. On a complicated glacier, various visual aids to memory are useful. Make a sketch to help you remember major features; if you have a digital camera, take a reference photo to view later on; bring a (recent!) postcard or photo taken from a distance.

Consider time of day in plotting your line of travel. Firm, frozen snow allows you to travel safely through very crevassed areas. Softer snow late in the day may dictate that you should stay away from such areas.

PREVIOUS TRACKS

A recent track can help you approach crevassed areas with more confidence. Someone else will probably have already found any weak bridges (sometimes by stepping into them!). The more heavily traveled the track, the more true this is. However, it matters what the makers of the track knew or could see. Climbers sometimes mistake covered crevasses for old trails! This is particularly easy in the fog or under new snow. Also, as discussed in Chapter 4, Routefinding and Navigation, a downhill track will usually be better informed than an uphill track. On glaciers, the passage of a few days can also change the appropriateness of tracks. A safe, conservative line can become progressively dicier as the season advances, crevasses open wider, or bridges thin and melt out. Even when following a well-worn track, continue to make your own independent analysis of conditions and risks, and change the route as needed to give suspect dips or visible gaps a wide berth and to avoid crossing bridges that no longer look sturdy.

THE IMPERMANENCE OF TRACKS

I once descended a heavily crevassed glacier with very soft, deep snow rather later on a hot day than I had planned. The track was well traveled, but most climbers had descended an hour or more earlier. I saw one very large roped team descending about a half hour ahead and hustled to catch up.

Approaching one particularly large crevasse, I was puzzled to see the track go straight up to a 3-meter (10-foot) gap and continue on the other side. There was no possibility that the previous party had leapt such a distance, but the track was unambiguous; no new trail or deviation. It was obvious that the bridge had collapsed just minutes before, presumably after the last party's passage, since there was no rescue going on. It was easy to go a dozen yards out of my way and end-run the crevasse, but it was a very dramatic case of a trail abruptly ceasing to be useful.

—Kathy Cosley

HAZARD ASSESSMENT

Glaciers present many potential hazards, but the most widespread and problematic is that of crevasses.

SURFACE EXPRESSION OF CREVASSES

Evidence of crevasses hidden beneath the snow can be very subtle and hard to recognize when they are close at hand. It is important to see and correctly interpret such evidence in order to take appropriate measures when crossing suspected snow bridges. Equally important is discerning similar-looking signs that do not indicate a hidden crevasse, in order to avoid needless detours or groundless fear. The following discussion of different ways hidden crevasses can appear on the surface, and how this surface expression varies with the seasons, is intended to help the reader pick up on these subtle clues and to accurately assess crevasse hazard.

"Saggers"

The daily pattern of intense daytime warming and nighttime refreezing typical of spring and summer alters the snow on the glacier. Snow covering large crevasses gradually deforms and sags under its own weight, before eventually falling in—occasionally beneath a climber's feet. During this process, the outlines of the crevasses become more and more apparent, like bones under aging skin (see Figure 77).

The sagging may be barely discernible early on. A change in snow color may be

Figure 77. *This "sagger" just to the right of the trail is the most hazardous type of crevasse. Climbers need to be alert to identify the risk. The weight of the overlying snow sags into the abyss beneath. Cracks in the snow just left of the depression give additional clues to the danger. Notice that the bridged crevasse runs parallel to open crevasses in the background on the left.*

the only visible evidence at first, as windblown snow or dust accumulates in the subtlest of depressions. Therefore, linear dips or changes in snow color or texture may be grounds for suspecting hidden crevasses, in which case you should approach them with caution (see

Rope Team Movement later in this chapter). However, snow presents an inherently uneven surface, and not every groove or change in snow color necessarily signals a bridged crevasse. Evaluate any dips you encounter in context, as follows:

■ Since crevasses are often grouped together roughly parallel to one another, look for other, similarly oriented depressions or snow patterns nearby. Also look for any open holes indicating the presence and overall orientation of other crevasses in the area.

■ Use your understanding of terrain considerations in determining the likelihood that your suspect is guilty, remembering that the tops of steep rolls—the beginning of acceleration—are particularly likely places for crevasses, while the least likely are flat areas at the base of steeper slopes.

■ In the case of an unusually large crevasse—perhaps 3 to 12 meters (10 to 40 feet) across—a snow bridge can appear as two smaller cracks, one on either side of the giant bridge; the cracks form as the bridge begins to sink and sag. The center part of the bridge may appear solid, but don't be fooled. If the entire area sags, most likely it is unsupported.

■ Small grooves oriented up and down the fall line, curving, branching, and/or very close together, are more likely signal patterns of water seepage within the snowpack rather than crevasses. Although crevasses certainly can be oriented along the fall line where the glacier stretches over a ridge or bump,

this is somewhat unusual. In any case, it is usually easy to differentiate these from meltwater patterns.

"Crackers"

Some crevasses show themselves more obviously as clean-cut, linear cracks with straight, smooth sides running down into the snow or ice (see Figure 78a). You can easily judge the depth and strength of the snow at its lip, so approaching these crevasses is much safer and more straightforward than is the case with saggers (see Figure 78b).

Figure 78a. *These midsummer crevasses are relatively clean and easily avoided, though recent snow has developed a bit of cornicing on the edges. Expect this new snow to have bridged some smaller holes nearby.*

Figure 78b. *This crevasse is safely approached even though it has a sunken "bridge." The clean, well-defined edge permits easy and quick inspection.*

Seasonal Changes in Surface Condition

The seasonal changes in the snowpack discussed in Chapter 6, Snow and Ice, also change the surface appearance of the crevasses hidden beneath the snow and the degree of hazard that they pose. Choosing the best travel route and risk management strategy depends on a good understanding of these seasonal influences. Here we look at seasonal conditions typical of only midlatitudes.

Autumn. Early autumn is typically the time when crevasses are most evident and visible. The long, hot summer days have melted and broken down overlying snow and bridges to their greatest extent, and nighttime freezing is intense. Travel may be circuitous, but the very strong frozen snow greatly reduces the risk of breaking through a snow bridge. The hard snow can be very slippery, however, so steep slopes above crevasses pose special hazards, and team self-arrest of a crevasse fall is very difficult, even on a gentle slope.

Winter. The beginning of winter is the most treacherous season to travel on glaciers. Shallow, windblown, and unconsolidated snow hides crevasses without effectively bridging them. Too weak to hold body weight but too light to sag, such snow hides the evidence and increases the likelihood of walking into an unsuspected hole. Later in winter, the snow becomes deep enough that bridges can again support the weight of a climber or skier, and travel once again becomes safer, although soft bridges over particularly large crevasses can still pose a hazard.

Spring. This is the season when the winter's snowfall has reached its maximum depth. Travel can be arduous (unless you use skis or snowshoes), but the thick snow cover makes glacier travel safer than in the midwinter months. Crevasse bridges are usually at their thickest and most substantial, and the snow begins to compress and strengthen under the influence of warming weather. Crevasses that later in the summer cause long detours are in springtime so deeply buried that you might never even suspect their existence. Travel from one point to another can be very direct.

Summer. As summer advances, the snow becomes ever more dense. Early morning travel on well-frozen surfaces and strong snow bridges is as easy as it gets. However, bridges also grow thinner and eventually collapse in the heat of summer afternoons. Crevasses gradually open and become more visible, making them easier to identify and avoid but also harder to jump across. Travel becomes more complicated and time consuming; open crevasses can force long detours or cut across an entire slope and bar progress altogether. Some well-known climbs on heavily crevassed glaciers, such as Liberty Ridge on Mount Rainier in the northwestern United States or the Linda Glacier on Mount Cook in New Zealand's Southern Alps, notoriously become impassible mazes of large, wide-open crevasses, typically becoming impracticable by midsummer.

In the ablation zone, glaciers eventually lose all their snow cover (climbers sometimes call the bare ablation zone a dry glacier). Ice climbers love to practice technique on the short, safely approachable walls often found in ablation zones. Watch out for rocks poised above these walls, and stay clear of unstable seracs.

OTHER HAZARDS

Glaciers harbor other hazards in addition to hidden crevasses. Here we mention two more significant hazards of glacier travel: seracs and moulins.

Seracs

As mentioned in Formation of Glaciers, above, steep or complex acceleration zones cause crevasse walls to break up into detached towers and blocks known as seracs, which the slow, inexorable movement of the glacier eventually topples over.

The fall of a serac is usually a noisy affair—huge amounts of ice can sweep a large area far below or trigger snow avalanches. Since the precipitating mechanism is the movement of the glacier itself, its timing is random and unpredictable, following no pattern according to season, weather, or time of day. The hazard is constant, though limited in area.

From a distance, serac zones may be easily recognized by the messy appearance of jumbled ice, by sheer walls where flakes of ice calve off, and by rubble and blocks in the runout zone below. It's especially important to note and remember the location of seracs because evidence can be subtle when you are actually in a runout zone; deep new snow can smooth and mask the rubble; and complicated terrain or whiteout conditions can hide the seracs above. Be alert to such signs as hard-to-explain patterns of mounds and bumps in a relatively flat area or chunks and boulders of hard ice. Remember also that runout zones can extend a long way from the serac zone itself.

Falling seracs often give no warning at all, though a major serac fall is sometimes preceded by frequent collapses of smaller bits of ice from the same location. Be especially cautious if you see this happening.

Many popular climbing routes unavoidably pass through or below areas of icefall. Some such routes, while reasonable for descent, pose unjustifiable risks for the much slower pace of ascent. If there is no way to avoid the hazard, minimize your risk by limiting the time you are exposed.

Passing under a serac on Mont Blanc du Tacul, France. The hazards of ice towers such as this can be difficult to gauge. The presence of fresh debris is a sign that you should move quickly or find another route if possible.

Too often we see climbers stop for a break smack-dab in the midst of huge ice blocks, seemingly unaware of how those blocks got there.

Moulins

This peculiarity of lower ablation zones on some large valley glaciers can be a significant hazard. Meltwater forms swift streams on the bare ice, which converge with other streams, eventually becoming quite large and digging deep channels. When the rushing water reaches a weakness in the ice such as an old crevasse, it flushes down, swirling and drilling. The resulting hole is called a *moulin* (French for "mill"). Erosion and melting widen and deepen the hole, which can develop into a very impressive abyss. Often moulins become long-term features lasting several seasons in one place—in some cases they are even marked on maps. Large ones can be suspected from a distance by the frightening roar of the water flowing into them. The dire consequence of losing your footing upstream from a moulin emphasizes the need for care when crossing large meltwater streams! Crampons or even roped belays may be advisable. Moulins can be harder to discern in winter, when snow often bridges them.

PROTECTIVE SYSTEMS FOR GLACIER TRAVEL

On most glaciers, climbers face the combined risks of falling into crevasses, as well as simply falling down the hill if the slope is steep and icy. The basic protective system for managing the crevasse hazard entails the party roping up and moving together, prepared to arrest a crevasse fall and to extricate the unlucky victim. There are a number of variations to this theme, which we discuss in this section. The falling hazard may need to be managed by other strategies, such as those in Chapter 6, Snow and Ice. In many places, the hazards of hidden crevasses and those of simply falling occur simultaneously; in others, alternately. Managing these changing hazards requires flexibility of technique, ability to transition efficiently from one strategy to another, and recognition of the greater risk at any given moment.

In this section we discuss how to match the appropriate protective strategies to different levels of crevasse hazard—how to assess and manage the concurrent risk of falling down the slope, preparing for glacier travel, and team movement on glaciers.

TO ROPE OR NOT TO ROPE?

The hazard posed by hidden crevasses on a glacier is highly variable, as is the risk of falling. Realistic assessment of these risks can reveal situations in which it is justifiable and even preferable to travel unroped on crevassed glaciers, although this is not the norm. Deciding when, where, how, and whether to rope up depends on snow conditions, season, mode of travel, and size and complexity of the glacier. It's easy to imagine scenarios in which the risk of hidden crevasses is small enough and/or the relative benefits of unroped travel are great enough that not roping up is preferable.

To cite one common example, ski mountaineers normally do not travel roped, even on very large, heavily crevassed, and complex glaciers covered with soft winter snow. This decision is justified by several factors: skis provide vastly more flotation than boots and spread the weight more evenly; moving fast downhill over snow bridges reduces impact on them; and skiers often descend by the same route they climbed, allowing them to assess the terrain and note hazards to avoid on the way down. The clincher, in truth, is the extreme difficulty and unpleasantness of roped downhill skiing versus the euphoria of unroped skiing.

But even in summer mountaineering, crevasse risk on a glacier can often be negligible or even nonexistent. A snow-free, bare ice ablation zone in the late summer or autumn is an obvious example; here, the rope is almost never used except when you anticipate the need for a belay. Another example might be a short traverse across a compression zone on a small glacier with highly visible crevasses, early in the morning with a good cover of dense snow frozen hard after a clear night.

CONTINUUM OF RISK AND PREPAREDNESS FOR HIDDEN CREVASSES

To help make this decision process clearer, think of crevasse hazard as spanning a continuum, with different protective strategies used in response to different levels of hazard. We give four examples here to illustrate the issues and decision-making processes involved.

Risk: Zero

Conditions are a bare ice glacier, free of snow.

Level of concern about hidden crevasses

is nonexistent because all crevasses are visible. The chief risk is of falling above a crevasse and sliding into it.

The strategy: travel unroped, unless you think you will want to belay at some point, in which case you may choose to rope up and travel on a shortened rope, as described in Chapter 6, Snow and Ice. However, you may want to put on your harness in advance of need, if you will want it later for belayed climbing or more hazardous glacier travel; having it on makes a later decision to rope up easier.

Risk: Low

Conditions are dense summer snow in a hard-frozen, early morning state, after a clear night.

Level of concern about hidden crevasses is very low, because snow bridges are quite strong. You would have to virtually walk or fall straight into an open hole. This last concern is not negligible, however—such firm snow means a slide is very hard to arrest, so losing your footing above a crevasse or other hazard is generally the more serious risk. Also, the team may be traveling in the dark hours before dawn, making it harder both to assess and to steer clear of hazards.

The strategy: rope up so that you can quickly deal with increasing crevasse hazard that you anticipate encountering later, due to daily warming or different snow conditions higher on the glacier. Keep eyes and brain alert to changing sources and levels of risk, and adapt your team's movement accordingly:

- Among frequent open crevasses or bridges, you typically travel roped together 9–11 meters (30–35 feet) apart, carrying no coils or rope in your hands.
- In obvious compression zones or other crevasse-free areas, you may prefer to walk very close together with coils in your hands for sociability, speed, or pacing.
- On steep slopes, especially above hazards, you may choose to short-rope or belay.

Risk: Moderate

Conditions are softer summer snow. Note that the same snow described as "low risk" in the morning, could enter the "moderate" category later in the day when the surface is no longer frozen.

Level of concern about hidden crevasses is moderate; punching through a weak bridge or into a hidden crevasse is a real possibility. At the same time, concern about falling on steep ground is reduced because the softer snow is less slippery.

The strategy: rope up and travel together 9–11 meters (30–35 feet) apart, carrying no coils or loops of rope in your hands. Consider tying stopper knots in the rope between climbers (see Roped Travel Strategies below), especially with a two-person rope team, unless you anticipate the frequent need to belay. You also might want to preplace prusiks on the rope (also discussed below), but only if you are fairly sure you will not want to adjust your rope length or belay (in our continuum of strategies, we advocate using stopper knots first, reserving preplaced prusiks for when the risk is high).

Risk: High

Conditions are soft or weak snow covering a heavily crevassed glacier, as in winter, spring, or early summer conditions with very soft snow and unusually numerous crevasses; extensive, sagging, and weak bridges; and early winter conditions with new drifting snow thinly bridging crevasses.

Level of concern about poorly bridged hidden crevasses is very high. The chance of bridges breaking and of climbers plunging through them or stepping into unseen crevasses is high and may be hard to predict.

The strategy: rope up and travel together 9–11 meters (30–35 feet) apart, carrying no coils or loops of rope in your hands; tie stopper knots between climbers, and preplace prusiks or cordelettes on the rope to facilitate rescue in case of a crevasse fall.

Limitations of Protective Systems

A thorough discussion of crevasse risk would be incomplete without a reminder that crevasse falls are dangerous even when you are roped to partners well trained in team arrest and crevasse rescue. Opportunities for injury abound, even if everyone manages the rope competently and the party is able to arrest the fall immediately. Ice axes and crampons can cause injury; big chunks of collapsing snow bridges can collide with a falling victim. Crevasse falls on steep terrain can be very hard to arrest, even by a large team. Your primary source of security among crevasses is avoidance, not the rope or other protective gear. Develop your skills of crevasse detection and avoidance and you will probably never have to use your rescue skills.

ROPED TRAVEL STRATEGIES

As our continuum discussion above illustrates, the decision to rope up is followed by further decisions about how to rope up and how to move together. These depend on your relative assessment of the risk of crevasse falls versus falling on steep slopes. The steepness of the slopes, the consistency of the snow, and the skill level of rope team members all play a role in determining the risk of falling on steep ground.

Determining Fall Hazard versus Crevasse Hazard on Steep Terrain

Unfortunately, the risk of falling on steep ground and the risk of falling into crevasses are not best managed in the same way. Crevasse hazard is best managed by keeping 9 meters (30 feet) or more of rope between climbers, while steep terrain is best handled either by belaying each climber individually or by shortening the rope, for the reasons described in Chapter 6, Snow and Ice.

Since the relative seriousness of these two risks can change often, flexibility in shifting from one strategy to another is important. For example, the risk of falling becomes quite serious when you are traversing a steep slope above an open crevasse and may call for a switch to short-rope or belay mode. Once you are past the steep terrain, the greater relative importance of crevasse fall risk may suggest returning to a longer rope and crevasse protection mode. This is why it is not always best to preplace prusiks on the rope, because this slows down the process of lengthening the rope or moving into belay mode and may cause a party to stick with an inappropriate strategy when a change is needed.

Soft versus firm snow. Soft snow hides crevasses and forms weak bridges, making unexpected crevasse falls more likely but also making it easier to arrest the fall. Conversely, while firm snow makes snow bridges more reliable and therefore unexpected crevasse falls less likely, it also makes arresting a fall more difficult and sliding falls more likely. This means that in choosing the best rope strategy, the firmness of the snow is at least as important as its steepness; firm snow above an open crevasse may call for a shortened rope or belay mode even if the slope is only moderately steep, while deep and soft snow conditions in the very same place make a fall down the slope less likely and glacier travel mode more appropriate.

Climber skill. Consider the relative strengths and abilities of all climbing team members when deciding where to belay, where to short-rope, and where to move together in crevasse protection mode. For example, a climber who is good at identifying crevasses and avoiding them is less likely to step in one, but the same climber might be less practiced at climbing steep slopes—falling down a steep slope may be relatively more likely for that person. On the other hand, a climber who never falls on steep snow or ice but has little glacier experience may feel most comfortable staying in glacier travel mode even on steep terrain.

Each member of a rope team has unique strengths and weaknesses. Even if this does not always result in obvious answers for glacier travel strategy, simply thinking about these factors is a good habit and will yield dividends in general. For example, it is typically best for the strongest and most experienced climber to lead, at least uphill, but that person may be more useful in the rear on the descent, to provide greater arresting power whether on steep slopes or against crevasse falls. However, poor visibility or routefinding challenges may cause you to want the most experienced climber out front on descent as well.

Large versus small teams. In crevasse protection mode, a rope team of three or more climbers typically ties in closer together than a team of two because of their greater collective arresting power. Thus a larger team may choose not to change the length of rope between them when negotiating steeper slopes, whereas a team of two might prefer to shorten up for the steep climbing.

Roping Up

When roping together for glacier travel, the team faces a whole list of tasks and decisions. How many climbers will be on one rope? What is the preferred spacing between climbers? Should stopper knots be tied between climbers? When should prusiks be placed on the rope? The team then must tie in and distribute and stow the extra rope according to the chosen rope strategy, as well as determine what rescue gear to carry and how it should be distributed among the party. In the following section, we discuss each of these tasks and decisions.

Choosing the number of climbers per rope. From a purely selfish point of view, more people on the rope to arrest our fall and haul us out would seem to be better. But the more people on a rope team, the slower and more cumbersome its progress, especially on variable or technical terrain. Obstacles slow the group more with each added person—the whole rope team must wait or slow down every time anyone reaches the difficulty. Rope management, coordination, and communication all become more complicated.

Imagine a group of six climbers traveling together on a glacier. They can rope up in a single team, in two teams of three climbers each, or in three teams of two climbers each. What is the optimum rope team size? In deciding this question, consider the following points:

■ **How technical is the terrain?** In technical terrain requiring belayed climbing, a rope team of two moves much faster than a larger team, so multiple rope teams of two are preferable to fewer rope teams of three or more.

■ **How great is the hazard of hidden crevasses?** The greater this risk relative to technical challenge, the more desirable it is to have more than two people on the rope. A rope team of three is still fairly mobile but has much better crevasse fall stopping power than a team of two.

■ **How firm is the snow?** If it is very firm, the risk of falling on steep slopes will typically outweigh the risk of crevasse falls, and small teams are preferable—they can more nimbly change into belay or short-rope mode than can a larger team. Go for teams of two. Conversely, if the snow is very soft, crevasse falls become more likely relative to slips, and a larger team of three may be preferable.

■ **What are the relative and absolute skill levels of the team members?** A group containing one experienced climber and three beginners is probably better off as a rope team of four, while four highly skilled climbers will be safer (and happier) as two teams of two. Large rope teams of five or more are generally too cumbersome and slow to be desirable; the decision to travel in such a large team is usually the result of being unable to split into smaller groups because of insufficient skill on the part of some team members.

Choosing the preferred spacing between climbers. In general, it is best to put no more rope between climbers than is strictly necessary, even if it would give rescuers more time to arrest before going into the crevasse themselves. Tying stopper knots is a better strategy than lengthening the rope between climbers where there is doubt about arresting power or concerns about crevasse falls. More rope usually causes more problems than it solves; more stretch and inevitable slack mean the victim falls farther and harder.

More rope between climbers slows progress by making it harder to coordinate movements when negotiating obstacles.

For most glacier travel in a typical alpine setting, a distance of about 9–11 meters (30–35 feet) is appropriate for a party of two. Three climbers on one rope should reduce this to 8–9 meters (25–30 feet) between climbers, while a team of four should shorten up to 6–8 meters (20–25 feet).

Tying stopper knots between climbers. Stopper knots—a series of knots in the rope between climbers—are extremely effective in helping to stop and to hold a crevasse fall. Knots create friction as the rope saws through the crevasse lip, and they "cork" in the resulting groove. Stopper knots are commonly tied when there are only two climbers on a rope team and conditions indicate a significant concern about crevasse falls. Larger rope teams usually have enough arresting power to make these knots unnecessary.

One caveat with this strategy: the rescuer cannot haul the crevasse fall victim out on the same strand that took the fall. Just as the knots increase friction to help stop a fall, they also increase resistance to hauling, and it is practically impossible to pull the knotted and weighted rope up through the snow. The rescuer deals with this by dropping a new strand or loop to the victim before setting up the haul. This is not necessarily a drawback, as such "dropped loop" haul systems have many other advantages as well (see Crevasse Rescue later in this chapter).

The butterfly knot is the preferred stopper knot. Its bulk and roughness in contact with the snow provide maximum resistance both on the surface and in the groove. Tie four or five knots in the rope, distributing them more or less evenly along the strand between climbers (see Figure 79). Each knot will use up about a

Figure 79. *Butterfly stopper knots tied in the rope. You can see by the deep tracks that the snow is soft—and crevasse bridges are correspondingly weak.*

half-meter (2 feet) of rope, so calculate this into your measurement of the rope between climbers.

Tying in and distributing and stowing the extra rope. Whatever the number of climbers on your rope team, distribute them by first finding the middle, then measuring outward—the average adult "wingspan" equals 1.5–2 meters (5–6 feet)—and tying knots (figure eight on a bight) at the desired distance between climbers. Strive to end up with an equal amount of extra rope at each end. This extra rope, carried by the end climbers, will be available for use in setting up a hauling system in the event of a fall.

Following this method, each member of a two-person rope team using a 50-meter (165-foot) rope and traveling with about 9–11 meters (30–35 feet) between them will carry another 20 meters (65 feet) or so of extra rope, while a three-person team traveling with about 8–9 meters (25–30 feet) between them will have each of the two end climbers carrying 17–18 meters (55–60 feet) of extra rope.

Clip the figure eight knots directly to the belay loop of your harnesses using two carabiners, reversed and opposed, typically one locking and one nonlocking carabiner, as shown in Figure 80a.

An alternative method is to tie in to the ends of the rope and shorten up to the desired distance by taking in coils as described in Chapter 5, Alpine Rock (see Figure 80b). Just as in a rock context, this method allows you to quickly drop or take in coils and to transition easily between

short-rope, belayed climbing, and glacier travel modes as appropriate to different sections of the climb. Thus it may be a better solution for a party of two expecting pitched technical climbing, for example, when crossing a short section of glacier en route to a steeper ice climb (see Figure 81).

Placing prusiks on the rope. We use the term "prusiks" here to denote cord tied onto the rope using a prusik or other friction knot, for use in crevasse rescue or

Figure 80a. *A figure eight knot on reversed and opposed carabiners is the recommended tie-in, unless you are at the very end of the rope, in which case tie in directly through the harness belay loop using a figure eight followed through.*

Figure 80b. *Once you have clipped in, you may coil up the slack in lap coils and tie off as shown here, then put the whole package inside your pack. Stowing the rope in your pack eases strain on your back and neck but slows transition to belayed climbing.*

Figure 81. *Kathy and Mike, roped up for a short glacier approach to a technical climb. They have both tied in to the ends and shortened the rope, leaving about 9 meters (30 feet) out for the glacier section ahead. Low crevasse hazard permits them to skip the step of preplacing their prusik loops on the rope. Instead, they keep them handy on their harnesses.*

other rescue and backup applications. A detailed description of the use of prusiks in crevasse rescue appears in Crevasse Rescue, later in this chapter.

Prusiks can be kept handy and placed on the rope after a crevasse fall, or they can be placed on the rope in advance of need, at the moment the party ropes up to travel on a glacier. The latter is what most U.S. climbers have traditionally been taught to do, because it facilitates a transition to crevasse rescue. However, it has a potentially serious disadvantage in that it hampers a rope team's transition to belayed climbing or quickly changing the length of the rope, which in turn interferes with the decision to change roped travel modes even when that would be best. Crevasse falls being quite rare, this disadvantage arguably outweighs the advantages in most situations. We personally recommend placing prusiks in advance of need only when you are reasonably sure you will not need to change your rope length—for example, when traveling for long distances on continuously nontechnical glaciers or when you think the danger of a crevasse fall is high.

Distributing rescue gear. A precise list of the equipment needed to effect a crevasse rescue is given in Crevasse Rescue, below. Whatever the size of the rope team, this gear must be distributed so that there will always be enough outside the crevasse to establish an anchor, set up a hauling system, and extricate the victim. On a two-climber team, both climbers must carry enough to accomplish this single-handedly. On a larger team, each end climber should carry this same equipment, while climbers in the middle of the rope may carry only prusiks and a few carabiners for self-extrication.

Rope Team Movement

The first climber on the rope has the job of reading the terrain ahead, identifying hazards, and putting in a track that avoids them. The other team members have the job of protecting each other, especially the lead climber, from injury in case of crevasse falls, as well as hauling each other out. The entire rope team must work together to move efficiently and safely, minimizing wasted time.

Stepping over and end-running crevasses. When you encounter crevasses, it may be possible to step over them, or you may need to walk around them. As you approach a potential crevasse crossing, walk fairly close to the lip to gauge the extent and strength of the bridge and/or the width of the gap you must cross. You may want to ask your partner(s) to walk a different line from yours as needed to keep the climbing rope perpendicular to the crevasse (alert partners will anticipate this and do it without being asked). In any case, they should be watchful and ready to arrest in case the edge is less solid than you expect, and they should be particularly careful to minimize the slack in the rope while you investigate.

Stepping over crevasses can be simple when they are "crackers" (see Surface Expression of Crevasses, above), but approach them carefully until you can verify that the crevasse walls and lip edges are solid and not overhung or soft. If a hop or leap is necessary, make sure to pull enough rope forward to allow you to clear the gap. When your partner is crossing, pay attention and be ready to lunge forward to keep the rope taut as he or she leaps. If the route across the crevasse uses a diagonal fin, those not on the fin should position themselves to keep the rope perpendicular to the crevasse.

"Saggers" and open holes usually require more investigation to determine the strength of the bridge, the exact location of the crevasse walls, and the direction the underlying crevasse runs. Treat them with caution, but also with curiosity. As you approach the hole, bridge, or suspected crevasse, probe aggressively with your ice ax or ski pole. Clear snow away and enlarge the opening until you can actually see the orientation and extent of the crevasse; then, assuming it is not too wide and you have found solid footing on the far side, gently take a big step across. Make sure your partner knows to take a big step with you and not bring you up short. In the case of a hole punched into a bridge by another climber's foot, it is usually best to step right over it rather than walk around it into unknown territory.

If a gap is too big to jump or a bridge too weak to hold body weight, you must end-run the crevasse or find a place where it is narrow enough or bridged strongly enough to cross safely. Walk along near the edge, with your partner(s) following a parallel line away from the crevasse. If the crevasse seems to end, investigate from the side to see how wide a berth you need to give it. Also step to the side to investigate any bridge or fin crossings and gauge their thickness and strength before you commit to using them. Keep the rope taut when crossing suspect features.

Threading through crevasses. End-running several closely spaced parallel crevasses involves many direction changes. The task of coordinating the team's movements while minimizing slack in the rope can test both patience and attention span. Look backward along the rope frequently, and be ready to accelerate briefly, slow down, stop, or even back up if needed to keep things moving along. With

When threading through crevasses, try to keep the rope perpendicular to the slot to limit fall distance. Hell's Highway, Mount Shuksan, Cascades.

practice, this becomes somewhat automatic, requiring less explicit instruction among partners.

Belaying crevasse crossings. In crevasse protection mode, the rope team members serve as a moving belay for each other simply by means of controlling slack and being prepared to self-arrest. The vast majority of the time, this alone is sufficient to stop a crevasse fall. If you question your ability to stop your partner's fall with a self-arrest, establish a fixed belay. Belays can take a variety of forms, depending on the terrain and how strong an anchor is needed.

For example, imagine a team of two is climbing a steep slope and encounters a poorly bridged crevasse that must be crossed. The first climber is very well protected by virtue of the fact that the other is downhill—it is difficult to pull a body uphill against gravity, so a crevasse fall would be stopped immediately. However, the last climber to cross will be at greater risk. Here, gravity works against efforts to arrest a fall. There is a significant danger that if the last climber falls in the crevasse, his or her partner may be pulled in as well. In this case, a belay is not needed for the first climber but may be appropriate for the last.

When a belay is judged necessary, use the quickest snow or ice anchor that you are sure will hold the potential fall forces, but also consider what happens after your partner does fall in. You may have to transition into a hauling system, so it is preferable not to be integrated into the anchor but to belay directly off the anchor. For this reason, boot-ax belays and unanchored body belays are not appropriate for belaying crevasse crossings unless you have enough other people to build an anchor once you stop the fall.

Maintaining efficient teamwork. OK, so now you are roped up to your partner(s) and ready to head uphill. Manage the rope to minimize the distance anyone might fall into a crevasse should they step in, and to move along with as little fuss as possible.

Moving together can be a frustrating experience with the potential to waste a lot of time, or it can be a beautiful example of teamwork. Experienced rope teams display an almost telepathic efficiency of movement and nonverbal communication, flowing effortlessly and continuously through even very complex and problematic terrain. The key to good teamwork is anticipation. Climbers need to know in advance each other's needs and movements and respond appropriately as a unit to changing circumstances. Even though it is the leader who investigates potential hazards and chooses the route, those farther back on the rope should scan ahead of the leader to make necessary adjustments in their position or rope tension without being told.

Holding the rope. When going uphill or on level terrain, hold the rope to the person behind you in your downhill hand. (Since there is nobody behind the last climber, that person holds the rope in front.) Feel the amount of tension in the rope, and adjust your pace to maintain a constant light tension.

If walking downhill, all team members (except the first) hold the rope in front. Each person is responsible for keeping the rope from slithering downhill and entangling the climber ahead. Watch the feet of the person in front of you while controlling the tension on the rope.

Keeping appropriate tension. No one likes to be pulled off balance, dragged along, or jerked unexpectedly. With the right amount of tension in the rope, each climber can sense and readily adjust to the other's stops or starts. The ideal amount of tension has the rope lying on the snow with a gentle curve, out of the way of the feet (see Figure 82).

Figure 82. *The leader and second hold the rope behind them to help them adjust to their partner's pace without jerking or pulling each other off balance. The rope tension in this photo is just right for normal glacier travel. When crossing crevasses, tension should be increased. Grand Plateau and Mount Tasman, New Zealand.*

Climbers in the rear must work to keep the amount of slack in the rope so that their partner ahead will be able to feel their movements without pulling or tugging on them. Do not flip loose rope aside to avoid stepping on it—this is a clear sign that you are going too quickly for your partner and generating excess slack in the rope ahead. It can be difficult to stay alert to this on traverses, where gravity keeps the rope to the side whether there is excess slack or not.

On the other hand, the team can go only as quickly as the slowest team member, so if you find yourself tugging on the rope behind, you may just have to slow down.

Moving smoothly. All you need to know in order to move smoothly as a group can be summed up in two rules:

1. Do not generate slack in the rope ahead of you.
2. When the rope behind allows you to move forward without tugging, then go ahead, unless doing so would cause you to break rule number 1.

Rule number 1 means that you must pace yourself to the person in front of you. If that person slows down, you must slow down. If that person stops, wait for him or her. Look to see why the climber has stopped. If you see him or her probing in the snow or investigating a crevasse, back up a step to remove slack and be ready to arrest if necessary.

Rule number 2 means that if the person behind you stops or slows, you must stop or slow down as well. Maintain gentle tautness on the rope behind by pulling lightly on it. Once it begins to slacken again, return to whatever pace it allows.

With these two rules, it is the rope itself that tells you all you really need to know. Try to dispense with unnecessary verbal or visual communication by learning to "read" the message in the rope. When you can anticipate your partners' needs according to the terrain and/or the movement of the rope, everything begins to flow much more smoothly.

Making direction changes. When you are zigzagging uphill, changing direction requires stepping over the rope behind and reversing the ice ax hand and rope hand. This transition can be a real time waster if done poorly, but when it is done well, each climber makes the turn without even breaking stride.

Do not use wrist loops. Nothing is a more annoying waste of time than everyone having to wait while one person struggles to get a tight wrist loop off a jacket sleeve and glove gauntlet and transfer it to the new hand. This is also an insecure moment for the person, paused in a duck-footed position facing the slope, distracted from maintaining balance and footwork. It is much better to get used to keeping a firm grip on your ice ax and have faith in yourself! Practice an exact sequence of rope and foot movements at the corner, as follows, until you can manage it without breaking stride:

1. Step over the rope as you make your outside corner step, as shown in Figure 83a.
2. Then, using your rope hand to

guide the rope under your feet, carefully step over the rope again with the trailing foot, as you turn your body and take the next step in the new direction (see Figure 83b). Do not wait until you have turned, or the rope will wrap around your downhill leg and become much harder to step over. Do not try to flip the rope over your head; this is

Figure 83a. *Turning to the left while stepping over the rope. First identify the outermost step at the corner. Still holding the rope in the downhill hand, step over the rope as you take that step (the rope is between the climber's legs in this photo).*

difficult when traveling uphill because the rope behind runs downhill from you.

3. Next, switch hands quickly but carefully so as not to drop your ice ax. This hand switch should occur just after you have stepped over the rope with both feet and while you are duck-footed facing the hill. Drop the rope, switch hands on the ax, and pick up the rope with your new downhill hand (see Figure 83c).

4. Finally, step through in the new direction, as shown in Figure 83d.

When you are descending, the rope running behind you extends up the hill; in this case, flipping it over your head is usually easier than stepping over it. For a smooth direction change, flip the rope aggressively with a wide, arcing movement of your rope hand to clear the top of your pack. A slight amount of tension on the rope behind you helps, as does turning your back squarely to the person behind you as you make the flip. Flip the rope before you turn your body. Only when the rope has cleared your pack should you turn into the new direction and change hands.

Do not try this if you have trekking poles or skis extending above your head! In that case, you have no choice but to step over the rope.

Figure 83b. *Still holding the rope in the downhill hand, turn the left foot in the new direction, stepping over the rope with that foot as you do so.*

Figure 83c. *Without moving the feet, switch hands on the rope and ice ax. Notice the unusual hand position on the ax, in preparation for turning it in a new direction.*

Figure 83d. *The final step brings the climber back into balance. Replace the ice ax and carry on in the new direction.*

CREVASSE RESCUE

A bit of perspective is in order before beginning this discussion. Like self-arrest, crevasse rescue procedures are extremely important to understand and practice extensively—they can be hard to remember, and rescuers are usually under great stress. But the need to haul someone out of a hole is extremely rare in normal, summer season, midlatitude mountaineering. In all our many years of nearly year-round climbing and guiding, we have had to extricate only four climbers from crevasses—two were on rope teams of our own and two from other parties we encountered on the mountain. Three out of these four cases were what most climbers would describe as "stupid mistakes," glissading into an open crevasse or cutting a corner that everyone else walked around. We ourselves have never (knock on wood) fallen into a crevasse from which we had to prusik or be hauled out.

This fact leads us to a number of conclusions. First, though rare, crevasse falls do happen and the responsible climber must know how to deal with them. This requires repeated and ongoing practice. Second, climbers must learn to avoid crevasses through routefinding and observation. And third, carrying specialized gear specifically for crevasse rescue (such as pulleys or ascenders) is generally not worth the weight. More versatile, multipurpose tools such as carabiners, slings, and cordelettes will do the job.

Crevasse rescue is a complicated affair that can be accomplished by a variety of techniques and procedures. Your choice among these can depend on many variables, such as team size, available equipment, crevasse configuration, surface snow conditions, and the possibility of injuries. Read through the descriptions below and practice the techniques, then mentally change the variables to see how this might affect what you would do in an actual rescue.

EQUIPMENT CONSIDERATIONS

Every crevasse rescue scenario requires a strong anchor. In ice you will build an anchor with ice screws or bollards; in snow, most typically you will T-trench an ice ax, hammer, or picket. Soft snow will require burying something larger, such as a pack, a pair of snowshoes, or a pair of skis. Think about the conditions you will encounter and bring what you will need to build a solid rescue anchor.

On a typical glacier route in normal summer conditions, such as one of the easier routes on Mount Baker or Mount Rainier in Washington State, a party of two should carry the following gear:

- **Rope:** a 50-meter, 8-mm to 9-mm rope is enough to set up a dropped-loop rescue system (described below).
- **Ice ax:** this must serve both to climb with and to T-trench as a rescue anchor.
- **Snow anchor (sometimes):** usually we simply plan to use our ice ax as the anchor. When crevasse conditions are particularly nasty, we sometimes carry another form of snow anchor, usually a 60-cm-long (24-inch-long) picket. If a backup to a T-trenched ax

or picket is needed, you can bury a pack or other object.

- **Ice screws:** one per climber.
- **Single shoulder runners:** two per climber; these have many uses, from anchoring elements to friction hitches.
- **Double runners:** one per climber.
- **Cordelette:** one 5-meter (16-foot); this has two uses—for the rescuer to transfer the load of the crevasse fall victim to the anchor, or for the crevasse fall victim to fashion a foot loop for prusiking out.
- **Locking carabiners:** four (including the one used for the tie-in to the rope).
- **Nonlocking carabiners:** three.
- **Prusik:** one 30-cm (12-inch) loop of 6-mm cord, sometimes called a "harness prusik," for prusiking or as part of the haul system.
- **Optional gear:** sometimes a few luxury items can be justified. These might include a mini-ascender such as a Wild Country Ropeman, an autoblocking belay/rappel device such as the Petzl Reverso, or an extra picket. All of these can be replaced by using other gear, but they make their various jobs a bit easier.

This list is only a guideline. You must practice crevasse rescue in order to determine exactly what you will do, how you will do it, and how much equipment you will need. Develop a "what-if" plan, and know how your selected equipment fits into it. Be picky about what you bring on your climbs and carefully consider every item. Base your decisions on your practice sessions and what you learn from them.

CARRYING THE EQUIPMENT

Place rescue and self-extrication equipment on the gear loops of your harness when you rope up in crevasse protection mode, so that you can easily reach it after arresting a fall or while hanging in a crevasse. Carry pickets inside your pack. If you decide to place prusiks on the rope as you rope up (see Figure 84a), place the harness prusik farther from your tie-in knot than the cordelette. The cordelette can be stuffed into a pocket, or daisy chained and clipped back to a gear loop as shown in Figure 84b.

Figure 84a. *When placing prusiks on the rope, start by forming the prusik knot in the middle of the cordelette (already on the rope in this photo), then pass the cordelette in a bight through the belay loop as shown.*

Figure 84b. *The climber has daisy chained the rest of the cordelette and stuffed the ends out of the way, in her harness gear loop. Place the harness prusik on the rope and clip it through a locking carabiner in the belay loop as shown. The harness prusik is farther away from the climber than the foot prusik (cordelette).*

If you do not preplace prusiks, carry them on your harness, at the ready. The small prusik can be girth-hitched around a gear loop, the cordelette stowed on a gear loop (see Chapter 5, Alpine Rock).

INITIAL STEPS OF A CREVASSE RESCUE

The self-extrication and hauling systems described later in this chapter are only a small part of a successful crevasse rescue. Here we discuss tasks that must be done before actual extrication. The first steps of crevasse rescue include the following:

- stopping the fall
- coordinating the actions of the rescuers
- building an anchor and transferring the victim's weight to it
- assessing the situation

Stop the Fall

When someone falls into a crevasse, the rescuer is usually pulled off his or her feet and dragged toward the crevasse. If the person holding the fall has any warning, he or she should dive in the direction opposite the crevasse, eliminating slack (there should not have been much there in the first place) and absorbing the forces of the fall as the rope goes tight. In softer snow, the friction of the rescuer's body being dragged along the surface and of the rope cutting through the snow will eventually stop the fall. In hard snow, stopping can be tough. Stopper knots in the rope will help enormously here. Once the fall has been arrested, the rescuer should brace and kick in the toes well to establish a strong, stable position to hold the victim and prevent further slipping.

Coordinate the Rescue

In cases involving more than one rescuer, once the fall is stopped everyone should take a moment to determine who will do what. Normally the person closest to the crevasse continues to hold the victim's weight, while the next climber comes forward and builds an anchor just on the crevasse side of the climber holding the weight. However, circumstances may favor another course of action, such as the near climber building the anchor or the anchor being built farther away. Discuss and decide what to do, and be sure everyone in the team understands his or her role. Rescuers moving along the rope should self-belay with harness prusiks on the rope, especially if there are other crevasses in the area.

With only one rescuer on the surface, decision-making is much simpler, though the overall task will be harder. Call loudly for help if there are any other climbers about.

Build the Anchor and Transfer the Load

The anchor is the single most critical element in crevasse rescue, essential for the survival of victim and rescuer alike. The rescuer can do little else until a reliable anchor has been established and the victim's weight transferred to it.

The anchor must be unquestionably strong. In the case of a haul, it must potentially hold several times the victim's body weight. The rope over the crevasse lip generates significant friction, resisting a haul. The greater this friction, the greater the total load on the anchor. This is true no matter how much mechanical advantage is built into the system.

A crevasse rescue anchor can be any of the snow or ice anchors described in Chapter 6, Snow and Ice. However, a crevasse rescue scenario introduces particular problems and constraints. The best procedure will depend on whether there is a single rescuer working alone or a team of two or more rescuers working together.

Single rescuer. A single rescuer will have to continue to hold the victim's weight on the rope and build an anchor at the same time—not so easy as it sounds! The entire procedure is much easier if there are knots in the rope helping to hold the victim's weight. In the description below, we assume that the anchor you have chosen is a T-trench, either a picket or an ice ax.

1. Once you have stopped the fall and your feet are well braced, dig a T-trench near your head or shoulders. Be thorough, and make your trench long and deep enough to seat your picket or ax completely. Then dig the second slot where the girth-hitched runner will lie, toward the load.

2. Attach a runner to the object to be T-trenched, and seat it into position (see Figure 85a). Pack snow into your trench. Clip a Münter carabiner in to the load end of the runner.

3. If you did not preplace your cordelette on the rope, you must do so now. Tie a prusik knot, using the middle of the cordelette on the loaded strand of rope near your harness. Tidy it as best you can.

4. Tie your cordelette strands into the Münter carabiner on your anchor,

using a Münter-mule releasable knot, as shown in Figure 85b. Although the releasable Münter-mule tie-off has many advantages (and practicing it before you leave for the mountains will make it less time-consuming and overwhelming in this high-stress situation), it is not critical. If you can't deal with it, simply clip your cordelette in to the anchor carabiner and snug it up with a limiting knot. The critical thing is to attach the cordelette to the carabiner securely.

5. Once you have tied your Münter-mule knot, carefully back off your stance, easing weight gently onto the anchor. Watch the anchor for movement and your prusik knot for slipping. Then get more aggressive and give the anchor a good tug to be sure it is solid. Once you know it will hold, take a deep breath and say a prayer of thanksgiving that you are no longer pinned to the snow. Unclip your tie-in knot from your harness and untie that knot.

6. Tie a new figure eight on a bight or clove hitch, to back up the prusiked cordelette. Clip it in to the anchor using either the same locker the cordelette is in or another if you have plenty of carabiners.

7. Uncoil your stowed or coiled rope and place the smaller harness prusik on the unweighted strand of rope, near the backup knot you just clipped to the anchor. Clip this prusik to your harness belay loop

using a separate locking carabiner. This prusik will be your self-belay while you work (see Figure 85c).

8. If you are not already tied in to the very end of the rope, do so now.

9. Back up your original anchor if necessary. T-trench or bury a second anchor behind and slightly to the side of your original anchor. It should be close enough that you can attach it to your original Münter carabiner (the one with the Münter-mule). Equalize the two anchors as best you can.

You are now ready to go on to the next step: assessing the situation. But before we discuss that, we need to back up and describe how best to get to this same place with multiple rescuers working together.

Multiple rescuers. The same tasks must be performed as those just described, but more rescuers can make everything easier, faster, and more secure. Here's what to do:

1. The rescuer nearest the crevasse (rescuer number one) continues to hold the weight, alone if possible, until the anchor is built. This is his or her only task.

2. The next person along the rope (rescuer number two) ties his or her small harness prusik on the rope (if it is not already there) and clips it to the harness belay loop with a separate locking carabiner. This rescuer then unclips his or her original tie-in knot.

3. Rescuer number two carefully approaches rescuer number one, sliding the harness prusik along the

Figure 85a. *Seating the picket in the T-trench with the help of the ice ax.*

Figure 85b. *In order not to drop your friend in any farther, tie your Münter-mule as snugly as you can.*

Figure 85c. *Attaching the short prusik to safeguard the approach to the crevasse lip. The cordelette/prusik is backed up by the rope tied in a clove hitch to the anchor.*

rope as a self-belay. The prusik protects rescuer number two from hidden crevasses and also allows him or her to help arrest if number one has a hard time holding the load.

4. Remaining prusiked to the rope, rescuer number two builds an anchor between rescuer number one and the crevasse, preferably about 5 to 6 meters (15 to 20 feet) from the crevasse lip. In some snow conditions, a single T-trenched anchor may be adequate, but usually two anchors are built near each other and equalized.

5. Once the anchor has been built, a cordelette is attached to the load strand with a prusik knot and then tied in to the master point with a Münter-mule knot, as described in **Single rescuer,** step 4, above.

6. Rescuer number one carefully eases off and transfers the load to the anchor, as described in **Single rescuer,** step 5, above.

7. Back up the cordelette by tying a figure eight or clove hitch to the anchor with the unweighted rope, just as described in **Single rescuer,** step 6, above.

Both rescuers are now free to move about. Remember that anyone working near the crevasse edge must be belayed, normally via a prusik self-belay.

TIPS: THE MÜNTER-MULE RELEASABLE KNOT

The Münter hitch is a friction device for belaying and lowering (see Chapter 5, Alpine Rock). The mule knot is a reliable way of tying off a Münter hitch (or any other friction device). The advantage of the Münter-mule is that it can be released under load. This knot has many uses in a variety of rescue situations. Here's how to do it:

1. Start the mule knot with a twist. "Cradle" all four strands coming from the Münter hitch (see Figure 86a).
2. Pass a bight through the twist, as shown in Figure 86b.
3. Snug the Münter up to the carabiner and back it up with an overhand around the load strand (see Figure 86c).

Figure 86a.   Figure 86b.   Figure 86c.

Assess the Situation

The next task is to establish communication with the victim in the crevasse, to assess his or her condition and needs. In the worst case, you may need to haul your partner out, but other scenarios may be more likely. If unhurt, your partner may need only to be lowered a meter or so (a few feet) to a snow ramp or an easy exit on foot or may already be ascending the rope and need only a helping hand to surmount the overhanging lip. He or she may even be able to climb the crevasse wall with a belay. Look for the simple solution.

In assessing the situation, don't become another crevasse victim yourself. As you move back and forth and work near the crevasse lip, it is all too easy to screw up in the stress of the moment. Establish the exact location and orientation of the crevasse, and make sure no one approaches it without being attached to the rope and self-belayed from the anchor (see Figure 87).

1. Self-belay as you approach the lip by sliding the harness prusik in steps along the rope. It's a good idea to also tie a limiting knot in the rope at an estimated distance from the anchor, to stop you at the lip should it collapse under you and the prusik slip.

2. Approach the crevasse opening a bit to the side of where your partner went in. Don't knock loose snow right onto his or her head. Look down and call out to establish communication and to determine your partner's condition. Also give a warning if you need to knock away bits of the lip to see what's going on.

3. Decide on your next step. From this point, you have basically four options:

Figure 87. Approaching the crevasse lip to check on the victim. Use your short prusik to self-belay to the edge. The next step is to place padding under the haul rope to be lowered into the crevasse.

Wait for your partner to prusik out. With any luck, while you have been building the anchor, your partner has been busy ascending the rope with prusiks. All you may need to do is help him or her at the lip where the rope is cut in. Work together. Prusiking through a snow lip is harder than it looks. You may need to tie a small "rope ladder" using the extra slack rope, drop a loop with a pulley for a short haul, or use other imaginative options to help.

Lower your partner. This is a good option where there is an easy route out of the hole, within reach of your extra slack rope. If you were able to tie your cordelette to the anchor using a releasable Münter-mule knot, this procedure will be very simple:

1. Explain your plan to your partner, and note the distance you will ultimately need to lower him or her.

2. Return to the anchor, and make sure you have enough rope free to cover the required distance (if not, you have no choice but to haul instead).

3. Untie the knot in the rope that is backing up your cordelette. Replace that knot with a Münter hitch in the rope, built on a second locking carabiner clipped to the master point of the anchor. Get this Münter hitch as taut as possible and then tie it off with a mule knot.

4. Carefully release the Münter-mule knot on your cordelette, so that the new Münter-mule in the rope takes the weight, then remove the

cordelette. (**Note:** If you did not tie a releasable knot on the cordelette but simply clipped it in with a limiting knot, you will now have to cut your cordelette in order to transfer the weight to the Münter-mule on the rope. Snug up your Münter-mule on the rope to reduce all possible slack before you cut the cordelette. Be extremely careful with sharp blades near the loaded rope strand; ropes under tension slice alarmingly easily.)

5. Carefully release the mule knot and proceed to lower using the Münter hitch. Fight and reverse the rope's tendency to twist.

6. When the rope goes slack and/or you want to check on your partner's position or status, retie another mule knot. Self-belay back to the lip to check on things, using your harness prusik on the unweighted strand.

Repeat these steps as needed until your partner is able to walk or climb out of the crevasse. Belay him or her if necessary, using the same Münter hitch you used to lower.

Transfer to a belay. A simple and easy solution is climbing out of a crevasse using crampons and ice tools, when possible.

1. Discuss the option with your partner and agree on what you will do.

2. Return to the anchor, untie the backup knot in the rope, build a Münter hitch direct belay on the anchor, and immediately begin to belay.

3. Remove the cordelette if it gets in your way; otherwise, just loosen it and let it slide along the rope as you bring your partner in.

4. If your partner needs help at the lip, tie off your Münter hitch with a mule knot, set up your harness prusik self-belay in the slack strand of the rope, and go to the lip to help.

Transfer to a haul. If none of the above options are feasible, you will need to "haul off" and build a system to hoist your partner out. This is the most complex solution, and there are several possible variations. We discuss a number of alternative hauling systems in the next section.

CHOOSE A HAUL SYSTEM

A bewildering number of methods can be used to pull someone out of a crevasse. This section describes two basic systems, the dropped loop and the direct haul. Both of these have countless variations, options, shortcuts, and refinements, and this is where things can get complicated. Unfortunately, with crevasse rescue, a one-size-fits-all approach simply does not work. Each rescue is different. Rescuers must adjust their strategy to their exact situation. The best solution is to practice, practice, practice. As you become skilled in and comfortable with the procedures, you will be better able to adapt them to the real world. If our years of teaching crevasse rescue have shown us anything, it is that this ain't gonna be easy.

The most complex part of the task—the

actual mechanical advantage systems—can be practiced in your living room by tying a rope to a sturdy piece of furniture. The initial steps of catching and holding a fall, building an anchor, and transferring the load should occasionally be practiced on real snow to work out the inevitable glitches. A real crevasse is not needed for this; you can set up practice situations using small features such as ridges or snowplow-cut road banks, but it is important to generate realistic body-weight force and have the rope actually on the snow surface.

Dropped Loop versus Direct Haul

In a dropped loop haul, the victim is pulled out on a loop of rope dropped to him or her by the rescuer. One end of the loop is tied off to the anchor and the other end is the one the rescuer(s) pull on. The rescuer lowers the loop with a locking carabiner on it, which the victim clips to his or her harness. This method allows the rescuer to pad the crevasse lip carefully before lowering the loop, which prevents the rope from cutting into the snow under load.

In a direct haul, the victim is pulled out on a single strand of rope, usually the strand that held the fall. This is the system more familiar to most U.S. climbers and is still taught in many climbing schools. Though it is visually simpler than a dropped loop—probably the reason it is commonly taught—this initial simplicity comes at a price, usually payable at the lip where the rope cuts deeply in.

Dropped Loop System Advantages

Whenever a dropped loop system is possible, it is preferable to a direct haul, for several reasons. The main virtues of the dropped loop stem from the fact that a new loop of rope is lowered to the victim. This allows the use of stopper knots, which a party of two should seriously consider whenever crevasse hazard is high. It also allows the crevasse lip to easily be prepared to perfection and the unweighted rope padded before the haul strand bears weight, unlike the direct haul, which uses the strand that was weighted and cut in during the fall. Yet another advantage of a dropped loop system is that the victim (if uninjured) can make the hauler's job much easier by pulling down on one strand of the loop.

Another important reason to prefer the dropped loop is that this method significantly reduces the forces applied to the anchor, compared to a direct haul, even if the weight of the victim and the mechanical advantage applied are identical. The reason for this is that the coefficient of friction at the crevasse lip, a considerable source of resistance, is not entirely transferred to the anchor in a dropped loop system, whereas in a direct haul, it is.

The only potential disadvantage to a dropped loop haul is that there must be enough rope available on the surface to reach the victim, pass through a carabiner clipped to his or her harness, and run back up to the surface, with an additional 2 to 3 meters (6 to 10 feet) left over to build in a mechanical advantage system. This is not a serious drawback if the rope is distributed in a normal way (see Roping Up earlier in this chapter).

Direct Haul Advantages

A direct haul appears to be a simple and fast solution, but the rope cutting into the crevasse lip during the fall introduces serious problems. It means that stopper knots cannot be used; it increases friction and load on the anchor during the haul; and the victim can be pulled into the lip and "corked" when he or she reaches the point where the rope is cut in—overcoming this corking normally requires extensive snow excavation or other imaginative solutions.

The most common and sensible rescue situation in which a direct haul may be best is one in which there are lots of folks to pull and the rope is not too deeply cut into the crevasse lip. (**Caution:** If the victim corks at the lip and no one realizes it, a lot of people pulling can do harm; documented incidents have occurred resulting in injury, anchor failure, and death.)

MECHANICAL ADVANTAGE "FOR DUMMIES"

The simplest crevasse rescue systems require the most pulling force. Your basic 1:1 "system" (hauling straight out on the rope with no mechanical advantage) typically requires four or more burly guys and gals to haul a victim up and out with sheer brute strength, plus someone to monitor progress at the lip. With less muscle at hand, you will need a mechanical advantage.

In a frictionless world, using a 3:1 mechanical advantage system you would need to pull with a force of 30 kg to raise a 90 kg load. When you pull, one-third of the victim's weight is being held by you, with two-thirds transferred to the anchor. In a 5:1 system, you hold one-fifth and the anchor the other four-fifths. For better or worse, the world is not frictionless. The friction of the crevasse lip as well as the carabiners used as pulleys contribute to the load that must be overcome in order to raise your victim. In general, with a direct haul system, the forces the anchor must withstand are typically about twice the weight of the victim and his or her pack. With a dropped loop system, the load at the anchor is about 25 percent less.

With all this friction, the average fit person will find it hard, but just possible, to raise someone of equal weight using a 3:1 system if the rope is not too cut in, whereas a 5:1 or 6:1 system will make the pull feel much more manageable. With two haulers, a 2:1 or 3:1 system is often adequate.

BUILD A HAUL SYSTEM

We begin this part of our discussion assuming that the victim's weight has been transferred to a good anchor and the rescuer has checked out the fallen climber's status and decided that a haul is necessary. Regardless of the haul system to be built, the first task, before leaving the lip, is to prepare it carefully to reduce friction during the haul.

Preparing the Lip

Clear away loose or overhanging snow. If you plan a dropped loop haul, prepare the crevasse edge just to the side of where your partner fell in. This will reduce the amount of snow you knock down on him or her as you work. Pad the lip with a pack, an ice tool, or another preferably slippery object to keep the haul rope from cutting into the snow once you begin to haul. If using an ice tool, secure it somehow (clip it to a stuffed-in trekking pole or to the strand the victim fell in on, etc.) so you don't lose it into the hole.

If you are using a direct haul, you may have to do some excavating. Don't chop at the snow with your ax, because you can cut the rope under tension. After you remove necessary snow, place your chosen padding under the rope just above the edge and wrestle or kick the padding out closer to the lip where it will do some good.

Whatever haul system you choose, anticipate the task of getting your hapless partner over the crevasse lip at the end; this may be your biggest challenge of all. A three-part strategy seems to work best. First, plan to create loops of rope to serve as a ladder at the edge, and think ahead to how you will anchor this. Second, you will probably need to remove a fair bit of snow from around any cut-in rope strands (do not use sharp objects for this!). Last, your partner should try to push away from the crevasse wall at the lip, freeing the rope from the snow. Once hauling is underway and your partner is moving toward the surface, someone must either stay near the lip and monitor progress, or the hauler(s) need to stop now and then to check on things, to avoid corking or hauling the victim into sharp ice axes, etc.

Dropped Loop 2:1

This very simple system is a good choice for three or more haulers and may be sufficient for even just two. The system consists of a "pulley" (a locking carabiner alone will serve) on a loop of rope, dropped to the victim and clipped in to his or her harness. One end of the loop is attached directly to the anchor, while the other end is used for hauling. The hauling end can be attached to a ratchet at the anchor or on the anchor strand (see About Ratchets, below) to allow haulers to let go for a rest. For a very short haul, this step may not be necessary.

Dropped Loop 6:1

This is a single rescuer's best choice. The first step is to establish a dropped loop 2:1. Then it is quite easy to increase mechanical advantage to 6:1 and to add a ratchet. A ratchet is needed in this case; the hauler must be able to stop, let go, and reset the haul point in order to take multiple pulls. Build the system as follows, starting from the position where the victim is hanging from the rope tied off to the anchor.

1. Create a loop with a locking carabiner clipped to it, as shown in Figure 88a. One end of the loop is the strand tied to the anchor; the other is "free" but

tied to the rescuer's harness to avoid accidentally dropping it in and losing the carabiner.

2. Drop the loop to your partner, as shown in Figure 88b. Instruct your partner to clip the carabiner in to his or her harness belay loop, and watch to see that it's done correctly and the carabiner is locked. Also check that there are no twists in this loop.

Figure 88b. *The loop is dropped to the victim, running over an ice ax to pad the crevasse edge. Anchor the ax to prevent it going into the hole and adding injury to insult! Be extra careful using crampons near the weighted rope.*

Figure 88a. *Creating a loop to drop to the victim. The end of the rope is tied in to the rescuer, both to prevent losing the end into the crevasse and to be used as a safeguard later. A locking carabiner is placed on the rope to be lowered to the victim.*

Figure 88c. *Extend the anchor point toward the crevasse. In this photo, a garda knot is assembled as the ratchet. The knotted rope on the left is the rope on which the victim fell into the crevasse.*

Figure 88d. *The completed dropped loop 6:1. The rescuer can now begin hauling.*

3. Tie a figure eight on a bight in the down strand (the one coming from the anchor) about 3 to 5 meters (10 to 15 feet) from the crevasse lip. This is where you will build your mechanical advantage system. Essentially this extends the anchor and creates a new master point closer to the crevasse.

4. Bring the up strand (the one coming from the crevasse) back to this new master point and clip it through a ratchet there (see About Ratchets, below), as in Figure 88c.

5. Place a prusik on the up strand as near the lip as you safely can, to create a "tractor point," then clip the haul strand exiting your ratchet to a carabiner at the tractor point as shown in Figure 88d, and you are ready to haul.

Direct Haul 3:1

This fast and simple system, also known as a Z-pulley or Z-drag, will almost certainly be too strenuous for a single rescuer, but it does offer enough mechanical advantage for two or more rescuers to use it efficiently. Build it as follows:

1. Back at the anchor, untie the figure eight knot or clove hitch that you used to back up the Münter-mule on the cordelette. Run that same strand of rope through a separate carabiner "pulley."

2. This system also requires a ratchet to prevent the rope sliding back down once you begin hauling. The cordelette can stay in place and serve as the ratchet, or you can place a new ratcheting device, such as a Tibloc (as shown in Figure 89), garda hitch, or autoblocking belay device (see About Ratchets, below).

3. Just as in the dropped loop 6:1 system, finish by placing a small harness-prusik tractor as near the crevasse lip as is practical and safe, then run the haul strand down from your ratchet and through a carabiner in this tractor. As you haul, watch the ratchet device to ensure it holds before you ease off to reset the harness prusik for another pull.

Figure 89. *A 3:1 direct haul system, using a Tibloc as the ratchet. Two rescuers can usually raise one victim with this system. The cordelette (to the right) has become slack and requires managing, or you can remove it, making it available for other uses.*

Adding Mechanical Advantage to a 3:1 Direct Haul

Mechanical advantage can be added to this system in a number of ways. It is common to add a 2:1 system, thus creating a 6:1 mechanical advantage system. We prefer a 5:1 system (see below), for three reasons.

First, in the 5:1 system there is only one prusik to reset periodically (a 6:1 direct haul requires two), so hauling is faster.

Second, a 5:1 system is more efficient. As a proportion of the friction inherent in the system, more mechanical advantage is preserved in a 5:1 system than in a 6:1.

Finally, in a 5:1 system, the load on the rope at the ratchet during hauling is roughly half that in a 6:1 system. This expands the range of ratcheting devices that can be used, because some devices add a great deal of friction if the rope is heavily loaded as it passes through them. When this strand is less loaded, the additional friction is dramatically reduced. For example, both the garda hitch and the autoblocking belay device are very effective, self-regulating ratchets, but they have a very high coefficient of friction. Reducing the load on the rope going into these devices reduces the problems this friction causes.

Direct Haul 5:1

Now that we have recommended this system so highly, here is how to build it. Note that the order of the various steps in this system is slightly different from those described so far.

1. Start as in the 3:1 system by placing the small tractor prusik and carabiner near the crevasse lip, but do not put the haul strand through this prusik. Instead, what goes into this prusik is a fixed length of cord coming from the anchor. You can use a portion of the rope, a second cordelette, or even a double runner. Anything will do, so long as it is at

least about 2 meters (6 feet) long. For convenience, we call this cordelette number two.

2. Clip the free end of cordelette number two into the anchor and then through the tractor prusik.

3. Now untie the knot you previously tied in the rope to back up the original Münter-muled cordelette, and place this rope through a "pulley" carabiner at the master point—this strand now becomes your haul strand (see Figure 90a). Build a ratchet for this pulley and eventually remove the first cordelette; or, again, the Münter-muled cordelette can stay in place and continue to serve as the ratchet.

4. Run the haul strand exiting the ratchet through a carabiner tied to the other end of cordelette number two, as shown in Figure 90b. The strand exiting this carabiner is your haul point.

5. Haul and reset, periodically checking on your partner's position and progress.

Figure 90a. *Converting a direct haul 3:1 to a 5:1 system. The cordelette (loose, in this photo) will "trade places" with the rope passing through the tractor. Finish as in Figure 90b.*

Figure 90b. *Complete 5:1 direct haul system using a Tibloc as the ratchet. We show a second cordelette in use here, but you could also use the free end of the rope or even a double runner.*

About Ratchets

As the name implies, a ratchet allows the rope to pass one way through a pulley, but not the other way. The ratchet can be either a prusik knot, a Tibloc, a Ropeman, a garda hitch, an autoblocking belay device, or another device. A variety of devices can be used for ratchets at the master point pulley (see Figure 91). Each device has its own peculiarities, which can make one preferable to another in different situations.

Prusik or Klemheist knot. A prusik knot is nearly always an acceptable option for a ratchet. Its main advantages are versatility: you almost always have the necessary tool (a small loop or cordelette of 6-mm or 7-mm cord). Another strong point is that it does not inherently introduce any more friction into the system. Finally, it is possible to switch from raising to lowering when using a prusik, something not so easy to do with other ratchets.

One disadvantage to a prusik ratchet is that it may slip or jam if you don't manipu-

late and supervise it. Being pressed into the snow, it can behave unpredictably and may not immediately grab when weighted. Each time a hauler wants to let go and reset, the hauler or someone else must push the prusik down the rope toward the load and ensure it grabs again. The prusik knot also can ride up the rope and jam into the pulley or pop through the carabiner.

The Klemheist is very similar to the prusik and has many of the same pros and cons. It is a better choice than a prusik when you lack cord but have webbing. It is a bit harder to loosen than a prusik, and for this reason it is not the best choice when both options are available to you (see Figure 92).

Tibloc. The Tibloc is a small mechanical ascender made by Petzl. Though it too bears some watching, it is somewhat more likely than the prusik to grab correctly on its own when the hauler(s) wish to release the rope, and it adds virtually no friction to the system.

The Tibloc's main disadvantage is that it

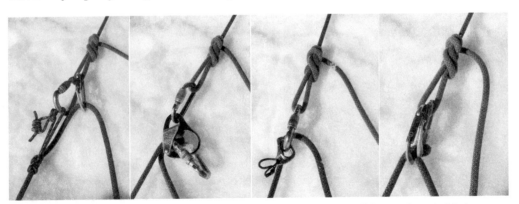

Figure 91. *Various ratchets (left to right): prusik, Reverso plaquette, Tibloc, and garda hitch*

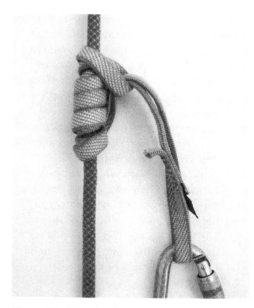

Figure 92. *The Klemheist is a good alternative to the prusik when you need to use webbing instead of nylon cord for a friction hitch.*

friction to the system. It should therefore be used only in systems in which the load on the strand entering the ratchet is reduced. This means it is effective in all dropped loop hauls or a 5:1 direct haul, but it is not a good choice in a 3:1 direct haul or a 6:1 direct haul (commonly found in some texts but not described here).

Second, it is easy to rig incorrectly and is rarely used in other contexts, so it has the potential to create uncertainty and doubt and requires a bit of practice. Finally, it is all but impossible to release a loaded garda, so transferring to a lower is complicated.

To rig a garda hitch, run the rope through two nonlocking carabiners as shown in Figure 93. These carabiners must

is an extra piece of gear to carry and one that has few or no other applications beyond crevasse rescue and self-extrication. Also, transitioning to a lower is harder when using a Tibloc than with a prusik.

Garda hitch. The garda hitch is made by looping the rope through two nonlocking carabiners. Like the Tibloc, the garda hitch is more reliable than a prusik (less likely to slip as it is reloaded). Unlike the Tibloc, it requires no specialized equipment and very little monitoring. It does have a few disadvantages, however.

First, if the rope being pulled through it is heavily loaded, the garda adds a lot of

Figure 93. *The garda hitch. The load strand is the one on the left.*

295

both be the same size and shape (modified D is best). Take the strand on the nonload side and loop it through the carabiner on the load side a second time.

Autoblocking belay device. An autoblocking plaquette style belay device (see Chapter 3, Preparation and Equipment) is probably the most trouble-free ratchet of all. Since it serves other functions, you are likely to have it with you in any case on a typical climb. Like the garda hitch, however, it adds significant friction in a high load situation, so the same limitations apply: use it only in a dropped loop haul or a 5:1 direct haul. It, too, is difficult to release under load, so transferring to a lower is problematic.

DESCENDING INTO THE CREVASSE

Certain unfortunate circumstances may force you to descend into the crevasse yourself; for instance, if your partner was unroped or needs first aid.

Before you descend, think about whether you have enough rope for a dropped loop system or will need to use a direct haul, because this will guide your actions inside the crevasse. If your partner is "corked" in a narrow crevasse, it is most important to raise him or her a few feet before doing anything else. The warmth of a human body will melt the texture of clothing and equipment into the ice and make it harder to break the victim loose, so the sooner you can budge the fallen climber, even just a little bit, the better. Even if you know you must use

a dropped loop system eventually—for example, because there are knots in the rope—you may still want to try to move your partner up half a meter (a foot or two) with a direct haul before you proceed any further. If you must descend into the crevasse:

1. Leave the backup figure eight knot or clove hitch in place at the anchor and arrange your rappel on the same strand with which you self-belayed to the crevasse lip. Set up a rappel device and backup on your harness (see Rappelling in Chapter 5, Alpine Rock). The backup is not optional in this case! You will need both hands free when you reach your partner.

2. Place a pack or other object at the lip, something large and rigid enough that the rappel rope will stay on it and not dig in. Otherwise you will have great difficulty getting out again.

3. Make sure beforehand that you have adequately cut away the overhang and cleaned up the lip so that the snow won't shift or collapse under this padding. If you are worried your padding might move or fall off the lip, secure it by tying it back to another anchor such as a dedicated picket or buried object.

4. Tie in to the end of your rappel strand, or tie a stopper knot to prevent rappelling off the end. If your partner is hanging free, tie this stopper knot just beyond the

distance you think you will need to reach him or her. If you err in this estimation, it is better to tie the knot too low than too high, because it will be very hard to untie it if you carelessly rappel onto it before you reach your partner.

5. Put on your crampons.

6. Begin your rappel, carefully backing over the lip to keep the rope running over the padding and to keep the padding from shifting. When you reach your partner, ease onto your backup to free your hands.

7. If your partner is injured, deal with any injuries as best you can, but be realistic! You cannot work miracles, and the most important task is to get your partner to the surface as quickly as possible. Try to stabilize the victim in a more upright position with an improvised "chest harness," as follows: Thread a shoulder runner through the shoulder straps of his or her pack. Tie a limiting overhand knot to get this as tight as possible, and clip a carabiner in here. Clip this carabiner in to the rope the victim is hanging on (if planning a dropped loop system, you will also need to run the dropped loop strand through this carabiner before you leave).

8. Once you have done what you can to help your friend, consider your hauling system before you ascend the rope. If you are using a dropped loop system, the strand you rappelled in on will become part of your dropped loop. Clip this strand (below your device, where it is unweighted) in to your partner's belay loop with a locking carabiner, being sure to also run this loop through any "chest harness" you might have created for him or her.

9. **Important!** Before leaving your partner, untie the stopper knot you used to protect yourself on the way down! Otherwise this knot will greatly complicate your hauling system later on.

10. Take from your partner any additional gear he or she has that you might need on the surface. Dress the victim warmly if needed and reascend the rope (see The "Texas Kick" Rope Ascending System, below).

11. Back on the surface, build your haul system and haul away. Take particular care that your partner does not jam at the lip.

SELF-RESCUE: WHEN YOU FALL IN

Not hurt? Good. Take a deep breath and look around. Crevasses are beautiful things and you may not get another chance for such an intimate view. Look to see if you can climb or walk out. You will need to decide what to do in a few minutes— prusik, climb out, or walk out. Also, if you are injured, you will have to factor this into your action plan.

Remove Your Pack and Secure Your Equipment

Your first task is to remove your pack and secure it. The simplest method is to girth-hitch a runner to the haul loop behind your neck and then clip that into the climbing rope, just above your tie-in knot. You can then simply take off the pack and let it hang from the runner.

If you had an ice ax or trekking pole in your hand when you fell in, chances are you dropped it. If you did not, secure it to the pack now.

The "Texas Kick" Rope Ascending System

There are many ways to ascend a rope, and some may be faster or less strenuous than the one we describe here, the Texas Kick. However, the Texas Kick is fairly simple, always works, and can be set up using the harness prusik and your cordelette.

Once you have dropped your pack, get out your small harness prusik loop and tie it to the rope with a prusik hitch. Clip this in to the belay loop on your harness, using a dedicated locking carabiner, not the same one you have used previously to clip in to the rope.

Attach your cordelette to the rope, also using a prusik hitch. This one goes between your harness tie-in knot and the harness prusik that you already tied. Tie a limiting overhand knot lower down in the cordelette, about 0.5 to 1 meter (2 to 3 feet) from where it attaches to the rope. This is the rung of your ladder, where you will place your foot (see Figure 94). Your ladder rung for your foot must be fairly short, so that standing in it gets you up fairly high compared to your harness prusik. Experiment to find the best length—this is shorter than you might think.

"Inchworm" up the rope, alternately standing on the cordelette to unweight the harness prusik and move it up the rope, then hanging on the harness prusik to unweight the cordelette and move it up the rope. Practice this at home by hanging a rope from a tree or some other safe and strong anchor. A few pointers:

1. Standing up in the ladder rung while loosening and raising the harness prusik can be strenuous. Start by getting your foot tucked right underneath your rear end, then straighten your leg while holding yourself in with your arms. This is much easier than starting with a straight leg and hauling up with your arms.

2. Hold yourself close in to the rope by hooking one elbow around it. Use your other hand to loosen the harness prusik and slide it up the rope. Slowly weight this prusik, watching it to make sure it grabs the rope without slipping.

3. Sit back down in your harness, relax, then loosen your foot prusik and slide it up as high as you can. Prop your feet on the crevasse wall to help unweight the prusik and get it as high as possible.

4. Repeat.

If you are quick, you may be able to ascend almost all the way to the snow lip

Figure 94. *Prusiking: Kathy has hung her pack on the rope with a garda hitch on a runner. This puts all the pack weight on the anchor and helps her to move the prusik knots up the rope.*

prusiks on the rope and begin climbing. Not only will it make the hanging less painful, it will help keep you warm and take your mind off morbid thoughts! Try not to be too violent in your efforts, however; you don't know what stage your partner has reached in holding your fall, building the anchor, setting up a haul, etc.

Placing an ice screw to "park" on. If you can easily reach the sidewall of the crevasse and if it is hard ice, you can help your partner a great deal by placing a single ice screw in the wall and clipping in to it with a runner or cordelette. This will reduce the danger of slippage while your partner is setting up the anchor. Of course, your partner can't know that you are doing this and will set up the anchor as if both your lives depend on it in any case.

Once your partner begins to haul, you will have to unclip quickly before he or she hauls you out of reach of your ice screw. Don't worry if you aren't able to get the screw out and have to leave it—it's a small price to pay, and if your partner is hauling you that quickly, you can be thankful indeed!

Assisting a haul. If you are being hauled out on a dropped loop system, you can help a great deal and stay warmer by pulling on the "down" load strand while your partner(s) haul on the "up" load strand.

before your partner has set the anchor and come to check on you. The rope will have cut into the lip, so at some point you won't be able to climb any farther without help from above. As you climb over the lip, you will have to extricate the original strand from the groove it has made. Use the shaft of your ax to gouge out the snow around the rope. Avoid using the adze to chop, because you can easily cut the weighted rope!

Even if your partner has everything well in hand and is quick in setting up a haul, it is still worth your while to set up your

WHAT NEXT?

When the fallen climber is out of the crevasse at last, you are once again a happy and reunited party! You may or may not be out of the woods; it depends on your problem list at this point. Injuries obviously have to be addressed right away and might require further first aid, evacuation, a call for a rescue, or a dip into the emergency rum barrel for a little stress relief.

The victim will probably be cold and doubly stressed. While rescuers were kept warm by running around and hauling for their lives, the victim was in another world. He or she was hanging in the shade, showered by snow and dripping water, probably wearing inadequate clothing since everyone was exercising vigorously before the crevasse fall; plus the victim's circulation was hampered by hanging in a harness. Do whatever you can to help get your partner warm again, especially if there was an injury or if the weather is nasty. Brew up a hot drink if possible, have something to eat (preferably strong, rich cheese), and add or change clothing.

Finally, have a look at what your partner fell into. Look around for surface clues that might have hinted at its hidden dangers. Learn from mistakes.

CREVASSE RESCUE PRACTICE

All of the essential skills can be efficiently practiced in a "mock" crevasse: any snow feature with a solid bottom, a vertical wall at least 3 meters (10 feet) high, a more or less level work area on top, and a snowy lip. The work area should allow a snow anchor to be built. Large wind scoops are often ideal. Watch out for other hazards, such as rockfall, real crevasses, or large blobs of snow that might fall on the victim. Though climbers occasionally practice crevasse rescue in real crevasses, consider this only if you have a guide or very experienced partner whose only job is to observe and advise and who is not a member of the rescuing team. If you use a real crevasse, always build a separate bombproof backup belay anchor. Use this and a separate rope to belay the victim, and also back up the rescue anchor.

Practice both single and multiple rescuer scenarios. Time yourselves; 30 minutes is a reasonable time from "jumping in" to having the victim back on the surface—20 minutes is even better. On guides' exams, candidates usually have to rappel into a crevasse, build an improvised chest harness to keep the victim upright, and prusik back up before beginning their haul. They get about 40 minutes to do everything, they have a limited (but reasonable) selection of gear, and they can't afford any mistakes (such as neglecting to lock carabiners). Go for it—see if you can beat them!

Appendix A. Guides Associations

The International Federation of Mountain Guides Associations (IFMGA, also known as UIAGM and IVBV) is an international organization containing the national guides associations of more than twenty countries worldwide. The IFMGA sets standards for the training and certification of mountain guides. Member countries' national training and certification programs must meet the international standard.

In many IFMGA member countries, only IFMGA certified guides may legally conduct professional mountain guiding. This is not the case in the United States. The American Mountain Guides Association is a member of the IFMGA and provides guides training and certification programs at the international standard. However, only a minority of American guides have participated in these programs as of the time of this writing. Most of these guides are certified in one or more disciplines: alpine mountaineering, rock climbing, or ski mountaineering. Certification in each discipline entails a series of courses followed by an in-the-field examination lasting several days. Only guides certified in all three disciplines are IFMGA certified. See the AMGA website listed below for an explanation of its training and certifica-

tion programs and for a listing of American certified guides.

Listed below are the guides associations of the main Alpine countries (France, Italy, and Switzerland) and those of the English-speaking member nations (Canada, Great Britain, New Zealand, and the United States). Other member associations are Aosta, Austria, Germany, Japan, Norway, Peru, Poland, Slovakia, Slovenia, South Tyrol, Spain, and Sweden. For information about these countries, contact the IFMGA Secretary:

Armin Oehrli, Secretary
IFMGA/UIAGM/IVBV
Phone: + 41-33-744-54-10
Email: *ivbv-uiagm@bluewin.ch*
www.ivbv.info

NATIONAL GUIDES ASSOCIATIONS

CANADA

Association of Canadian Mountain Guides
Box 9341
Canmore, Alberta T1W 2V1
Canada
Phone: 403-678-2885, Fax 403-609-0070
Email: *acmg@acmg.ca*
www.acmg.ca

FRANCE

Syndicat National des Guides de Montagne
210, rue François Guise
F-73000 Chambéry
France
Phone: +33 (0) 4-79-68-51-05
Fax: +33 (0) 4-79-68-65-90
Email: *sngm@wanadoo.fr*
www.sngm.com

GREAT BRITAIN

British Association of Mountain Guides
Siabod Cottage, Capel Curig
Conway, North Wales LL24 0ET
United Kingdom
Phone: +44 (0) 1690-720-386
Fax: +44 (0) 1690-720-248
Email: *bmg@mltb.org*
www.bmg.org.uk

ITALY

Collegio Nazionale Guide Alpine Italiane
Via Petrella 19
20124 Milano
Italy
Phone: +39-02-2941-4211
Fax: +39-02-2941-7650
Email: *guidealpi@tiscali.it*
www.guidealpine.it

NEW ZEALAND

New Zealand Mountain Guides
  Association Inc.
Executive officer, P.O. Box 10
Aoraki, Mount Cook 8770
New Zealand
Phone and fax: +64-3-434-2355
Email: *info@nzmga.co.nz*
www.nzmga.co.nz

SWITZERLAND

Schweizer Bergführerverband
Geschäftsstelle Hadlaubstrasse 49
CH-8006 Zürich
Switzerland
Phone: +41-1-36053-66
Fax: +41-1-360-53-69
Email: *sbv@awww.ch*
www.4000plus.ch

UNITED STATES

American Mountain Guides Association
PO Box 1739
Boulder, CO 80302
USA
Phone: 303-271-0984
Fax: 303-271-1377
Email: *info@amga.com*
www.amga.com

Appendix B. Rescue

We hope you will never need to rescue or be rescued. In our more than 25 years of climbing and almost as many years of guiding, we have had little need, thankfully, to execute or call for rescues, even for other parties. Still, it is important to be prepared and to have a clear idea of your priorities—just in case.

Most rescues are trivial affairs. Someone sprains an ankle and has to be carried out piggyback; someone strains his or her back and you have to carry his or her pack. In a rare instance, you may be called upon to take part in a more complex rescue scenario. Whether you must take charge or merely help out, the following should help you make the best use of available resources while avoiding added risk.

INITIAL STEPS

KEEP CALM

Whenever you approach an accident or injury, your first priority is to maintain a calm state of mind in which you can weigh options and risks while keeping the big picture in mind. Nothing is so urgent that you can't take a moment to breathe and collect yourself before acting.

SAFEGUARD YOUR PARTY

Your primary duty is to safeguard yourself and those not yet injured. The best of intentions don't justify risking other lives, including your own, for the sake of someone who is already hurt. Something bad has happened to that person; don't make it worse.

Look first for signs of ongoing hazards before you move in to check out the accident and injuries. If rockfall, avalanche, or other hazards threaten further injury to either the victim or rescuers, you may need to seriously consider the wisdom of attempting a rescue at all. If you do proceed, you may have no choice but to move the victim to a safer place, no matter what injuries he or she might have sustained, and to do so as quickly as possible. If the hazard no longer exists, take your time and do not move the victim unnecessarily.

Rescue situations are often inherently stressful and confusing for everyone involved. People tend to neglect their own safety as they focus on the injury or accident. Careless mistakes are more likely than usual. Protect yourself and others by expecting this and taking preventive measures. When on exposed terrain, even if it is easy ground or a large ledge, make sure that everyone is anchored in or otherwise secured.

DECIDE WHETHER TO SELF-RESCUE OR SUMMON OUTSIDE HELP

A helicopter rescue or competent evacuation by a search and rescue team—if readily available—can save lives and improve outcomes. However, in many cases, such outside help will be slow to reach you or less competent than you are. Depending on the degree of the victim's injury, you may be able to evacuate the injured person more quickly or effectively without outside help.

In deciding whether or not to self-evacuate, compare the quality and timeliness of outside help with your own resources. Consider also the impact on the injury and the safety of the party.

SUMMONING OUTSIDE HELP

If you decide to seek outside help, there may be various ways to get it.

Send a Note Out

You can send one or two of your group out with a note and instructions for a rescue party (see Convey Crucial Information, below). Do not rush this effort: before the messengers leave, make sure they know exactly what they must accomplish and exactly how they will accomplish it. They may need to take the map; do you have another? If not, note down all necessary information about your location before you relinquish any maps.

Use a Phone or Radio

In an emergency, use your radio or cell phone judiciously. Your spouse, parent, and boss will truly appreciate hearing that you will be delayed and that they don't need to panic. However, batteries have limited lives. Conserve them when possible. Be sure you know the phone numbers or radio frequencies you need (also see Chapter 3, Preparation and Equipment).

Create a Signal

If you do not have a cell phone or radio, if there is no one you can send out, and if you are within view of a trail, road, or—possibly—other people, signal for help. Good signaling devices include flashlights, camera flashes, mirrors, flags, surveyors tape, etc., or you can shout or whistle to be heard.

The universal distress signal used in the mountains is six signals per minute followed by a minute of pause, then repeated. The universal reply is three signals per minute, a minute of pause, then repeated.

If you are spotted by an airplane or helicopter, signal to those on board. Both arms lifted in the air in a V signals the need for a rescue. One arm up and one arm down signals that no rescue is needed.

Convey Crucial Information

A rescue party will need certain information from you. Anyone you call or radio will need the following information; messengers going out for help should write down this information and take it out with them when they leave.

- **Your exact location:** give a clear and unambiguous description. If you lack unmistakable landmarks, give the grid reference of your location (see Global Positioning System in Chapter 4, Routefinding and Navigation). Better still, provide both.
- **The time the accident occurred:** as near as you can determine.
- **How many people were involved**
- **The nature of all injuries**
- **Vital signs for all the injured people:** monitor these periodically, and also indicate any changes you observe.
- **Any anticipated problems:** or anything that may get worse, such as hypothermia.
- **What you think you will need:** does the person need to be carried out on a stretcher? Will the terrain allow that? Can the victim ride out on horseback? Are medical attention and a helicopter necessary?

HELICOPTERS

Helicopter rescue capabilities vary greatly throughout the world. Many alpine areas, most notably in Europe and the Canadian Rockies, have developed mountain rescue with helicopters to an impressive degree, and you can be plucked via winch or sling from even very steep and technical terrain where the helicopter cannot land. Other areas may not be as well set up for this, and you will have to get to reasonably flat terrain where the helicopter can land and the victim can be loaded on board and flown away. It will help if you know how to prepare for the arrival of the helicopter, how to behave around it, and how you can help the pilot.

PREPARE FOR THE HELICOPTER'S ARRIVAL

Identify a possible landing zone. It should be flat and big enough to accommodate the rotor disc (the circle described by the spinning rotor) without the rotors getting too close to the ground, trees, etc. A rotor disc is typically 11 to 14 meters (35 to 45 feet) in diameter. A helicopter must always be approached from downslope or on level ground, never from above, where the spinning rotor disc is near the ground and hard to see. For this reason, landing zones in hollows with only rising ground surrounding them are not a good choice.

The pilot needs an idea of wind strength and direction. To help him or her discern this, rig a wind indicator out of lightweight material or surveyors tape tied to a stick, tree, or cairn. If necessary, prepare the site by flattening snow. Rotor wash is very powerful; remove, tie down, or anchor any small packs or other objects that could blow away. Protect the injured person's face from flying dust and debris. Put on glasses or goggles so that you'll be able to see the pilot. Everyone except the victim, and any others necessary for the victim's support, should stay well away from the landing zone. Make sure everyone who will approach the helicopter knows basic safety rules (see below).

TAKE PRECAUTIONS WHEN THE HELICOPTER GETS THERE

As the helicopter approaches, stand or crouch on or near the proposed landing site with your back to the wind. As the helicopter descends, crouch or kneel and do not move until the pilot signals you to do so. Do not be surprised if the helicopter lands very close to you; this is common. When working with helicopters, make sure everyone knows and follows these simple safety rules:

- Do not rush. Move calmly and deliberately.
- Do not approach the helicopter until signaled to do so by the pilot.
- Never approach a helicopter from the rear or from upslope.
- Carry packs and all other equipment in your hands and below the waist— nothing should extend above your head.
- If a hat or anything blows away, let it go!

If you are not to board, then after loading the injured party, move away from the helicopter (toward the front!) and crouch again. Do not move until the helicopter is in the air and on its way.

CARRYOUTS

Alas, most of the time you will have a much less thrilling and glamorous prospect: that of carrying a victim out yourself! Carrying someone piggyback style can be very taxing on steep ground or for any distance, but if the nature of the injury allows it, this may be the fastest and easiest option. Taking turns with another rescuer, you can go a long way without stopping much. Another

fast and simple solution, lacking other options, is to simply drag a victim for a short distance, if you are on snow. A couple of other methods may be more useful for carrying a more seriously injured person or for handling greater distances.

COIL CARRY

Use the rope to create a "backpack" in which to carry a victim, as shown in Figures 95a and b. Carrying a victim on your back is not easy. Take lots of breaks. On steeper terrain, use another rope and

Figure 95a. *Building the coil carry. Make large, round coils, shoulder-to-ground length, and tie off the ends.*

Figure 95b. *Twist the coils into a figure eight and wear it as in this photo. Note the location of the coil tie-off, just in front of the shoulder, below the clavicle. The victim's legs will go through the opening on either side of the hips. Add a sternum strap with a sling and carabiners for more comfort.*

two belayers to arrange quick belays for protection.

LITTER CARRY

Another option for carrying a seriously injured person is to create a rope litter. Try to re-create the macrame shown in Figure 96. Carrying a person in a litter is exhausting. You will need a dozen or more people to move anybody a significant distance. Be sure you have sufficient help before you commit to a plan involving a litter carry.

RESCUE INSURANCE

Rescue is expensive, especially when it involves helicopters. In some parts of North America, National Park or Forest Service personnel do the rescuing. Taxpayers normally foot the bill in these areas. In other places, local volunteers carry out rescues, which are usually free of charge to the injured party.

In many other countries, climbers pay

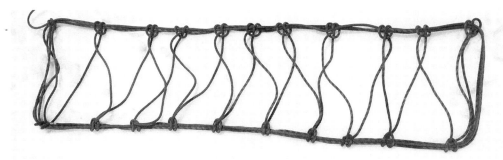

Figure 96. *The ends of the zigzags are clove hitches, through which the rope is passed as you create the rail. Place padding under the victim for comfort and to give the stretcher more rigidity.*

307

for their own rescues. In the Alps, where professional rescue is readily available, the victim typically pays. However, good rescue insurance can be purchased at a very reasonable cost, with coverage lasting several days or a year. Ask in the tourism office or guides bureau of any mountain town.

COMMUNICATION

In the United States, the Federal Communication Commission (FCC) regulates radio communications, and many commonly used frequencies require a license. Other countries have similar restrictions. In spite of this, in a true emergency, do whatever you have to do regardless of regulation.

Anyone with a ham license (or without it in an emergency) can use the range of 2-meter band frequencies (144 to 148 MHz) dedicated to amateur radio operators. Repeaters maintained by ham clubs greatly expand the range of handheld radios. Most repeaters are open for any licensed amateur to use, and the Internet lists many regional frequencies. Amateur radio operators are always happy to help anyone in need. A ham license is easy to obtain by passing the required exam. Study up, pass your test, and get your call sign. It's fun.

Government authorities, huts, and other local operations also use frequencies that you may be able to reach in an emergency, but they lie outside the legal amateur range. Transmission on these frequencies is blocked on most 2-meter band radios sold in the United States, though most radios can be modified to allow transmission. Such modification is illegal but may be ethically justified because of the possibility of emergency need. Government agencies are understandably protective about the frequencies they use, so it may be very difficult or even impossible to find out what they are. In some areas, local guides may be able and willing to help you.

In some climbing areas around the world, use of 2-meter band handheld radios is quite common, and calling out for help with them can be fairly easy. In the main climbing areas of the Alps, the entities responsible for rescue monitor certain frequencies, and these are readily available by asking or from the Internet. The French mountain rescue agency is called the Peloton de Gendarmerie de la Haute Montagne (PGHM). In Switzerland, several individual helicopter companies conduct rescues. Look under REGA, Air Glacier, or Air Zermatt for phone numbers and radio frequencies.

Bottom line: if at all possible, carry something with which to call for help. If you carry a radio, get a ham license and be sure to note down any useful frequencies, repeaters, government agencies, etc., before you head into the hills. If you carry a cell phone, find out whether or not there is adequate cell coverage in your climbing area to make it useful, and know the appropriate emergency response phone numbers.

Appendix C. Rating Systems

Throughout the world, several different systems are used to describe climbs and to rate their difficulty.

NORTH AMERICAN RATING SYSTEM

The North American rating system is relatively simple and includes two types of information: the technical difficulty of the hardest move or pitch and how long the climb normally takes to accomplish.

TECHNICAL DIFFICULTY

In the North American system, the technical difficulty is called the class.

Class 1	Hiking.
Class 2	Hiking on very rough, though generally not very exposed, ground, such as scrambling in talus and boulders.
Class 3	Scrambling on exposed, broken terrain. Most climbers either solo on class 3 or move together on a shortened rope (see Chapter 5, Alpine Rock).
Class 4	Climbing usually with short belayed sections, but also occasionally roped but moving together.
Class 5	Technical, high-angle climbing, usually belayed; this class is further broken down into decimals from 5.0 to 5.15.

North American climbers also use difficulty ratings for waterfall ice (WI) and for mixed climbing (M). The designations WI 2–WI 9 indicate the maximum technical difficulty on water ice, assuming "good" ice conditions, while M1 to M10 (and higher) indicates the difficulty of a mixed ice and rock pitch. Alpine mountaineering routes very rarely get an ice rating any harder than about 5. The systems used for rating waterfalls and mixed climbs are reasonably consistent throughout the world. A grade 4 waterfall in Banff is about as hard as a climb of the same rating in Colorado, France, Scotland, or New England.

LENGTH

In the North American system, the length of the technical portion of a climb is known as its grade. Expressed as a roman numeral, it indicates the amount of time a competent party will take in good conditions.

Grade I	several hours
Grade II	about half a day
Grade III	most of 1 day
Grade IV	1 long day
Grade V	1–2 days
Grade VI	more than 2 days

The North American system works well for pure rock or waterfall ice climbs, but without a more detailed verbal route description, it does not adequately indicate the overall difficulty of an alpine route. Difficulty in the mountains includes such factors as commitment, risks, complexity of routefinding, difficulty of placing protection, amount of moderate ground, and vertical distance to be covered.

FRENCH ALPINE RATING SYSTEM

The French system, widely used outside the United States, does a better job with the complicated factors of the alpine environment. Its increasingly widespread use suggests it may become the international language of the future for guidebook rating systems.

The main distinction between the North American and French rating systems is that the French includes a seriousness rating, as well as a description of overall technical difficulty. The seriousness rating, expressed as a roman numeral, denotes such things as remoteness, possibility of retreat, difficulty of the approach or descent, and objective hazards.

SERIOUSNESS

I   A short, relatively safe route; little belaying needed; not remote; with an easy descent.

II About 4 to 6 hours of climbing; usually some belayed pitches; skill in routefinding and hazard recognition required; descent may involve rappels or technical climbing; few objective hazards.

III A longer route, requiring most of a day; extensive belaying; possibly remote or difficult to retreat from; tricky descent.

IV A long day with much technical terrain; requires very good skills, experience, and fitness; complex descent; some objective hazards.

V   A long, committing route, sustained and often remote; retreat difficult; potential for significant objective hazards.

VI A very long and difficult route that can be completed in 1 day by only the best climbers; difficult technical climbing with tricky or minimal protection; retreat entails danger; serious objective hazards.

VII Harder still. Like grade VI above, but longer. The best climbers take several days on these routes.

OVERALL DIFFICULTY

The overall difficulty rating describes the amount of technical climbing and the degree of difficulty.

F   Facile—Easy: Easy climbing, little or no belaying, well protected. May involve crevassed but straightforward glaciers.

PD Peu Difficile—A little difficult: Moderate climbing, usually requires some belaying, possible rappel on descent. Exposed scrambling, crevassed glaciers.

AD Assez Difficile—Fairly difficult: Belayed climbing, in addition to large amounts of exposed but easier terrain. A wide range of protective systems are needed.

D   Difficile—Difficult: Climbing at a fairly high standard. D routes either involve many hundreds of meters of moderate climbing or a harder but shorter route.

TD   Très Difficile—Very difficult: TD routes usually have very long sections of hard climbing. Climbers need to move very fast and be very efficient to keep to guidebook time.

ED   Extrêmement Difficile—Extremely difficult: ED routes are further broken down into ED 1 to 4. The 1938 route on the North Face of the Eiger is considered ED 2.

TECHNICAL DIFFICULTY

The French technical difficulty rating, like the North American class 5 decimal system, is the simplest and easiest aspect to quantify. It indicates the hardest technical moves on a route. For rock, it uses the numbers 1 to 9, subdivided by the letters a, b, and c. The chart below compares the French technical difficulty rating to the North American technical difficulty rating.

French	North American
2	4th class
3	5.0–5.3
4a	5.4
4b	5.5
4c	5.6
5a	5.7
5b	5.8
5c	5.9
6a	5.10a
6b	5.10c–d
6c	5.11b
7a–c	5.11d–5.12a
8a–c	5.13b–5.14b
9a	5.14d

The technical difficulty of alpine ice is described by indicating the angle of maximum sustained steepness. If the angle is more than about 55 degrees, routes are often given a waterfall ice difficulty rating, using the same numbers as the North American water ice and mixed rating systems.

FRENCH ALPINE RATING SYSTEM EXAMPLES

A typical rating for an alpine climb will include any of the above information deemed relevant to the ascent. For example, the Traverse route on Mont Blanc involves more than 1370 meters (4500 feet) of ascent and 2400 meters (8000 feet) of descent on large, crevassed glaciers, with some moderately steep snow or ice slopes to 45 degrees and 3rd-class rock on the descent. It also involves high altitude; the summit is more than 4800 meters (15,770 feet) high. It is rated III PD +, 45°.

The Southeast Arete on the Index, also in the Chamonix area, is a six-pitch rock climb. The hardest moves are equivalent to about 5.7 in the North American rating system, but most of the climbing is much easier 5th class. A 30-minute walk and easy scramble from the top of a chairlift gets you to the start of the climb, and the descent is a long rappel followed by some 3rd- and 4th-class down-scrambling. It gets a rating of II, 4b.

To bring this closer to home for the North American climber, we have rated some familiar climbs using the French system.

Tetons

- Grand Teton, Exum Route: III, AD-, 4 (rock)
- Black Ice Couloir: IV, D, 4 (ice/mixed) 60°
- Irene's Arete: II, AD+, 5c

Sierra Nevada

- Mount Whitney East Buttress: III, AD, 5a
- Mount Whitney, Mountaineers Route: II, PD-, 2
- Mount Sill, Swiss Arete: III, AD-, 4
- North Palisade, U-Notch Couloir: III, AD, 3 (rock), 45° (snow/ice)

Cascades

- Mount Baker, Coleman Glacier: II, PD-
- Mount Stuart, North Ridge: III, D-, 4c
- Forbidden Peak, West Ridge: III, AD-, 3
- The Tooth, South Face: I, PD, 4c

Canadian Rockies

- Mount Louis, Kain Route: III, AD+, 5a
- Mount Athabasca, North Face: III, D-, 4 (mixed) 55°
- Mount Robson, North Face: IV, D+, 3 (ice) 55°

NEW ZEALAND ALPINE RATING SYSTEM

Ever independent, New Zealanders have developed their own overall difficulty rating system for the Southern Alps. This system uses a number, augmented with the occasional plus or minus sign. For the difficulty of the hardest move on a route, the Kiwis use the Australian rock system, rating routes with a number from about 10 for very easy North American 5th-class rock to somewhere about 34 for the hardest climbs.

NEW ZEALAND ALPINE RATING SYSTEM COMPARED TO FRENCH ALPINE RATING SYSTEM

NZ 1 = F/PD-
NZ 2 = PD/AD-
NZ 3 = AD/D-
NZ 4 = D/D+
NZ 5 = TD
NZ 6 = ED

Glossary

Abalakov anchor—A type of ice anchor made by drilling intersecting holes into the ice, then threading and tying a section of nylon cord or webbing. Invented by the Russian climber Vitali Abalakov, these anchors are commonly used as rappel anchors.

ablation zone—The area of a glacier below the firn line where annual summer snowmelt exceeds the winter snowfall.

acclimatization—The process by which the body gradually adapts to the decreased oxygen of high altitude.

accumulation zone—The area of a glacier above the firn line where annual winter snowfall exceeds summer snowmelt.

acetazolamide—A drug that has been shown to help reduce the symptoms of acute mountain sickness (AMS) by increasing respiration.

ACMG—Association of Canadian Mountain Guides.

aiming off—A whiteout navigation technique of deliberately erring slightly off-course in order to intercept a handrail or other identifiable feature that can be followed to the desired destination.

air mass—A large parcel of air extending over hundreds of kilometers, fairly homogeneous in temperature and moisture content.

AMGA—American Mountain Guides Association.

acute mountain sickness (AMS)—A common group of symptoms caused by too rapid ascent to high altitude.

antibotte—A plastic or rubber plate that fits into the frame of a crampon to prevent wet or sticky snow from balling up under the sole of a climbing boot.

application—Using the right technique, at the right time, in the right place.

arête—The French term for ridge, usually designating narrow and sharp ridges of snow or rock.

ataxia—Impairment of balance, a common symptom of high-altitude cerebral edema (HACE).

autoblock hitch—A friction hitch characterized by easy release under load.

autoblocking belay device—A class of plate-type belay devices useful for direct belays off the anchor, where the rope runs freely in one direction and locks in the other direction. Some models are also useful for rappelling and belaying the leader. Also known as a plaquette.

beacon, avalanche—A radio transceiver allowing rescuers to locate buried avalanche victims.

belay loop—A closed nylon loop incorporated in the design of many climbing harnesses, used for belaying and rappelling.

bergschrund—The highest crevasse of a glacier, where the glacier ice pulls away from the permanent snow and ice plastered to a steep wall above.

black ice—Dirty, dark, and usually very hard, old ice.

bollard—A type of ice or snow anchor built by chopping a mushroom- or teardrop-shaped groove. The rope or a sling is placed in the groove and used as an anchor. Most commonly used as a rappel anchor.

butterfly knot—A knot tied on a bight of rope to create a small loop.

cairn—A human-made pile of stones usually marking a route, summit, or key location.

clinometer—A device used to measure the angle of the slope, often incorporated in some compasses.

clove hitch—An adjustable hitch most commonly used to clip in to an anchor.

col—A high pass.

cold front—Cold air displacing warm air. Often associated with squally weather and thunderstorms; usually followed by improving, if chilly, weather.

compass bearing—The compass direction from one point to another.

compass heading—The compass direction in which you are currently traveling.

compression test—A snowpack bonding test that uses downward force applied to an isolated column of snow via a shovel blade to measure resistance to collapse.

compression zone—A part of a glacier where the angle of the underlying bedrock lessens and the glacier decelerates and compresses.

contour tangent method—A whiteout navigation technique using change in fall-line direction (the contour tangent) as an aid to determining location on a map.

convective lifting—The force causing an air parcel to rise as long as it is warmer than the surrounding air.

cordelette—A 5-meter length of cord used in anchor building and rescue systems.

coriolis force—A force whose effect is mostly seen on large, slowly moving systems such as weather systems or ocean currents. The coriolis force is the result of the earth's spin in combination with its roughly spherical shape.

cornice—A snow lip overhanging the lee side of a ridge; formed by the wind transport of snow.

couloir—The French term for "gully," which applies to narrow or broad gullies as well as narrow, concave ice faces.

"cracker"—A type of open crevasse characterized by sharp, clean, and well-defined edges. Climbers can safely walk right up to the edge of "crackers" to inspect or step over them. Contrast to "saggers."

cyclonic lifting—The gentle lifting of air in the center of a low-pressure system.

cyclonic storms—The storms that typically accompany low-pressure systems.

daisy chain—A runner-strength loop or webbing sewn with many small loops, used to clip in to anchors. More commonly used in aid climbing than mountaineering.

declination—The deviation between true north (the geographic north pole) and the magnetic north pole, as measured from a particular location.

dexamethazone—A steroid that can be used to treat high-altitude pulmonary edema (HAPE) in an emergency. Used in conjunction with descent.

direct belay—A belay in which the friction-generating device is attached directly to the anchor. When a second is belayed with a direct belay, the fall force is transmitted directly to the anchor, not to the belayer.

dry glacier—The snow-free lower part of a glacier, where all of the winter's snow has melted off and all crevasses are open and visible.

easting—The first segment of numbers in a grid reference; defines the east-west axis of a location. *See also* northing.

ERNEST—An acronym applied to anchor building; stands for **E**qualized, **R**edundant, **N**o Extension, **S**table and Secure, and **T**imely.

figure eight follow through—A knot commonly used to tie a climber in to the end of a climbing rope.

fireman's belay—A method of protecting a rappeller by pulling on the ropes from below.

firn—The German word for "névé." *See also* névé.

firn line—The theoretical line dividing the accumulation zone and the ablation zone.

fishermans bend, single and double—A knot used to join two ends of rope.

flat figure eight—A variation on the flat overhand.

flat overhand—A knot commonly used to join the ends of two rappel ropes.

foehn wind (chinook)—A strong, warm, downslope wind on the lee side of a mountain range, typically occurring during periods of heavy precipitation on the windward side.

foot penetration—The depth to which a weighted foot sinks into the snow. Used in conjunction with other observations as an aid to assessing snow stability.

French technique cramponing—A method of cramponing in which the soles of the boots are kept roughly parallel to the ice.

frontal lifting—The lifting of warmer air as it is pushed up and over cooler air in a front.

garda hitch—A hitch made with two carabiners. The garda hitch acts as a ratchet, allowing the rope to be pulled through in one direction but not the other.

girth hitch—Commonly used to attach a sling to a tree or to join two slings together to make one longer sling.

"global" technology compasses—Compasses that employ a specific type of compass needle that allows them to be used in both the northern and southern hemispheres. Compasses without this will function well in only one hemisphere.

graupel—Rimed snow crystals, often round, typically associated with cold fronts in the mountains.

grid reference—The coordinates used to define a specific location.

guidebook time—The amount of time a party competent for the route will take without making significant routefinding or application errors.

high altitude cerebral edema (HACE)—Swelling in the brain caused by maladaptation to high altitude. A dangerous condition that can be fatal if left untreated or ignored.

ham radio—Also known as amateur radio, ham radio refers to a range of radio frequencies assigned in the United States by the Federal Communications Commission (FCC) for noncommercial, civilian use by amateur radio operators.

handrail—Any linear feature that can be identified on a map and followed in the field.

High altitude pulmonary edema (HAPE)—The dangerous buildup of fluid in the lungs caused by maladaptation to high altitude. A dangerous condition that can be fatal if left untreated or ignored.

hectoPascals (hPa)—A measure of air pressure; 1 hPa equals 1 millibar. Average sea-level air pressure is about 1013 hPa.

high—An area of relatively high air pressure characterized by stable, clear weather.

HMS carabiner—A large locking carabiner with a broad curve at the gate opening end. Designed for use with the Münter hitch and for use as a master carabiner. Also called a Münter or "pear-shaped" carabiner.

hyperbaric chamber—A portable, airtight bag in which HAPE or HACE victims can be placed for treatment. Air is pumped in to simulate a lower elevation. A Gamow bag is one example.

IFMGA—International Federation of Mountain Guides Associations. An international organization whose members include most of the national guides associations around the world, of which the ACMG and the AMGA are examples.

in-balance position—A stance on a slope in which the foot of the uphill leg is forward and above the downhill foot.

katabatic winds—Cool, downslope winds caused by sinking cool air. Common on large valley glaciers.

Klemheist—A friction hitch commonly used with webbing; functions much the same way and in the same applications as a prusik knot.

known point—A designated map location selected as an intermediate as part of a route plan or whiteout navigation plan.

lapse rate—The rate of temperature change in a rising parcel of air. Dry air changes at about 10° C per 1000 meters of elevation gain or loss, while saturated air changes at about 6° C per 1000 meters.

LED headlamp—More energy efficient than headlamps that use incandescent bulbs, though the light-emitting diode (LED) typically is not as bright.

lenticular cloud—A lens-shaped cloud formed when water vapor in the air condenses into a cloud as it is forced over mountains.

low—An area of relatively low air pressure that typically gives rise to cyclonic lifting, frontal systems, and unstable, wet, or stormy weather.

mailon—*See* quick link.

marginal crevasses—Crevasses that form on the edges or margins of glaciers, formed by the tensile stress created by the faster-moving center ice "pulling away" from the slower ice at the edge of a glacier.

master carabiner—A carabiner used at the master point of an anchor to which other carabiners can be attached.

master point, anchor—In a complex rock or ice anchor, the single point at which the various anchor components are joined. The master point is also typically the clip-in point.

melt-freeze metamorphism—A gradual process whereby snow grains on the ground become transformed through alternating warm daytime temperatures and nighttime freezing into rounded, icy grains.

meridian lines—The lines inside the circular housing of a compass that designate true or grid north.

millibar (mB)—A measure of air pressure. *See* hectoPascals (hPa).

moat—The gap that forms between a rock wall and a snow slope, formed by creep of the snow downhill as well as by melting of the snow from the relative warmth of the rock.

moulin—A hole in the ablation zone of a glacier where running surface streams drop into the bowels of the glacier.

moving together on a shortened rope—A technique for shortening the rope and carrying it with tied-off coils in order to efficiently carry the rope on easy terrain and keep it ready for a quick transition to belayed climbing.

mule knot—A hitch used for tying off ropes in a way that allows them to be released under load. Often used with the Münter hitch.

Münter carabiner—*See* HMS carabiner.

Münter hitch—A hitch that provides friction for belaying or lowering. Often used with the mule knot.

Münter-mule—A Münter hitch tied off with a mule knot. Useful in rescue, in which a heavy load can be managed with the Münter hitch but also needs to be tied off in a releasable manner.

névé—This term is used to describe several things: the snow above the firn line of a glacier, in the accumulation zone; the dense melt-freeze metamorphosed snow typical of summer in the alpine regions, on or off a glacier; in some areas, also a common term for a large accumulation basin high on a glacier, usually relatively flat and crevasse-free. Also known by its German term, firn.

nifedipine—A drug frequently used to treat hypertension that is also useful for the emergency treatment of HAPE. Used in conjunction with descent.

NOAA weather radio—Periodic weather bulletins and forecasts continuously broadcast by the National Oceanic and Atmospheric Administration in the United States on dedicated radio frequencies, usually in the 162-mHz range.

northing—The second segment of numbers in a grid reference; defines the north-south axis of a location. *See also* easting.

occluded front—A cold front that has overtaken a warm front. Occluded fronts usually appear similar to warm fronts.

orographic lifting—The lifting of air as it is forced by wind to rise over mountains and ridges.

out-of-balance position—A stance on a slope in which the foot of the downhill leg is in front of the uphill foot.

periodic breathing—A benign but bothersome symptom of incomplete acclimatization to altitude in which normal breathing rhythm is disrupted during sleep.

pieds à plat—A French term meaning "feet flat." A general term for flat-foot cramponing technique.

pied en canard—A French term meaning "duck-footed." A flat-foot cramponing technique used on moderate slopes.

pieds troisième—A crampon technique used on moderately steep terrain, with one foot sideways and the other on front points.

piolet—French for "ice ax."

piolet ancre—A French term meaning "ice ax anchor." A secure technique for steep ice in which the ax is swung and placed overhead with the pick digging into the ice.

piolet appui—A French term meaning "ice ax support." A group of three ice ax techniques—piolet manche, piolet panne, and piolet poignard—useful on moderate to fairly steep terrain.

piolet canne—A French term meaning "ice ax cane." An ice ax position used for support on low-angled slopes.

piolet manche—A French term meaning "ice ax shaft." An ice ax technique for firm snow at about 40 to 60 degrees in which the climber's hand grasps the shaft of the ax just below the head and pushes the pick into the snow.

piolet panne—A French term meaning "ice ax adze." Similar to piolet manche, but with the climber's hand over the adze.

piolet poignard—A French term meaning "ice ax dagger." An ice ax technique used on steep, firm snow with the head of the ax held at head height and the pick "stabbed" into the snow.

piolet ramasse—A French term meaning "ice ax 'gather'." An ice ax technique for moderately steep snow or ice in which the climber holds the shaft across the body, using the spike as a balance point.

piolet traction—A technique for using two ice tools on very steep ice.

plaquette—*See* autoblocking belay device.

plunge step—A fast technique for descending soft snow by facing outward and digging the boot heels in with each step.

polar front—The boundary between the polar air masses and the tropical air masses; frequently the breeding ground for cyclonic storms.

pre-equalized anchor—An anchor that uses a cordelette or sling clipped to several anchor components and brought together to a master point via a tied knot. Also called static equalization.

prerigged rappels—A time-saving method of setting up a rappel with all team members attaching their rappel devices to the climbing rope at the same time, though they rappel separately.

probes, avalanche—Long collapsible poles used to find an avalanche victim.

prusik knot—A friction hitch usually tied with cord around a rope of greater diameter.

quickdraw—A short length of nylon webbing with a carabiner at each end; used to connect the climbing rope to protection.

quick link—A steel ring with a threaded opening, commonly used for threading rappel ropes.

rales—The rough and raspy breath sounds of someone with HAPE.

rappel ring—An aluminum or steel ring used for threading rappel ropes.

redirected belay—Belaying a second off the harness, with the rope redirected through a carabiner on the anchor.

repeater, radio—Remote device that receives a radio signal and retransmits it at a higher power level, allowing a low-power radio to communicate over long distances. Many repeaters are owned and operated by ham radio clubs.

resection—A navigation technique that uses bearings from multiple, visible, known points to determine location. Also known as triangulation.

Ropeman—A small ratcheting device used for rope ascending and in some rescue and hauling systems.

route plan—A series of information-gathering and planning steps used to prepare an ascent, gauge progress, and stay on route and on schedule.

running belay—An anchor, either artificial or natural, anchoring a rope team to the mountain as team members climb simultaneously.

Rutschblock test—A test measuring the bonding between layers within a snowpack, which uses the weight of a skier to collapse an isolated block of snow.

"saggers"—Crevasses bridged by sagging snow; the actual edge of a "sagger" crevasse is hidden and difficult to locate, and the bridge strength often is difficult to assess.

scree—Gravel, dirt, and small rock debris.

self-equalizing anchor—An anchor that uses a sling to bring together a number of anchor components in such a way that the individual components share the load equally, even when the direction of pull changes.

serac—Ice towers formed by intersecting crevasses patterns; often unstable.

short pitching—Belayed climbing on a shortened rope with tied-off coils to protect short sections of difficult or exposed terrain.

short-roping—A protective technique widely used by mountain guides in which the team moves together on a very short amount of rope. Short-roping allows a stronger climber to provide some protection and help to a weaker climber through pacing, modeling, close monitoring, a solid stance, and quick responses.

shovel shear test—A test measuring the bonding between layers in a snowpack using the relative resistance to shear stress by pulling on an isolated column of snow.

slab avalanche—An avalanche that fractures and releases as a cohesive slab, leaving a distinctive fracture line at the start zone.

snow crystal—What a snowflake is called when it is in the air; once it is on the ground, it is known as a snow grain.

snow grain—A snowflake that has reached the ground.

snow stability—The relative likelihood that avalanches will or will not initiate.

Spectra—A very strong and light synthetic fiber used in cordage, webbing, and some fabrics, usually in conjunction with nylon.

stopper knots—Knots tied into a rope for glacier travel to help stop and hold a crevasse fall. The butterfly knot is recommended for this purpose.

T-trench—A snow anchor created by burying an ice tool, picket, skis, or other long object in the snow.

talus—Broken rock debris, ranging in size from boulders down to small rocks; larger than scree.

terrain belay—A direct belay using a terrain feature such as a rock horn or block.

Tibloc—A small ratcheting device used for rope ascending and in some rescue and hauling systems.

topo—A climbers' diagram depicting features of a climbing route; used for routefinding.

triangulation—See resection.

triaxial loading—Loading a carabiner in three directions. Triaxial loading increases the odds that fall forces could pull straight out on the gate, the weakest part of the carabiner.

Tri-cam—Small and light camming device used for protection and anchor building on rock.

transition—The process of changing from one protective system or mode of movement to another; for example, from short-pitch climbing to belaying full-length pitches.

tying off coils—A method of carrying and securing coils when climbers are moving together on a shortened rope, short pitching, or short-roping.

UIAGM—Union Internationale des Associations des Guides de Montagne. The French-language acronym for the IFMGA.

UTM grid—A metric coordinate system (Universal Transverse Mercator) used in most parts of the world, defining locations on the globe using zones and a square kilometer grid. Commonly used to define GPS waypoints.

VHF radio—Small, lightweight, handheld, very high frequency units useful in the mountains for rescue or for communication between groups. The VHF frequency range is also known as the 2-meter band because the wavelength is about 2 meters long.

warm front—Warm air displacing colder air. Usually associated with wet and warm weather.

water knot—Also a bend, this knot is used for joining webbing.

waypoint—A location on a map that is defined by a set of coordinates; used to refer to locations in the context of a GPS route.

whiteout navigation plan—A type of route plan, or component of a route plan, that will allow for travel in very poor visibility or bad weather.

whumph—The sound caused by the sudden collapse of layers within a snowpack, usually an indication of poor stability.

Wilderness First Responder—A level and type of first-aid certification designed to be useful to backcountry travelers. WFR courses are typically about 8 days long and require renewal every two or three years.

wire-gate carabiner—A type of carabiner that uses a steel wire for its gate. Frequently small and very light, these have the added advantage of not freezing up in cold and wet conditions.

wind slab—A relatively dense and stiff layer of snow formed by the deposition of wind-blown snow.

Bibliography

American Alpine Club. *Accidents in North American Mountaineering.* Golden, CO: American Alpine Club Press, 2003 (published annually).

Brenstrum, Erick. *The New Zealand Weather Book.* Nelson, New Zealand: Craig Potton Publishing, 1998.

Chouinard, Yvon. *Climbing Ice.* San Francisco: Sierra Club Books, 1982.

Cox, Steven M., and Kris Fulsaas, eds. *Mountaineering: The Freedom of the Hills.* 7th ed. Seattle: The Mountaineers Books, 2003.

Fasulo, David. *How to Climb: Self-Rescue.* Helena, MT: Falcon, 1997.

Ferguson, Sue, and Ed LaChappelle. *The ABCs of Avalanche Safety.* 3rd ed. Seattle: The Mountaineers Books, 2003.

Fredston, Jill, and Doug Fesler. *Snow Sense.* Anchorage, Alaska: Alaska Mountain Safety Center, 2001.

Gadd, Will. *Ice and Mixed Climbing: Modern Technique.* Seattle: The Mountaineers Books, 2003.

Hackett, Peter, MD. *Mountain Sickness, Prevention, Recognition and Treatment.* Golden, CO: American Alpine Club Press, 1980.

Houston, Charles. *Going Higher.* 5th ed. Seattle: The Mountaineers Books, 2005.

Lawrence, Letham. *GPS Made Easy.* 4th ed. Seattle: The Mountaineers Books, 2003.

Leave No Trace, Inc. *Leave No Trace.* Boulder, CO: Leave No Trace, Inc., series of minimum-impact booklets.

Lewis, Peter, and Dan Cauthorn. *Climbing: From Gym to Crag.* Seattle: The Mountaineers Books, 2000.

Long, John, and Craig Luebben. *How to Climb: Advanced Rock Climbing.* Helena, MT: Falcon, 1997.

Lowe, Jeff. *Ice World: Techniques and Experiences of Modern Ice Climbing.* Seattle: The Mountaineers Books, 1996.

Luebben, Craig. *How to Climb: How to Ice Climb!* Helena, MT: Falcon, 1998.

—. *How to Climb: Knots for Climbers.* 2nd ed. Helena, MT: Falcon, 1993.

—. *Rock Climbing: Mastering Basic Skills.* Seattle: The Mountaineers Books, 2004.

McClung, David, and Peter Schaerer. *Avalanche Handbook.* 3rd ed. Seattle: The Mountaineers Books, 2006.

Powers, Phil, and Clyde Soles. *Climbing: Expedition Planning.* Seattle: The Mountaineers Books, 2003.

Rebuffat, Gaston. *100 Finest Routes in Mont Blanc Massif.* Paris: Denoël, 1974.

Renner, Jeff. *Northwest Mountain Weather, Understanding and Forecasting for the Backcountry User.* Seattle: The Mountaineers Books, 1992.

Selters, Andy. *Glacier Travel and Crevasse Rescue.* 2nd ed. Seattle: The Mountaineers Books, 1999.

Soles, Clyde. *Climbing: Training for Peak Performance.* 2nd ed. Seattle: The Mountaineers Books, 2008.

Tremper, Bruce. *Staying Alive in Avalanche Terrain.* 2nd ed. Seattle: The Mountaineers Books, 2008.

Twight, Mark, and James Martin. *Extreme Alpinism, Climbing Light, High, and Fast.* Seattle: The Mountaineers Books, 1999.

Index

About the Authors

Mark Houston and Kathy Cosley began climbing in the late 1970s in the Cascades range of Washington State, where both grew up. Their subsequent climbing and guiding careers have included extensive travel and ascents in the Andes of South America, the Himalaya of Nepal, the European Alps, and the Southern Alps of New Zealand, as well as throughout the United States and Canada. They have contributed to the development of guides training and certification through their involvement with the American Mountain Guides Association from the late 1980s to the present. Both are mountain guides internationally certified by International Federation of Mountain Guides

Associations. They have run their independent mountain guiding service since 1994. They currently reside in Bishop, California, and have been married since 1986.

THE MOUNTAINEERS, founded in 1906, is a nonprofit outdoor activity and conservation club, whose mission is "to explore, study, preserve, and enjoy the natural beauty of the outdoors. . . . " Based in Seattle, Washington, the club is now one of the largest such organizations in the United States, with seven branches throughout Washington State.

The Mountaineers sponsors both classes and year-round outdoor activities in the Pacific Northwest, which include hiking, mountain climbing, ski-touring, snowshoeing, bicycling, camping, kayaking, nature study, sailing, and adventure travel. The club's conservation division supports environmental causes through educational activities, sponsoring legislation, and presenting informational programs.

All club activities are led by skilled, experienced instructors, who are dedicated to promoting safe and responsible enjoyment and preservation of the outdoors.

If you would like to participate in these organized outdoor activities or the club's programs, consider a membership in The Mountaineers. For information and an application, write or call The Mountaineers, Club Headquarters, 7700 Sand Point Way NE, Seattle, WA 98115; 206-521-6001. You can also visit the club's website at *www.mountaineers.org* or contact The Mountaineers via email at *clubmail@mountaineers.org.*

The Mountaineers Books, an active, nonprofit publishing program of the club, produces guidebooks, instructional texts, historical works, natural history guides, and works on environmental conservation. All books produced by The Mountaineers Books fulfill the club's mission.

Send or call for our catalog of more than 500 outdoor titles:

The Mountaineers Books
1001 SW Klickitat Way, Suite 201
Seattle, WA 98134
800-553-4453
mbooks@mountaineersbooks.org
www.mountaineersbooks.org

The Mountaineers Books is proud to be a corporate sponsor of The Leave No Trace Center for Outdoor Ethics, whose mission is to promote and inspire responsible outdoor recreation through education, research, and partnerships. The Leave No Trace program is focused specifically on human-powered (nonmotorized) recreation.
Leave No Trace strives to educate visitors about the nature of their recreational impacts, as well as offer techniques to prevent and minimize such impacts. Leave No Trace is best understood as an educational and ethical program, not as a set of rules and regulations.
For more information, visit *www.LNT.org*, or call 800-332-4100.

OTHER TITLES IN THE MOUNTAINEERS OUTDOOR EXPERT SERIES

ROCK CLIMBING ANCHORS: A Comprehensive Guide, *Craig Luebben*
CLIMBING SELF-RESCUE, *Andy Tyson & Molly Loomis*
ROCK CLIMBING: Mastering Basic Skills, *Craig Luebben*
ICE & MIXED CLIMBING: Modern Technique, *Will Gadd*
CLIMBING: Training for Peak Performance, 2nd Edition *Clyde Soles*

OTHER TITLES YOU MIGHT ENJOY FROM THE MOUNTAINEERS BOOKS

MOUNTAINEERING: The Freedom of the Hills, 8th Edition
The Mountaineers
The climber's bible—complete, authoritative instruction in an easy-to-use format.

**MEDICINE FOR MOUNTAINEERING
& Other Wilderness Activities, 6th Edition**
James Wilkerson, M.D.
A classic since 1967, this book starts where most first-aid
manuals stop. Written and edited by a team of climber-
physicians, this is the perfect companion to
Mountaineering: The Freedom of the Hills.

EXTREME ALPINISM: Climbing Light, Fast, & High
Mark Twight & Jim Martin
This master class centers on climbing the hardest routes with
little gear and high speed.

ALTITUDE ILLNESS: Prevention and Treatment, 2nd Edition
Stephen Bezruchka
Stay healthy at high heights — includes current information on
preparing for and adapting to altitude.

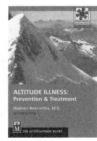

**The Mountaineers Books has more than
500 outdoor recreation titles in print.**
Receive a free catalog at
www.mountaineersbooks.org.